Hello,
Friends!

Hello, Friends!

STORIES FROM MY LIFE AND Blue Jays BASEBALL

JERRY HOWARTH

Published by ECW Press
665 Gerrard Street East
Toronto, Ontario, Canada M4M 1Y2
416-694-3348 / info@ecwpress.com

Editor for the Press: Michael Holmes and
Laura Pastore
Cover design: David A. Gee
Cover photograph: © Joseph Michael
Photography / www.josephmichael.ca
All interior photos are from the author's
personal collection.

To the best of his abilities, the author has related
experiences, places, people, and organizations from his
memories of them.

LIBRARY AND ARCHIVES CANADA CATALOGUING
IN PUBLICATION

Howarth, Jerry, author
    Hello, friends! : stories from my life and Blue
Jays baseball / Jerry Howarth.

Issued in print and electronic formats.
ISBN 978-1-77041-498-3 (hardcover)
ISBN 978-1-77305-353-0 (HTML)
ISBN 978-1-77305-354-7 (PDF)

    1. Howarth, Jerry. 2. Sportscasters—Canada—
Biography. I. Title.

GV742.42.H69A3 2019   070.4'49796092
C2018-905287-2   C2018-905288-0

The publication of *Hello, Friends!* has been funded in part by the Government of Canada. *Ce livre
est financé en partie par le gouvernement du Canada.* We acknowledge the support of the Government
of Ontario through the Ontario Book Publishing Tax Credit, and through Ontario Creates for the
marketing of this book.

PRINTED AND BOUND IN CANADA   PRINTING: FRIESENS   5   4   3   2   1

To my loving wife, Mary,
and our two loving sons, Ben and Joe.
Ben and Megan live in Chicago, with their two sons,
Coleson and Emmett. Joe and Kathy live in Toronto
with their son, Wesley.

To Joan Levy Earle, who
inspired me to write this book.

To Ann Tersigni, who spent countless
hours refining this book for all to enjoy.

To Michael Holmes and everyone at ECW Press, who
have been like family to me.

I could not have done this without you.

CONTENTS

FOREWORD BY PAUL BEESTON, PRESIDENT EMERITUS OF THE TORONTO BLUE JAYS

He was not in attendance when the Blue Jays played their first game on April 7, 1977, against the Chicago White Sox, and in an official capacity, he has not attended any Blue Jays games, post the 2017 season. But in between the first pitch of the 1982 season on April 9, when the Blue Jays entertained the Milwaukee Brewers (after broadcasting three Blue Jays games in 1980 and 20 games in 1981), and the last pitch of the Blue Jays 2017 season on October 1, against the New York Yankees at Yankee Stadium, no person witnessed more Blue Jays baseball than Jerry Howarth. And no one is more qualified to detail those 36 seasons, completely unvarnished, than Jerry Howarth, the seemingly forever voice of the Blue Jays.

From the start of spring training until the last out of each season, Jerry was in the booth to chronicle the fortunes of the club. Certain seasons were bad, many were good, and some were great! Jerry had a front row seat to them all.

While Jerry had energy, personality, curiosity and attention to detail, he was also ubiquitous. His friendships in the game are myriad. They span the players, the manager, the coaches, the umpires, the front office of all clubs, fellow broadcasters and telecasters, and most importantly, the fans. How many happy birthdays, happy anniversaries, and, yes, condolences has he conveyed on behalf of the Blue Jays? How many fans has he chatted with over his 36 years? How many tickets has he set aside for Blue Jays fans when the team was on the road? And it is through these relationships and experiences, totally written from Jerry's perspective, that makes this book an essential read for all baseball fans in general, and Blue Jays fans in particular.

With Jerry's immense capability to paint the picture with the spoken word, without edits, this narrative allows Jerry with reflection and consideration to tell his story, his version of what he experienced and what he observed.

If I had to characterize Jerry with one word, I would simply describe him as a gentleman. He embodied the golden rule to do unto others as you would have them do unto you. Rarely angry, 99 percent of the time positive, always willing to treat anyone he meets as a friend, or potentially a great friend, Jerry is unique. He is proud of his religion, his family and the Blue Jays. While not born Canadian, he became a citizen of our country and made a conscious (or unconscious) decision to make Canada and Toronto a better place.

I can think of no one person more capable or qualified to tell it as it was. Blessed with a great sense of humour, including the ability to laugh at himself, he always took his work very seriously, but also knew that he was fortunate to be working in a game. You never had the impression that Jerry had a job. No, it was a passion, and he was fully aware and thankful of how fortunate he was to be in the position he held for 36 years.

So relax, and enjoy. Tom Cheek, Jerry's longtime partner and friend, said of Joe Carter's historic home run: "Touch 'em all, Joe, you will never hit a bigger home run!" I can confidently say to take license with Tom's call. "Read it all fans, you will never get a more insightful read."

I love baseball and I love the Toronto Blue Jays, but I don't write about them. I write about leadership, and I was up against a deadline for my first book when I heard the news: Jerry Howarth was retiring.

I felt stunned, then emotional, then grateful for what he had given us all. I put the book aside and began writing what I know: a profile of someone who uses their gifts to celebrate and empower others. A profile of a leader.

I missed my deadline, but it felt good to celebrate someone whose career had touched me so significantly. I posted it online, hoping it would make my dad smile, and tried not to think about how different the upcoming season would sound.

Sure enough, the post made its way to Jerry, who reached out with a profoundly kind note. A few weeks later came a request I consider one of the great honours in my life: would I allow him to include it in his book? That couldn't be more

Jerry: asking someone of whom most people have never heard to contribute to his book.

Most of the leadership on the planet comes from people who don't see themselves as leaders — people who say they're just "doing their job" but do so in ways that serve and strengthen our communities. They teach our children, staff our coffee shops, drive our buses, and in some rare cases they create shared experiences over the airwaves — experiences that bring families, cities, and sometimes even entire countries together. That's leadership. That's Jerry Howarth.

What Jerry Howarth Taught Me about Leadership

Jerry Howarth is the radio voice of the Toronto Blue Jays, who were born six weeks after I was in 1977. My father was at each one of those births and has loved both of us ever since (I think). Naturally, his love of the Jays became mine.

Jerry joined the Jays' broadcast team five years later in 1982 — around the time I remember first hearing the Jays on the radio in the car or at the cottage with my dad. I had never been to a baseball game, and it would be a while before we'd get them on television, so major league baseball was created for me through the voice of Jerry and his broadcast partner, Tom Cheek. I didn't know what my baseball heroes looked like, but I knew what it sounded like when they played.

Seeing my first game live wasn't exactly a letdown, but I wasn't used to having to watch the game instead of Tom and Jerry painting images in my mind. There weren't stories and lessons during the breaks in the action. There was no explanation of obscure rules or insights that helped you better appreciate the beauty of what had just happened on the field. There were just people yelling and eating.

Live baseball didn't have a voice. And to me, baseball was supposed to have a voice.

You see, if you're a baseball fan, you don't remember moments — you remember the calls of those moments, how they were described as they happened. As such, the voice of your team is the voice of your memories.

I witnessed Jose Bautista's "bat flip" live, yet my memory of that moment still features Jerry's call: "Fly ball, deep left field! Yes sir! There. She. Goes!"

When I heard the news of Jerry's retirement, I went online to watch his call of that moment again. The goosebumps came, as they always do. But for the first time, I realized something: in the absolute bedlam that followed — in the midst of that deafening roar that I swear shook the concrete beneath my feet — Jerry Howarth didn't say another word for almost a full minute.

I recently heard what has become one of my favourite leadership insights: "In your life, you will be given countless opportunities to shut the hell up. Seize every single one that you can."

To have the power to be heard yet recognize your voice is not called for is a powerful skill for any leader, and there was Jerry Howarth demonstrating how it was done.

It suddenly occurred to me: it's likely that only my mother and my father have spoken more words to me in my life than Jerry Howarth. If I've grown up to share leadership insights, surely some of them were influenced by this man. What other leadership skills might he have helped teach me?

Shine by Reflecting the Light of Others

I've been moved to tears several times over the years by Jerry's work on a broadcast. Not because of a win or a loss, but by his stories and tributes to people who love the game.

Jerry loves people who love baseball, and part of what made him so beloved was his commitment to using his platform to celebrate the contributions of others to the game, their teammates, and their communities.

During almost every game, there was a birthday wish to an elderly fan, congratulations to a production assistant on the birth of their child, even a get-well-soon to the mother of a clubhouse manager. Jerry seemed acutely aware that while the focus was always going to be on the millionaires on the field, there was an entire community of people who helped put them there.

Midway through his final season, I listened as he gave a half inning–long tribute to a former umpire who had just passed. I could hear him choke up as he described this man's dedication to the game, the impact he had had on the people around him, and how baseball was better because he had been a part of it. By the end, I was crying myself.

Jerry didn't talk about what baseball meant to him — he showed it through his commitment to highlighting those who contributed to the game and didn't have a microphone.

Sometimes the best way to shine is to reflect the light of others. Just ask the moon.

Honour Your Team by Honouring other Teams

Jerry is pretty obviously a Jays fan. But in the 30 years or so I can recall listening to him on the radio, I can't remember him ever saying, "we" when talking about the Jays. Jerry wasn't a member of the Blue Jays — Jerry called Jays games.

When Alan Trammell and Lou Whitaker turned a magical double play to kill a Jays rally, you could hear the admiration of a baseball fan in Jerry's voice, not the disappointment of a "homer." You'd hear him celebrate the skills of individual Jays not with hyperbole, but with honesty, giving credit where credit was due. Kevin Pillar was not "the greatest centre fielder in baseball," he was "one of the game's best centre fielders, along with perhaps Tampa Bay's great Kevin Kiermaier." In the days before replay, when an umpire blew a call in the Jays' favour, Jerry would tell you.

That respect he showed opposing teams and players, along with his willingness to describe what actually happened rather than what the audience wanted to hear, gave his voice tremendous credibility.

Respect and honesty, even to your competitors, and even when it's not necessarily to your advantage, will often earn you a lot more respect than chest-beating, denying failures, and exaggerating accomplishments.

Empower without Fear

I didn't realize that Joe Siddall is a broadcaster because of Jerry Howarth.

When the 2014 Blue Jays season began in April, I remember listening to Jerry's new broadcast partner and thinking, *Wow* . . .

is Jerry ever carrying this new guy. I figured the new addition to the booth was an experienced broadcaster struggling with some understandable nerves.

Turns out, "the new guy" had never been in a broadcast booth before. In February, Jerry had seen an article discussing the death of Joe Siddall's 14-year-old son, Kevin, from blood cancer. He sought out Joe's email address and sent him a note of condolence. Joe immediately sent his thanks, saying, "I look forward to seeing you when you come to Detroit this season." He then added the joke, "or maybe in the broadcast booth one day."

Jerry responded, "How about now?" before submitting Joe's name to the director of programming as his potential new partner. Two weeks later, Joe Siddall was a broadcaster.

At the time, Jerry Howarth was 68 years old and had been broadcasting Jays games for 33 years. He had every right to demand to work with a pro. Instead, he chose to advocate for someone he knew would make his job more difficult. Then he worked to make that person better.

When I learned of this story, I couldn't help but think of a former CEO I met while he was on his retirement trip. I asked him about what he was most proud of when he looked back over his career.

"Drew," he said. "I created a company filled with people who could do my job. I created a company where absolutely everyone wanted my job. But you know what? Not a single one of them wanted to take it away from me. They knew that every day I was in that role, I was going to try to find a way to make them better. I wanted to empower others without fear one of them would make me pay for it. The less fear I had of that happening, the less I had to be afraid of."

Empower without fear. You're creating allies, not threats.

Screw Tradition

There is no sport that venerates its past like baseball. Unwritten rules over a century old still dictate how the game is played and how players act. To be frank, baseball continues to do things that don't really make sense because "it's tradition."

For instance, keeping team names that are profoundly insulting to entire cultures.

But Jerry Howarth hasn't used team names like "Braves" or "Indians" for over 25 years. After the Jays beat Atlanta's team in the 1992 World Series, a member of a Northern Ontario First Nation wrote Howarth a letter pointing out how deeply offensive those names and long-used expressions like "powwows on the mound" actually were.

Moved by the letter, Jerry wrote back and promised he wouldn't speak the names on the air again. He's kept that vow. Other broadcasters have cited his example and chosen to do the same. Everyone should.

To break with baseball tradition when you rely on the game for your livelihood takes a certain type of person. Taking a stand against something the majority feels "isn't that big a deal" usually comes with consequences. But some fights need fighting.

What happens when someone charges the mound? At first they charge alone . . . but by the time they get to the real fight, they've usually got a whole team behind them.

There are certain things in our society calling us to charge the mound. Someone has to take the first step and get the benches moving.

Goodbye, Friends!

Throughout this entire piece, I've simply said "Jerry." As I wrote, I found myself asking, "Why do I feel I have the right to talk like I'm a friend of his?"

I suppose it's because he told me to. He told us all to. Every single night. One hundred and sixty-two nights a year — it was always the same greeting:

"Hello, friends! This is Jerry Howarth! And welcome to Blue Jays Baseball!"

He told us we were friends . . . and then he acted like someone with whom you'd want to be friends.

It's hard to say goodbye to your favourites. But goodbyes are a part of sport. I'm 40 years old, and thanks to my dad, I've been a Jays fan for 40 years. I've watched a lot of the greats say goodbye: Bell, Barfield, Alomar, Halladay, Encarnacion, Bautista.

They were all Jays.

To me, Jerry Howarth was *the Jays*.

Thanks, my friend. You touched 'em all.

PREFACE

Hope springs eternal.

While the English dictionary defines the above as "It is human nature to always find fresh cause for optimism," the real definition for ardent baseball fans is simply the start of spring training. Whether you are a Blue Jays season-ticket holder or a casual fan on the periphery, by the time late winter rolls around, everyone, either mentally or physically, wants to somehow leave the cold and frigid winters for the warmth of a baseball game in Dunedin, Florida. You feel warmer just listening to a Blue Jays game on radio, or watching it on TV, or reading about it online or in the newspaper when pitchers and catchers first report to camp.

Every year tells its own story. For me, there is always that anticipation and excitement that *this could be the year*, and baseball fans in every major league city feel exactly the same way. That's the beauty of baseball. Not many people — except for the editors at *Sports Illustrated*, as it turned out — thought that the Houston Astros would win the 2017 World Series. But they did, upsetting the team with the highest payroll in baseball.

The old adage "you can't buy a World Series" proved ominous yet again.

Remember just a few years ago, the Blue Jays were picked to win the World Series by Las Vegas oddsmakers. That did not quite work out. However, the opposite was true when the Blue Jays went to spring training in 2015, judged by many as a .500 team. That is exactly what they were after 102 games — 51-51 — but they were on their way to winning the American League Eastern Division Championship and came within two games of advancing to the World Series.

This is why I love spring training and the uncertainty of what the season might hold — there are no guarantees. Play the games and see what happens; it's better to be surprised than disappointed. Every game, I took a fresh white canvas in my mind and artistically painted it to the best of my ability for our audience. Then at the end of the broadcast, I would initial it in the lower right-hand corner and look forward to painting another blank canvas the next day.

It seems like only yesterday.

Late one evening in October 1981, I found myself seated on the right side of a plane that just hours before had left Salt Lake City, Utah. Looking out the window at the bright lights of Toronto, I was seeing my new home through new eyes. I was so excited: this was my opportunity to broadcast a full season of major league games on the radio. At the same time, there was a natural curiosity about where this would lead. I had no idea how long I would be staying in Toronto, but I was not concerned or worried. All I knew was that tomorrow I would be introduced as the new Toronto Blue Jays radio announcer, joining veteran Tom Cheek in the broadcast booth. A dream come true. Rarely do people who played sports all year round like I did as a kid get a chance to turn a passion into a career.

Growing up in the San Francisco Bay Area, I played baseball from Little League through high school. I even played one college game at the University of Santa Clara where I went 1 for 2. My one hit was a triple to right-centre field before the competition caught up to me. Hey, I hit .500 in college! As a boy, I would lie in bed at night, listening to baseball, basketball, and, yes, even hockey on the radio (with Roy Storey calling the San Francisco Seals against the Seattle Totems in the 1963 WHL championship). Without ever realizing it, I was being drawn to a love for sports broadcasting.

As I got off the plane that night and headed downtown, I was grateful for this new challenge, even if it would be only a two- or three-year experience in Toronto. Little did I know that when 2017 came to an end, I would be celebrating 36 years calling Blue Jays games on the radio for my first and only team.

CHAPTER 1

THRILL OF A LIFETIME

I was born in York, Pennsylvania, on March 12, 1946. A month later, my parents moved to San Francisco so my dad could start a new job working in refrigeration and air-cooling systems. He was an excellent mechanical engineer and would be starting a new company with one of his close friends. My older son, Ben, graduated from Purdue in 2000, with a degree in electrical engineering. Skilled engineers, my dad and Ben both excelled in math and science. Somehow, those genes skipped right past me. All I do is watch baseball games.

Within a year and a half, my sister, Anita, was born. Shortly after, we moved to Santa Rosa, 60 miles north of the Golden Gate Bridge, to escape the expensive downtown San Francisco area. By the first grade, sports were already starting to become a part of my life. One day, during recess at St. Rose's Catholic School, we were playing with a soccer ball that sailed over the fence into the shrubs. Everyone thought that ended our game. Except me. I climbed over the fence to get that ball, not even considering the consequences. Suddenly, I was in the principal's office surrounded by smiling nuns, including Sister Kevin, who gently reminded me that it was probably not a good idea to climb fences to retrieve soccer balls. Better to wait and ask someone to get it for you. They loved me, and I could feel that.

In the fifth grade, sports would again leave its imprint on my life. In the midst of a hard-played game of football on the playground, a pass came my way. I jumped to catch it at the same time as my classmate, Rod Thorn. That was the last thing I remember. I came down hard and hit the blacktop face first. I was lying there, knocked out, with my four front teeth nearly knocked out, too. My mother quickly arrived on the scene and rushed me straight to our dentist, Dr. Nordstrom. He used what looked like bubble gum to push my front teeth back into the roof of my mouth and said to come back in a week.

The next week, after removing the gum-like substance, he put ice cubes on my teeth and asked me if I could feel anything. I said no. He said to come back in another week and if I didn't feel anything at that time, he would have to remove my four front teeth and put in a plate of false teeth. The following week, he repeated the test. When I winced and jumped a little bit, he smiled at my mom. My teeth could be saved. Little did I know I would become a broadcaster, where bouncing your tongue off the roof of your mouth rather than a plate is so much better for your *ar-tic-u-la-tion*.

After the fifth grade, we remained in Santa Rosa but moved out to the country to an area called Rincon Valley. I would ride my bike to school, a mile each way. Right beside the school was a fire station. I was enamoured with the big red fire trucks and would stop by to see them. The firemen were very gracious and always welcomed me. On weekends they taught me how to play chess, checkers, and shuffleboard. That was where I first learned to compete.

We moved from Santa Rosa to Novato when I was in the middle of the sixth grade. This allowed Dad to cut his commute to San Francisco from an hour to thirty minutes. It was also in these middle school years that I began playing a lot of baseball and basketball. I even tried to referee a basketball game on the playground as an eighth grader, but at the end of it I vowed *never again*. I couldn't please anyone. My friends were all staring me down and complaining. Because of that brief experience, I have a much greater appreciation for umpires and their hard task calling games.

On radio, I let home plate umpires call the 300 balls and strikes per game, without being judgmental on certain borderline pitches. Plus, TV angles from centre field can be very misleading, even with the updated "strike zone" boxes on the screen. I have said many times on the air: "Umpires are required to start from a state of perfection and then they are asked to improve." I have also noted, perhaps somewhat controversially, that I have never seen the Blue Jays lose a game because of an umpire's call. There are too many other innings and missed opportunities that lead to defeats.

It was also in the sixth grade that I went to Kezar Stadium in downtown San Francisco to watch my first 49ers games. My parents were season-ticket holders on the 35 yard line about 30 rows up. Perfect seats for a youngster to see the game. At the end of the 1957 season, the 49ers had a playoff game at Kezar against the Detroit Lions. I was 11 years old. Dad got me a ticket on the goal line in the very front row. Sounded pretty good until I realized I couldn't see the other half of the field because the players were standing in the way.

The 49ers led 27–7 early in the second half, with the winner to play the Cleveland Browns in the NFL Championship game the following week. Final Score: Lions 31, 49ers 27. It broke my heart. A few days later, I wrote a five-page essay on that game as part of an in-class assignment that allowed us to pick any topic. When the bell rang for recess, all my classmates went out to play. But not me. I wish I still had that essay because I know in my heart of hearts that my love for sports and writing and eventually broadcasting began with those five pages.

Meeting Willie McCovey

Middle school then led to four wonderful years at Novato High School, which happened to be just 500 yards up the street from where I lived. Sports continued to consume my time. I was the backup quarterback on the junior varsity football team for a season; and a guard on the freshman basketball team before moving full-time to baseball. Baseball was dominant. I played with my high school team all four years, then semi-pro baseball in the summer and on a winter ball team in nearby Fairfax. This was with and against some of the best athletes in the area. I put in the work to try to get better at playing third base and centre field, batting leadoff, and stealing bases, as well as improving my overall conditioning.

One of my most memorable experiences occurred when I was 16 years old, standing on the first tee at the Santa Rosa Golf and Country Club where my father was a member. I grew up on the golf course, caddying for Dad. I played in my first junior tournament when I was 10, finishing second and winning a little five-inch trophy. Now, six years later, I had no idea what surprise Dad had in store for me. During the week, he had mentioned that on Sunday there would be a celebrity golf tournament. He wanted me to caddy for a celebrity he had specifically chosen for his foursome, but he wouldn't tell me who it was.

On Sunday, I was on the first tee waiting to see who would show up. "Jerry, I want you to meet the man you are going to caddy for today. You know who he is. This is Willie McCovey." I was stunned and so happy at the same time. My father knew just how special McCovey was to me. First, he was a star with Willie Mays and the San Francisco Giants. And, second, as luck would have it, Dad and I were there on July 30, 1959, for McCovey's major league debut as he had just been called up from the Giants Triple-A team in Phoenix, Arizona.

That day at Seals Stadium, playing first base, Willie became just the eighth player in history to go 4 for 4 in his major league debut, on his way to becoming the National League Rookie of the Year. Willie had two triples and two singles, lining baseballs off the left, centre, and right-field walls. He did all of that against future Hall of Famer Robin Roberts, of the Philadelphia Phillies.

Years later, I shared this story with another future Hall of Famer, Joe Morgan, who is from the East Bay. Joe grew up in and around Oakland. "Jerry, my dad took me to that game, too!" When Interleague play began in 1997, I met and befriended Phillies third-base coach and fellow Californian John Vukovich. I mentioned to John that both Joe Morgan and I had seen Willie McCovey's first game with our dads. "My father took me to that game!" What are the odds that three fathers would bring their sons to a historic game like that and years later all three sons would make it to the major leagues? That's why I love baseball: you never know what you're going to see when you go out to a game.

So there I stood on the first tee with one of my heroes. Dad would later laugh and say that Willie and I were in the woods all day talking baseball, trying to track down his many long drives that sliced and hooked miles away from the fairways. Willie was a gentle giant — no pun intended. He talked softly about his collection of 5,000 jazz albums — yes 5,000 — that he listened to at his home in Mobile, Alabama. It was his way to relax and enjoy his quiet time away from baseball.

Willie was six-foot-four, 210 pounds, and the first major league All-Star I had ever spent time with. At the start of the tournament, Willie wore a bulky blue sweater until the fog finally lifted around the fourth hole. Willie took off his sweater, revealing a tight-fitting blue shirt. I remember staring at his huge, muscular arms. I had seen Willie from the stands but never this close, and it was a moment that has stayed with me throughout my career. I began to realize at a very young age how and why so many major league players are stars in this game. They are so gifted physically. You cannot appreciate that from the stands. If they combine hard work with year-round dedication, they become the very best at what they do.

A Much-Needed Wake-Up Call

In high school, I was spending way too much time on sports and not enough time on my classwork. Every year on my report card there would be one A in physical education and a couple of Bs. The rest of my grades were Cs. I even got a D in algebra. Honestly, I didn't think too much about it. At the end of my third year of high school, I was at my girlfriend's house one day when her report card arrived in the mail. Her dad asked, "Kris, how did you do?" Her answer: "I have all As and one B."

"Jerry, how did you do?" That one simple question helped turn my life around. I was embarrassed and mumbled: "Oh, my report card hasn't come in the mail yet, Mr. Schoof, so I don't know." When I left her house later that day, I vowed that I would never be ashamed of myself like that again because of my own lack of effort.

In my last year of high school, I worked as hard as I possibly could, and I earned all As and one B in the first semester. In my last semester, I had all As, proving that I could do anything in life if I truly applied myself. I needed that embarrassing wake-up call. I hadn't given much consideration to furthering my education after high school. I was content to look for a job, make a few bucks and then go from there. If I hadn't made that quantum leap forward academically at that precise moment in time, there is no telling where life might have taken me.

CHAPTER 2

DEVELOPING AN INTERIOR LIFE

In June 1964, I graduated from high school. As young students at the time, we began hearing about the Vietnam conflict that could lead to war. We had no idea where Vietnam was, nor did we care. That is, until my father reminded me that there was a military draft. The army could send me directly to Vietnam from high school. But if I continued my education and went to college, I would receive a Class II deferment from the draft. I finally had the grades to do that, which made my decision so much easier.

Going to the University of Santa Clara was one of the best things that happened to me in my young life. I had heard about a Jesuit education and how good it could be. My freshman year, September 1964, I moved into Walsh Hall. There I met the Jesuit priest living in that dorm, Father John Shanks, S.J. (Society of Jesus), who lived on the first floor. Every dormitory had a resident priest. Fortunately for me, Father Shanks was also the head of Sodality, which was a Christian group on campus I knew nothing about.

My parents were in the middle of a divorce when I was a few months removed from high school. My mom and dad were a mismatch from the beginning. It was one of those World War II marriages you so often heard about: you met someone and six weeks later you got married. Some of those marriages worked, but many more did not. My parents' clearly did not. Suffice it to say, I grew up around conflict and fighting and anger and alcohol. Our worst family times were during the holidays when everyone ended up fighting with each other by the end of the night. I would lie awake in bed at night, listening to the uproar in the house and telling myself that I would avoid conflict at all costs for the rest of my life. That I would not drink. That I would learn to walk away.

After meeting Father Shanks that first week, I told him about my parents. He invited me along with many other freshmen students to a silent retreat, which the Jesuits were famous for. At first, I was hesitant about going on the retreat; I told Father I would not be attending. When he asked me why, I told him it was Thanksgiving, and I wanted to be home. He knew I didn't mean that and firmly asked me to reconsider. Fr. Shanks knew this was what a Santa Clara education was really all about, especially for young students like me trying to find a new beginning and shed the past. So I said yes. The silence made you listen. That quiet time in turn allowed you to reflect and meditate. It was a necessary part of helping me to grow as a person, and it couldn't have come at a better time.

During that retreat, Fr. Shanks would speak to all of us. Then we would go outside on our own to meditate and think about what he had to say. Later we could ask him questions in a group setting. The retreat included a general confession on Saturday night, where one by one we would wait in the hallway and then go into a room where Father sat in the far corner with his back to us. He would hear our confession. Then he would make a few comments, and we would leave the room for the next person in line.

When it was my turn, I went into the room and knelt down. I proceeded to ask for forgiveness in a few general areas. Father knew me by the sound of my voice. He asked me if there was anything else I wanted to say. That's when I suddenly let it all out about the built-up hatred I had for my mother. How I felt she contributed to the lack of love and happiness in our family. I was crying like a baby. Father gently said to me: "Try not to look at your mother as you think she should be. Look at her as she is. Then love that person to the best of your ability." It was a moment of truth that I have kept in my heart ever since. I said thank you and walked out of that room with my head down, still crying as I quietly walked past everyone in line. When I left the building I went right to the beach. I looked up into the sky and thanked God for that moment. My mom and I have had a cordial relationship ever since.

With that, I returned to Santa Clara as a new person, trying to "know thyself," as Father used to say. The goal was to develop an interior life that would sustain and ground me through whatever ups and downs the future might bring. I graduated from Santa Clara in 1968, with a bachelor of science in commerce, majoring in economics and minoring in philosophy. But my real degree was an awareness of who I was spiritually. In my freshman year, Fr. Shanks told me that I had just one of my four burners going on the top of a stove. Over the next four years, it was my intent to fire up those other three burners because I knew I had it in me. He wanted me to work hard every day so when I put my head on the pillow at night, I could say, "Thank you, Lord, for this day and for letting me love, praise and serve you with it."

Seven years later, in the summer of 1975, I was in my second year broadcasting for the Triple-A Tacoma Twins. We went into Arizona to play the Phoenix Giants. At the time, Fr. Shanks was teaching in Phoenix at Brophy High School. We had lunch together and celebrated the start of my new career. He knew how much I appreciated him as a mentor and father figure. A year later Father was killed in a small plane crash on a mountaintop in Arizona. He came into my life and went so fast. Along with my father, he was easily the most influential person in my life. He inspired me to be the person I am today.

Tom Brogan

November of that first year rolled into January and baseball try-outs. That was in part why I went to Santa Clara: I wanted to play baseball for the Broncos. I had a small academic scholarship to attend St. Mary's in Moraga on the east side of the Bay Area, but Santa Clara had just played in the finals of the 1962 College World Series. The school had a renowned baseball program. It was where I wanted to play, knowing full well the odds were long. During the tryouts, I moved to second base and competed with two others for the position on the freshman team. In our practices, we scrimmaged against the stars of the varsity team.

Our freshman coach was Bill McPherson, who was also the assistant football coach at Santa Clara with legendary head coach Pat Malley. Who knew that as a freshman, I would be playing baseball for someone who would years later leave Santa Clara and win five Super Bowl rings as a defensive-line coach for the San Francisco 49ers? In our scrimmages against the varsity team, one player who reached out to say hello to me was second-year Bronco Mike Port. Mike later became a significant member of the Boston Red Sox and California Angels front offices and eventually worked in the Commissioner's office. The practices and scrimmages continued, and I played a lot. But I could see the competition was getting fierce. Now I was just trying to make it as the backup second baseman.

During a short break at practice one day, I was standing in right field with my back to the infield. I was talking with a group of teammates, when suddenly I felt a tap on my shoulder and turned around. "Hi, Jerry. My name is Tom Brogan. I wanted to say welcome to Santa Clara and have fun playing baseball here. We are happy to have you with us. Enjoy your education here — I know I have." With that, Tom trotted back to first base. I do not know what prompted our star first baseman to make that trip to the outfield just to say hello to me. Tom was a third-year player; he could hit and he could field. Here I was trying to make the freshman team. That moment has stayed with me the rest of my life, and here is why: Tom was affable and unassuming and a leader on the team. He led by example with his character and work ethic, on the diamond, in the classroom, and on campus as well. Everyone knew Tom Brogan. Santa Clara has a mission church right in the middle of the campus with a daily Mass in the mornings. I attended a few times during the week. Tom would go every day. He would arrive at 7:15 a.m. and sit alone at the back of the church. Then Fr. Shanks would say Mass at 7:30 a.m. I asked Father why Tom was always there 15 minutes before Mass started. Father said he had asked Tom that very question. Tom's answer was simple. "I want to sit quietly in the back of the church for fifteen minutes and just listen to God, in case He wants to talk to me."

That summer, I came home one day from a practice and my dad handed me the *San Francisco Chronicle* sports section. He asked me if I knew the player in the article. The Broncos had travelled to Hawaii to play in a tournament. On a day off, the players had gone swimming out in the ocean. One player got caught in the undertow and was swept out to sea and drowned. It was Tom Brogan. He was 21. I couldn't believe it. Nor could anyone else who knew him.

When I came back to school for my second year, you could feel Tom's absence across the campus for months. I knew all the grieving players from the previous year. It was decided that to honour Tom, there would be a Tom Brogan Day on campus in February. A celebration would be held at Buck Shaw Stadium, where we played our games. The Broncos would play Stanford. Tom's parents came up from Los Angeles, where Tom was born and raised. Mr. and Mrs. Brogan had had Tom later in life, and he was their only child, which made it even sadder.

I had been cut from the freshman team after playing in just one game, and I decided it was time to move on. I had been working for a brand new campus radio station called KSCU that had just gone on the air during the evenings. I was already in my second year covering sports for the campus newspaper and was asked to broadcast a five-minute show each night to get some experience. The radio work was interesting. I was assigned to cover the afternoon game against Stanford. Tom's parents were introduced before the game. There wasn't a dry eye in the house. It was all so sad. And so unbelievable for all of us that this could happen to someone so young. The game itself made it even sadder as Stanford dominated the Broncos inning after inning, piling up an 8–3 lead going to the bottom of the 9th inning. And then it happened.

A base hit; then another one; then an error on a made-to-order double-play ground ball hit to shortstop as a run scored; two more hits led to two more runs. Then Joe Karlin — who couldn't run at all with a leg injury — was forced to pinch hit and drew a walk on four pitches. All of a sudden, Stanford's lead was at 8–6 with two outs and two on for Rod Austin. Rod was a strong right-handed hitting outfielder. He was another outstanding person on campus who had known Tom well. Rod hit a mammoth three-run home run to deep left-centre field to dramatically win the game, 9–8. Buck Shaw Stadium erupted. Tom's parents were crying and so was everyone else, including me. After taking in all the euphoria, I ran across campus and wrote out my script for the radio show that evening. It was one of the most meaningful radio shows I have ever broadcast and easily the most gratifying. Tom Brogan will live forever in Santa Clara history. He definitely helped put my young life into perspective.

Caddying in the U.S. Open

In June 1966, I went straight from the classroom to the fabled Olympic Club in San Francisco, where I had the good fortune of caddying in the U.S. Open. Dad knew a lot of people at the Olympic Club. He was able to get me into the caddy shack. This was at a time when golfers at the U.S. Open were required to take the caddy from the home course rather than bring their own. I caddied for a Connecticut pro, Mike Krak, who had qualified that year. Mike was a good golfer and an even nicer person — a perfect fit for me. I enjoyed caddying in the practice rounds. It was there I saw the great Ben Hogan up close on the greens. I also saw what the yips were all about.

Earlier in his illustrious career, Hogan had been in a very bad car accident and nearly died. There was a lot of nerve damage. Yet he remained one of golf's greatest. But when he stood over putts, his hands twitched and moved back and forth. He had to back off the putt and take a deep breath. Then he would get back over his putt again. It definitely affected his putting, or he would have won that Open.

Having said that, he still finished fifth overall, tied with an amateur who was actually in the caddy shack with me to begin that week. But the Olympic Club said to that caddy: "This is your home course. Even though you are just nineteen, we want you to play and not caddy." And so a young Johnny Miller played. He was paired with Hogan that last day as both finished tied for fifth. Two of the greats. My golfer did not make the cut, so I had a free pass the final two days. I made a point of seeing everyone from tee to green. That 1966 U.S. Open was a famous one: Arnold Palmer led Billy Casper by seven shots with nine holes to play. Casper caught Arnie to force an 18-hole playoff on Monday. Palmer had a two-shot lead after nine only to see Casper catch him again and pass him for an unbelievable come-from-behind win of that prestigious Open.

Switching Majors

After that summer, I went back to Santa Clara for my third year, where I began writing full time for the campus newspaper, covering all sports as both a sideline reporter and a columnist. It was so enjoyable. I dreamed of working in sports journalism at an elite level, like Curry Kirkpatrick, my favourite columnist with *Sports Illustrated*. Writing has always come easily for me;

I like expressing myself this way and always have. Santa Clara did not have a course in journalism, so the best avenue for me to follow my writing dreams was to write for the school paper.

When I first arrived at Santa Clara, my major was accounting. I had enjoyed my first two years studying and learning the principles of accounting. I could do the work, and, for all intents and purposes, a career as a chartered accountant was where I was headed. I was fine with that. That is, until I began my third year and took intermediate accounting. *Hello!* I hit a wall. As hard as I tried, I just could not solve any of the problems. Each day, I asked my friend Jim Pagandarm to help me with the assignments. It was fortunate that he lived right across the hall in our dorm. In retrospect, perhaps not so fortunate for Jim, with all the trips he had to make to help me. Finally, I said to myself during that first semester: *Jim should be the chartered accountant. I should be something else.* I promptly switched majors to economics, which I enjoyed. Jim later became a very good chartered accountant. Follow your heart — I have always lived by that.

In my senior year, I finished up as one of the sports editors for the campus newspaper. I wrote a weekly column following all of our teams. Interestingly enough, the campus radio station, KSCU, continued (and to this very day), but I did not. That didn't bother me at all. Writing was first and foremost for me at that time. The thought of a career in broadcasting never crossed my mind. I was also in my fourth and final year of the ROTC (Reserve Officers' Training Corps) program. Many of us wanted to be officers in the U.S. Army. This way, we avoided the draft, did not have to attend a rigorous Officer Basic Training course, and would be leaders in Vietnam rather than be led. For us, ROTC was the "paved highway through the jungle" toward becoming an officer.

All that was left now was to graduate. I did so in June 1968. I invited Mrs. Gertrude Schwedhelm, my fourth grade teacher, to share the moment. She believed in me. I never forgot that. It was my way of saying thank you for all she had done. Her graduation gift to me was a book of poetry that I still treasure.

CHAPTER 3

TWO LIFE-CHANGING MOMENTS

After graduation, I spent the summer at Ft. Benjamin Harrison in Indianapolis, Indiana, where I began my training in the Adjutant General Corps, a non-combat branch of the U.S. Army. For that I owe a debt of gratitude to my good friend and fellow Santa Clara alum Roger Epperson. In the summer after our third year in ROTC, we were required to go to Ft. Lewis, Washington, for six weeks of army training. It was part of the four-year program. I did not realize just how significant one aspect of that program was until Roger set me straight before I left. He was a year ahead of me in school and was in ROTC.

"You can go to Ft. Lewis, Jerry, and put in the time like everyone else. Then when you graduate a year later as a commissioned officer, you will most likely be placed in one of the three combat arms — infantry, armour, or artillery — and sent to Vietnam. However, Ft. Lewis has what they call a Distinguished Military Student Award. There are only six of them. Those six students get to choose their branch upon graduation, which means they do not have to go into any of the combat arms. I want you to work as hard as you can each day and win one of those six awards." At the end of my six weeks, I was named one of the six Distinguished Military Students and chose the Adjutant General Corps. Roger had come through for me in a big way.

After my summer in Indianapolis, I received my orders to report to Frankfurt, Germany. There I served two years at V Corp Headquarters. I spent my first year working with top secret documents. The second year, I was in charge of running five departments. During that time I lived with a German family, spoke German, and visited 18 countries. Those two years were just what I needed to mature and broaden my horizons in a way I could never have imagined. At work, I learned what it meant to be responsible, accountable, and disciplined while focused on the job at hand. The Russians had just invaded Czechoslovakia. A lot of tension was in the air among the NATO nations. There I was, right in the middle of it. It caught me by surprise and taught me to concentrate.

I left Germany in August 1970, saying a tearful goodbye to the Krueger family I lived with and would never see again. But it was time. I remember looking out the window during my flight back to the U.S., smiling and being so grateful for everything. Upon landing stateside at Fort Dix, New Jersey, I quickly turned down a promotion to become a captain. That would have meant serving a year in Vietnam. I wanted no part of that. My active duty career was now over. I was en route to law school in San Francisco, crossing the country in my brand new bright yellow 1970 Volkswagen Bug, where, unbeknownst to me, I would meet my future wife.

Law School

By September 1970, I was back in the Bay Area. My dad strongly suggested that I go to law school to continue my education, and so I chose the University of California at Hastings Law School in downtown San Francisco. I welcomed this. Hastings was unique. After World War II, many law schools introduced a policy of mandatory retirement for their professors at age 65. All the Bay Area law schools, such as the University of California at Berkeley and Stanford University, were doing this. Many very qualified law professors were suddenly out of work. Hastings stepped in and put itself on the map with a key decision for the school's future: they would hire all of these professors and let them continue teaching.

In my first semester, I took torts from Professor William Prosser, who wrote the book that we used in class. Two of my other classes were exactly the same: Richard Perkins, who taught criminal law, and Richard Powell, who taught property, both wrote the books that we were studying from. That was a little intimidating, to say the least. These professors clearly were not ready to retire, and we all benefitted from having them as teachers and patient mentors. I enjoyed my first semester in a very large freshman class of 400. Cal-Berkeley and Stanford took fewer applicants in the first year, but they made a point of trying to help all of them graduate. Hastings took the opposite approach: they took in many more students at first but had a much higher turnover rate. This was perfect for me: I did not have the marks to get into the other schools.

At the semester break, I had done very well, including an 88 percent in torts, which had me smiling — big time. I was very comfortable in my first year. I went to class in downtown San

Francisco during the day and drove back to my small, affordable apartment up on the hill near the University of San Francisco in the evening. USF also had a law school, which is where I studied at night. It turned out to be the perfect situation.

In the middle of January, while studying at the USF law library, I would hear this clicking sound every night. I'd look up from my law book but never see anything, so I'd go back to my reading. Until one night, when I saw *her*. A very nice looking young lady was wearing high-heeled shoes. When she got up to take a break from her studies, she would pound those heels into the tile floor with her quick-paced walks. It was funny enough to make me laugh. A couple of weeks later, Charlie Sledd, a friend of mine and a first-year law student at USF, was coming down the library staircase with someone just as I was walking up. "Jerry, I want you to meet a friend of mine, Mary McMorrow, who is my classmate here." *The heel clicker.* Charlie knew I loved baseball. He also knew that Mary, who was from Kalamazoo, Michigan, was a big fan of the Detroit Tigers. He just felt he should introduce us and that we would click. No pun intended. He was right.

When Mary told me not only that she loved the Tigers, but that outfielder Al Kaline was her favourite player, the light went on to see if I couldn't immediately impress her. As luck would have it, on April 23, just two months after we had met, the Tigers came to Oakland to begin a weekend series with the A's. I took a chance and called the A's and asked what hotel the Tigers were staying in. I called the Edgewater Hyatt and asked for Al Kaline. The next thing I knew, someone picked up the phone. "Is Al Kaline there?" I asked. "Yes, this is Al." Well, to say that I was shocked and surprised to even get through to this future Hall of Famer is an understatement. I might add: those days of a complete stranger talking to a player on the road are "long gone!" as Tigers radio announcer Ernie Harwell would say with his famous home run call.

"Al, my name is, Jerry Howarth, and my girlfriend, who is from, Kalamazoo, Michigan, is celebrating her birthday today [I lied!] and you are her favourite player [not a lie]. Would it be possible for you to come over and say hello to her during batting practice tonight?"

"That would be fine. I will see you both tonight."

When I got off the phone, I called Mary and said, "Are you sitting down? I just talked to Al Kaline, and you're going to meet him! Tonight! Now, I know you told me your birthday is July 14, but let's pretend it's tonight."

Around 5:30 p.m., as I was walking down the steps with Mary at the Oakland Alameda Coliseum, I saw Al Kaline in the batting cage. After he took his last swing, he was headed over to the Tigers first-base dugout, where I gently waved my right arm in his direction, hoping he would realize I was that crazy fan who had called him earlier that day. Al came over and we talked for a few minutes. He couldn't have been nicer or more gracious. At the end, he said, "Mary, nice to meet you," and he trotted out to right field. Wow.

That was in 1971. Years later in 1982, when I joined the Blue Jays on radio, I talked to Al about that night on the field, and while he didn't specifically remember it, we became longtime batting practice pals, meeting on the field every time the Blue Jays and Tigers played. A true Hall of Famer.

Mary was the second oldest of five. Her father, George, was a longtime professor of Philosophy at Nazareth College, located right in their backyard in Kalamazoo. Her mother, Betty, was a fifth grade teacher and later was a reading specialist for 20 years. Knowing her background — and trying to impress her — I took Mary to the San Francisco Symphony on our first date to see legendary conductor Seiji Ozawa. On our second date, I took her to see a Giants game at Candlestick Park. I haven't taken her to another symphony since, but I have taken her to a lot of baseball games! That was 46 years ago. They say opposites attract — they are right about that. Mary reads over 100 books a year while I read maybe three or four, unless they are books about playing duplicate bridge; she does all the cooking while I do all the "postgame shows," cleaning up the kitchen and dishes; she loves to communicate with everyone in every possible way while I don't even own a cell phone and love my quiet time. I tell people I am an extroverted introvert while Mary is the true extrovert.

The 49ers Call

In February 1971, well into my second semester and just a month after Mary and I had met, my life's journey abruptly took a turn. It's funny how it goes; you can call it divine intervention, luck, good fortune, following your heart, or whatever else you want, but a simple phone call changed my life forever.

For the longest time growing up, my dream was to watch a 49ers game on the sidelines. I wanted to hear the violence and mayhem and see the contact and really experience an NFL game up close and personal. When I returned from Germany, I began that quest by calling and sending out letters and notes to people I knew who had some connection to the 49ers front office.

In the process, I discovered that my college roommate's father knew Lou Spadia, who was the president of the 49ers.

Dave Beswick and I played baseball against each other in high school. At Santa Clara, we were teammates on the freshman team and later roommates. It was his dad, Dan, who opened the door. As I was studying in my apartment one afternoon in February, my phone rang.

"Jerry, this is Lou Spadia, president of the San Francisco 49ers. I have heard from everyone except the Pope about you and your desire to see one of our games on the field. Well, I can't do that for you, as there's an NFL policy against it, except for members of the media and photographers. I also don't have any openings here in our front office, as we have just a few employees. But I would like to meet you. Can you come in next Tuesday?" When I hung up the phone, I left law school.

Yes, the very next day I went to the Hastings admissions office with a letter I had typed the night before, explaining that I wanted to take an immediate leave of absence to pursue something in sports. I didn't know what that was, but could I have my seat back in September if things did not work out? They took my letter and said that would be fine. I never went back. I tell young people all the time: when your heart jumps, follow it. When I hung up the phone that day with Lou Spadia, my heart jumped. I knew right then I had to pursue something in sports because that is where I felt I was supposed to be. I am also very big on two words: *no regrets*. I have none about leaving law school the way that I did.

The following week, I went downtown and had a great visit with Mr. Spadia. He was as nice as he could be, introducing me to those in his front office, and I left knowing I had made the right decision: I was going to have a career in sports. In hindsight, I can't believe my good fortune in meeting Mary literally days before suddenly leaving school in the middle of my second semester. We had known each other only a month before I impulsively decided to leave Hastings. I was lucky and blessed to have met someone who has been the rock in our relationship from day one. We were married later that year, in 1971, in Kalamazoo, Michigan, before 300 people. My mother and her husband were there. The other 298 were from Mary's side of the family. That day I got to know a lot of McMorrows, Cagneys, Northams, and Sheridans.

So there I was having just left law school with no job. When I explained to my dad what I had just done, he told me to leave the house. He was angry and upset that I had not told him I was leaving school and that I had not finished my three-year commitment and had nothing to fall back on. My father had been through the Great Depression of 1929. He fought in World War II as a communications officer in the U.S. Navy, aboard the submarine *Guardfish*. He was very good at what he did. I knew what his response would be when I told him I was dropping out, but I also knew I had to leave. I loved sports. I knew there was something out there for me — I just didn't know what.

CHAPTER 4

HANDLING DISAPPOINTMENT

I immediately began to look around for a job in sports. I wanted some gainful work but something I liked, too. As luck would have it, that all fell right into my lap just a few short months after leaving law school. On June 1, 1971, my alma mater, Santa Clara, hired me as their first-ever athletic department fundraiser to run the Bronco Bench Foundation, which encourages the development of well-rounded student athletes at Santa Clara. I thank two key mentors for this opportunity: head football coach Pat Malley, who hired me, and alum Sal Sanfillippo, who loved the Bronco Bench so much that he became their volunteer business manager when he retired. Pat needed some help, and I was at the right place at the right time. That first year I made $8,400. A raise the next year took me to five figures! Making $10,000 seemed like a fortune.

I met a lot of people in my new capacity that summer. I realized that the best approach to meet and greet people as a new and young fundraiser was to take full advantage of Santa Clara's football history. The Broncos had played in the Sugar Bowl in 1937 and 1938 and the Orange Bowl in 1950. There were many SCU grads in the area who had witnessed this history and now had the money to donate to the football program. It didn't take long to put together a fifteen-minute slideshow with so many great black-and-white photographs from those years, taken by the team's legendary trainer Henry Schmidt. I took the show and presented it to all the service clubs in San Jose and Santa Clara. This taught me a lot. I gradually gained confidence in speaking before large groups of people, never dreaming that someday I would be doing that for a living.

One evening in late September, I was at home in our little apartment when I turned on the radio and heard the broadcast of our Santa Clara football game on a small 250-watt station, KPEN-FM. My heart jumped, but not for the reason you might suspect. At once, I began to realize what a plus this could be to a young fundraiser. I could get my name "out there" in my new circles by simply being on our broadcasts to let people know about our program. I envisioned alumni saying, "Jerry, come on in. I just heard you on the radio. Let's talk money for Santa Clara." I was into fundraising and wanted to be the very best.

The games were broadcast by a Santa Clara alum who was an insurance salesman in San Jose. He donated $1,000 each year to the athletic department to be the team's play-by-play announcer. I met with him and explained my idea for boosting our fundraising efforts. Much to my disappointment, the broadcaster said no. I asked him a couple of times as the weeks went by, but I still got no for an answer. Then one day at Buck Shaw Stadium, where our football team was playing, we crossed paths. "Jerry, I know you're disappointed that I am not letting you join me on the radio. But you and I have the same problem: neither of us has a major league voice." I was so surprised at the time, but in hindsight, he was right. It was one of the best things ever said to me in my young life.

The next day and without a trace of anger or resentment, which has never been my style, I went out and bought a tape recorder and a microphone with our wedding funds. My intentions were to try out my voice and call some football and basketball games. For the next two years while I continued to raise funds for the program, I seized every opportunity to sit on top of press boxes or on a folding chair above the field and tape our Bronco football games. During the basketball season, I would be at the end of press row doing the same — all with my best friend, Mike Rewak, whom I "recruited" to be my stats man and security blanket. After each game, I would listen intently to every word back in our apartment. At once, I could hear all the mistakes I was making. In my first-ever taping at one of our basketball games, I distinctly remember saying the name of our point guard "Alan Hale" 41 times in the first half alone. I realized I could substitute "Hale" or "Alan" or "The tall Santa Clara point guard" to add much-needed variety.

I had a decision to make. I had always been a good writer, and a career as a feature writer at *Sports Illustrated* had long been my dream. I could take the journalistic path and find my way to *Sports Illustrated* someday, which would have been fine with me, or I could explore the world of broadcasting, which was the much greater challenge. Remember, I had already been told I didn't have a major league voice; now, listening to myself on tape, I knew I could be better. In Robert Frost's words, I chose the road not taken.

As my two years working at Santa Clara and taping games drew to a close, I asked friends to hear the tapes. All I had were football and basketball tapes; for some reason, I never taped any baseball games. Funny how life goes. One of our basketball coaches at Santa Clara, Dan Fitzgerald, who later became the head basketball coach at Gonzaga University, asked me to play one of my basketball tapes for him. After listening for a few minutes, he turned it off and said, "Jerry, you are very good. It's time to take this around to radio stations and get on radio. You can do it." With that boost of confidence from Dan, that's exactly what I did.

So Good to Be a Logger

I took my tapes to a few local radio stations in the Bay Area, hoping for my "big break." The search included a drive over to Stockton, some 50 miles east of San Francisco, and a visit at KJOY radio, the station that carried the University of Pacific football and basketball games. I envisioned myself happily in that role as a college radio broadcaster, but unfortunately, there were no openings. So I decided to pursue baseball on the radio, starting with the Triple-A Pacific Coast League. I called Phoenix and Tucson and a couple of other teams. Nothing. The Eugene Emeralds were in the league, too, and one of my best friends at Santa Clara, Bob Spence, was on their team.

"Come on up. You and Mary can stay with Pat and me. We will make room for you, even with our young kids running around everywhere." We drove up to Eugene and spent a week there. It opened up the door I needed. Spence had arrived as a freshman with me at Santa Clara and was hailed as "the next Ted Williams, out of San Diego." Bob had the sweetest left-handed swing and power to go with it. Two things stand out from that trip. First, I was finally taping baseball games for Bob's team in Eugene after two years of recording football and basketball games. It felt very comfortable, albeit with some comic relief. I played a call late one night in Bob's apartment after a game, with Bob, Pat, and Mary listening. I did not tell them what was coming. "Here's the pitch to the big left-handed hitting Bob Spence. There's a LONG drive to DEEP right field! Back goes the right fielder to the wall . . . it's GONE! (long pause here) NO! It's off the wall! Spence into second with a double." When Bob heard the call, he burst out laughing. So did the rest of us. We couldn't stop. Bob still has that tape. I gave it to him as a thank you for having us up that week. From humble beginnings. That call taught me to slow down and lag and not get caught up in friendships.

The second thing that stands out from that trip to Eugene is the pivotal role the Emeralds' veteran radio broadcaster, Hal Weimeyer, had in helping to advance my career. Hal had broadcast baseball games for years in the minor leagues. He was friendly and open to my being there with Bob and the team. I told Hal I was looking for an opportunity to start a radio career calling games in the Pacific Coast League. At that time, save for the rare exception, only Triple-A games were broadcast on the radio. There weren't too many opportunities. "Have you called Stan Naccarato, the general manager of the Tacoma Twins? He is on his second radio announcer in the past two years, and I know he still isn't happy with his situation."

Within days, I called Stan and flew to Tacoma, Washington. I spent four days at Cheney Stadium, taping games in the press box with members of Stan's board of directors listening right behind me. At the end of that week, Stan called me in and said the board liked my work. They wanted me to be the team's announcer the next season, in 1974. But because it was late August, he could do nothing for me until the following April. He suggested that I head across town and meet with Doug MacArthur, who was the longtime athletic director at the University of Puget Sound, to see if UPS might hire me in the interim.

Doug and I met in his office in the UPS fieldhouse. He asked to listen to one of my tapes. It was from a Santa Clara basketball game. After a few minutes, he asked me to turn it off. He looked me right in the eyes and said, "Jerry, you are going to be a very good broadcaster." It was music to my ears. Doug wanted me to replace him as the Loggers football and basketball announcer. He no longer had the time to run the department and broadcast all those games, which he had been doing for years. All he asked for in return was that I help him raise money for his athletic department while I used this opportunity to improve behind the microphone. I happily said yes. The following 24 months, I was able to broadcast both UPS and high school football and basketball games as well as two full seasons of Triple-A baseball on the radio. And I was able to help Puget Sound's athletic department grow and prosper. It was a perfect fit.

Before leaving the Bay Area to begin my broadcasting career in Tacoma, I reached out to my dad to tell him the good news. Although only two years earlier he hadn't agreed with my decision and had been disappointed that I didn't consult him before abandoning law school in the middle of my first year with no job prospects in sight, he could now see that I had made the right choice. He gave me a hug with some great advice: "When baseball starts next spring, you call every game as if it were a major league game." I proudly honoured my father by doing just that.

CHAPTER 5

STARTING MY BROADCASTING CAREER

Tacoma turned out to be such a great experience for a young, fledgling broadcaster trying to break into the profession. Mary had just graduated from law school and had found a job as a deputy prosecuting attorney for Pierce County. She thoroughly enjoyed beginning her legal career, and her salary kept us going through those early years. I was only making $250 a month and $25 a game. But it was not about the money. It never is if you are doing something you love to do.

I was so happy to finally get the chance to broadcast games, and on September 3, 1973, I went on the radio for the first time in my life as a play-by-play broadcaster. It was the first football game of the season, billed as "The Sound against the Rock." The Puget Sound Loggers were hosting the fabled Slippery Rock from Pennsylvania. Many who grew up on the west coast, including myself, thought Slippery Rock was a fictitious school. That was certainly not the case. For that team, coming out west was the trip of a lifetime. The two teams were down on the field getting ready for the kickoff before a packed house of some 2,500 fans who poured into the stadium. Up in the stands some 25 rows from the field, I was sitting right next to Doug MacArthur.

It wasn't a radio booth per se, but rather a table in the last row. That didn't matter to me at all. I was ready. The Loggers kicked off to Slippery Rock. Midway through the second quarter, Doug said on the air: "I hope all of you are enjoying your new 'Voice of the Loggers,' Jerry Howarth." I gulped. Every now and then you hear that someone was so nervous they had "an apple in their throat." Well, that day I had an apple in my throat, but I was able to get through that first game without a hitch. To top it all off, Puget Sound beat Slippery Rock. I still have that broadcast, thanks to Marc Blau and the Tacoma Sports Hall of Fame, who found it years later.

In the spring of 1974, I started broadcasting my first Triple-A season at Cheney Stadium for the Tacoma Twins. I smiled when someone told me that all the lights had come from the old Seals Stadium in San Francisco. I had sat under those same lights as a kid with my father, watching the Giants play. It seemed meant to be that I was starting my baseball-broadcasting career under those same bright lights.

During that season, I experienced a moment that still resonates with me today. I called a foul ball down the left-field line and paused. Right then, I heard a voice in my head say, "Without me, this is meaningless." I called the rest of that game and went home that night with those few words still echoing in my head. The next morning, I got in my car and drove downtown. I went into a quiet and empty church and dropped to my knees, thanking God for speaking to me the night before. I made a promise to myself that for the rest of my career, wherever it took me, I would offer up each broadcast to Him. It's a promise that I continue to honour.

Another memorable on-air moment took place that season, but it was a lot lighter. My first blooper. I had filled up many notebooks with words to build my vocabulary, trying to use just the right word at just the right time. Words like *azure* for a special coloured sky, *pandemonium* for a crowd's reaction, or looking around at a ballpark filled with kids in their various team uniforms and seeing a *kaleidoscope of colours*. Then there was this: "Left-handed hitting Bobby Jones at the plate for Spokane. Here's the pitch. It's lined up the gap into left-centre field. Centre fielder Randy Beach races over. He dives headlong and can't quite make the catch as he's lying motionless on the field. The ball goes all the way to the wall. Bobby Jones pulls into second with a double as Randy Beach lies prostate in left-centre field." Whoops.

The next night, as I was going up the stands to the radio booth, this little girl came running over to me.

"Are you Jerry Howarth, the Tacoma Twins announcer?"

I proudly thrust out my chest. "Yes, I am."

"My dad thinks you're hilarious."

Sometimes you can broadcast a blooper and not even know it. I came home one night after a game only to hear Mary laughing.

"What's so funny?"

"I heard you talking about all the promotions coming up this weekend and then you finished by saying: 'So tomorrow, come on out early and pick your seat.' I could just picture all those fans picking their seats."

I have not used that particular phrase since.

Recreating Games

That first season calling Twins games brought me a surprise. I was told that I would be recreating all 72 road games. There wasn't enough money to cover my expenses, so the Twins would go on the road while I remained back in the station. I was disappointed. I felt like I would be broadcasting only half the season, which would hurt my development, let alone the fact that I had never recreated games before.

If a game started at 7 p.m., we would go on the radio at 7:30 p.m. We had a stringer on site at each game who would write down the result of each at-bat and then call Connie Hill at our station to tell her what happened. I would then recreate those at-bats. After the first game, it dawned on me that I needed some ballpark sounds. I bought two small wooden souvenir bats to click together whenever there was a ball put in play, I brought in my own tape recorder with organ music to play during pitching changes, I looped a crowd noise in the background for ball-park ambience, and I gently reminded our engineers not to bring up a cheering crowd when the Twins scored because we were the visitors.

Recreating those 72 games was the best thing that could have happened to me as a young announcer. It taught me to ad lib, think on the fly, make adjustments within the course of a game, let the crowd noise come in for long periods of time when the other team scored, and have inflection in my voice. I had to try to see the game in my own mind. This was truly a radio classroom that I wouldn't trade for anything. It was the only year I had to recreate games, and what I got out of it was priceless. The following season, I cut a deal with our radio station and our local newspaper. I would broadcast all the road games, then, after the games, I would write all the game stories and send them back to the *Tacoma News Tribune*. I gave all the money I made from the newspaper to our station to pay for my road expenses. I was able to call all 144 games live during my second season. It was well worth it.

Painting Pictures for Ginny Redfield

During the summer of 1975, in my second season with Tacoma, we arrived in Phoenix, Arizona, to play the San Francisco Giants' top farm club. The Phoenix Giants always had a good team and this year was no exception. Being from San Francisco I was looking forward to making this first trip into the desert. Before the game as I was preparing for the broadcast, I heard the organist playing some great songs. Because there was no enclosed radio booth, I could see there was a gentleman sitting right beside her as she played. I went over to both and introduced myself.

Ginny Redfield had been playing the organ for the fans for years. She was blind and really enjoyed going to all the games throughout the season. Her husband, John, was retired and enjoyed watching the Giants and listening to Ginny play. During our conversation, Ginny asked, "Jerry, would it be all right with you if John brings me over to sit next to you once the game starts, so I can hear you call your innings? Then I'll come back and play between the innings?"

Ginny sat next to me for the 10 games Tacoma played that year in Phoenix and for the following three years when I came in with our Salt Lake City teams. She loved hearing the games, and I enjoyed painting the pictures for her. "The right-hander goes into his windup to face the left-handed hitter," or "There's a foul ball that sails over the first-base dugout into the crowd about five rows up, caught by a big burly fan with his bare right hand!"

I would name the position of the player for her instead of just saying a player's name. "There's a ground ball up the middle, fielded by second baseman Billy Smith, who turns and throws to first for the out." I wanted Ginny to see the movement of the ball off the bat. "That ball is lined down the left-field line, hooking into the corner fair by a foot for a base hit!" or "A ball blooped softly into shallow right-centre field just dropping in for a base hit." I had no idea how beneficial this later would be in my profession. Those calls for Ginny then are still my calls today for everyone else.

My Mentor Don Hill

Looking back over my two years in Tacoma, there was one gentleman who took me under his wing like a son. He shared with me daily his thoughts and ideas. After listening to my every word the night before, he would give me his constructive criticism the following morning. He made me so much better. His name was Don Hill. His wife, Connie, had helped me with the recreations during my first broadcasting season. After a long and distinguished career broadcasting Triple-A games in Louisville, Kentucky, he had come out to Tacoma to broadcast Tacoma Giants games from 1960 to 1965. Then he spent six more seasons with the Tacoma Cubs before he retired. From the first day we met, Don and I formed a loving and caring friendship that lasted until the day I was at his bedside in Tacoma when he passed away. Although in his 60 years calling minor league games, he had filled in for only three big league games for the St. Louis Cardinals, Don was grateful for all the games he did call rather than resentful for the major league games he did not call. But he saw something in me that perhaps he knew he didn't have, and I appreciated how he taught me the fundamentals.

When I finally made it to the Blue Jays as their full-time broadcaster in 1982, I called Don and told him we did it together and that I couldn't have done it without him. He was so happy for me and told me that while he never made it to the major leagues, my games would be his games.

CHAPTER 6

A GLIMPSE INTO THE FUTURE

At the end of my second season in Tacoma, I found out that the Triple-A Salt Lake Gulls assistant general manager, Sammy Gehring, had had a stroke and could not continue in his job. The team was looking for help. I felt this could be an opening to both work full-time for a team and be their radio broadcaster. The Salt Lake City opportunity was a blessing in so many ways, and I have Tom Sommers to thank for that. Tom was the Angels' farm director back in 1975. He happened to be in Salt Lake City one day when the Gulls hosted the Tacoma Twins for a series. There were no radio booths at that time in the small press boxes. You just sat among the writers and you broadcast.

As luck would have it and unbeknownst to me, Tom stood right behind me for five days, listening to my broadcasts. At the end of that series, he introduced himself and told me I had a career in broadcasting. He told me to keep working at it and stay patient, and that someday I would realize my dreams of becoming a major league broadcaster. I thanked him for his encouragement and told him I would stay in touch. When the sudden opening came up in Salt Lake, it was Sommers who called owner Art Teece. Tom told Art he had a person in mind who could both help run the team with Art's son-in-law, Rainer Krowas, and broadcast all the games. Soon after that, Art called me in Tacoma and offered me the job.

Mary and I immediately packed up and moved to Salt Lake City. From this point forward, baseball would also go hand-in-hand with family. I would start not only my third year as a broadcaster, but also my first year as a dad. We had signed up for adoption with Catholic Charities as soon as we moved to Salt Lake City. Within 10 months, we were blessed with our first child, a week-old baby boy whom we named Benjamin George, born October 3, 1976. Twenty months later, we welcomed our second week-old baby boy, Joseph Michael, born June 26, 1978. While raising our two sons, Mary also worked for the Utah attorney general during our six years in Salt Lake City. It was work she enjoyed and where she made many friends.

Salt Lake provided me with a wonderful opportunity to help run a Triple-A team. The work included lining up in-game promotions, licensing billboard and radio advertisements, selling tickets, and broadcasting the games on KALL radio, one of the top stations in the market. The previous season, the Gulls had drawn just 70,000 fans. In 1976, the team won 90 games to reach the Pacific Coast League Championship Series, drawing a franchise-record 240,000 fans. Art Teece was named the *Sporting News* Minor League Executive of the Year.

The winter meetings that year were in Los Angeles. Part of that week included a dinner at Angels Stadium in Anaheim, where the Angels honoured Art for his achievement. I had the pleasure of flying over to be a part of that. I met the legendary singing cowboy and Angels owner, Gene Autry. What a thrill to talk to someone I had seen so many times on television. He was a gentle soul who was so happy to be in baseball. Before the dinner as everyone was milling around and mingling, I quietly slipped out of the room and made my way to the third floor, where the broadcast booths were located. Luckily, I found an attendant who was still working, and I asked him if he would let me into the home radio booth so I could see what it looked like. He said sure and to take my time. I walked in and went straight to the front row and sat down where I knew Dick Enberg and Don Drysdale called the Angels games on radio. It was a beautiful night with a full moon overhead. I remember it like it was yesterday. For five minutes, I quietly sat there, looking out over the field. "I can do this. Someday, I will call major league games right here." Six years later in 1982, I did just that — one booth over to the left.

Applying for the Blue Jays Job

As I hit the ground running with the Triple-A Salt Lake City Gulls in 1976, major league baseball announced the addition of two teams to the American League. The state of Washington would soon welcome its first major league club, the Seattle Mariners, located just a short distance away from Tacoma and my former Triple-A radio job. That other expansion team getting ready for the 1977 season was the Toronto Blue Jays. But it was the major league opportunity in Seattle that really excited me: Tacoma is a small city just outside Seattle, much like Hamilton is to Toronto. With that, I felt very confident I would get that job. I realize now, of course, that I was way too naive thinking that Seattle was a shoo-in for me to begin my major league career.

You can imagine, however, how excited I was when I interviewed for the job with Mariners general manager Lou Gorman. In our conversation, he was as nice as he could be. He also very nicely told me that I was not chosen for the job. I was so crestfallen and disappointed as I sat in our living room in disbelief. Mary looked at me. "I think you should apply to that other team."

I said, "No, I am not interested." I had put all my eggs in one basket and couldn't see past that.

Mary repeated her suggestion with a little more earnestness. "I really think you should apply to that other team."

"Okay," I said. "Where is Toronto? Where's our atlas?"

She laughed and said, "It's downstairs. Go get it." When I opened it up, I immediately went to the back and started to go down the list of cities alphabetically until I got to the letter T. It read: Toronto, Ont., Canada. I had no idea what the Ont. stood for, but I did know where Canada was. Now I had my instructions, turning to page 195 and running my finger to D4 and down to No. 3. There was Toronto. I glanced to the opposite page and saw Salt Lake City. I closed the atlas. "No, I'm not going there. It's too far away, and it's in another country."

Mary laughed out loud. She was very familiar with Toronto and Canada. She was born and raised in Kalamazoo, Michigan, not too far from Toronto. Here I was showing my ignorance, having spent way too many hours growing up playing sports instead of paying attention in the classroom. "Okay. I will send my tape and resume to this new Blue Jays team." One day, a month later, I was sitting down on the sofa, sorting through our mail. Much to my surprise, I saw a yellow envelope with HEWPEX Sports Network in the upper left-hand corner with Toronto, Ont. beneath it. By this time I knew what the Ont. stood for. My heart jumped again. Always a good sign.

"We hope you are the Jerry Howarth who sent the Blue Jays a tape and resume. The Blue Jays sent us your tape, which we really liked. But the paperwork somehow got lost. Could you please send us more about yourself." It was signed Len Bramson and Sue Rayson. I jumped off the sofa and yelled to Mary: "It's me!" The next day I sent my resume and background to HEWPEX and waited. It took another month before I received another HEWPEX envelope. There was an announcement inside. The network had signed Tom Cheek and Early Wynn to be the Blue Jays radio broadcasters for the 1977 season. There was a note at the bottom from Sue. "Thanks for sending your information, Jerry. Please keep in touch."

I did not hear from Sue again for three and a half years.

Basketball and the Utah Pros

Three seasons broadcasting Salt Lake Gulls games gave me five full seasons of Triple-A radio play-by-play experience. I felt it was time to branch out and expand my resume. Other broadcasters were moving to the major leagues with a lot more experience in other areas than I had. As fate would have it, there was a new team on the block that summer in 1978. A brand new Western Basketball Association League had just been founded that included a team in Salt Lake City called the Utah Pros. Its new owner was a gentleman from Salt Lake named Bill Maxwell.

Bill and I hit it off immediately. He was thrilled with his new basketball team that would now play out of the Salt Palace in downtown Salt Lake, but Bill did not have any experience running a sports team. I asked him if he would consider letting me take on some of the duties as an assistant general manager and be the team's radio broadcaster, too. He quickly said yes. The WBA was like the Continental Basketball Association, where players had one more opportunity to prove they could cut it in the NBA. The team travelled to cities I had never been to before, from Las Vegas to much smaller Great Falls, Montana. That's where I met an up-and-coming young coach who was just getting started. His name was George Karl.

The Pros had a very good first season, drawing thousands of fans to the Salt Palace. I was so happy with another year on the radio and was already looking forward to the next year. What's more, there would be a little magic to end my first season in basketball. Because Bill was the owner of the Utah Pros, he had access to four seats and two floor passes to see that year's 1978–79 NCAA Final Four, played in Salt Lake City at the Special Events Centre. Yes, THAT Final Four! Larry Bird and the Indiana State Sycamores against Earvin "Magic" Johnson and his Michigan State Spartans. I sat with Bill and his family Saturday afternoon as Bird and company beat a very good DePaul team coached by the legendary Ray Meyer. Then we saw the Spartans beat Pennsylvania. On Monday night with my floor pass, I stood right under the basket as Michigan State defeated Indiana State, 75–64, dealing Indiana State its only loss all season. The Sycamores were 33-0. Magic had a game-high 24 points while Bird scored 19. What a memory. What an NCAA Championship game. Bird and Magic.

Chance to Broadcast Oakland A's Games

During my season with the Pros, I took an impromptu flight to Oakland that almost landed me my first major league job. I had heard from friends in the Bay Area that the Oakland A's were looking for a third announcer to join veteran play-by-play man Red Rush and his partner Hal Ramey for the 1980 season. Hal was also the MLS's (Major League Soccer) San Jose Earthquakes radio broadcaster, and there was an overlap between his two seasons. I called the station that carried the A's games on KXRX radio in San Jose and told them I would like to talk to them about the possibility of filling the role of third announcer at their station. They said fine. With a break in my Pros schedule, I flew to San Jose where I sat down with Red Rush to discuss the major league opportunity.

Red was very cordial and friendly. We had a good 30-minute chat about his background and the situation they were facing for the upcoming season with Hal, and how I might fit in. He liked my broadcasting background in the Pacific Coast League. He mentioned that I was the only candidate for the job. Red told me to come back tomorrow and we would work out the details. I was so happy. I could see myself commuting to Oakland and other cities, getting my break to start what might be a very long run as a broadcaster where I had grown up.

I went to see Red the next day and sat right across from him in his office. He held in his hand a yellow legal pad. On it he had written down the 40 games that Hal could not make due to his soccer commitment. He handed me the pad to review. "Jerry, here are the 40 games where there is a conflict with Hal's schedule. But Hal has just told me that he will take red-eye flights and crisscross the country to do all 40 of these games along with his soccer games. We won't be needing a third broadcaster." I could not believe what I had just heard. I left his office and KXRX, got in my rental car, and drove away. Within about 500 yards of the station, I pulled off to the side of the road and stopped the car. I cried my eyes out for about half an hour. The job had actually been handed to me and then taken away.

I will say this: three years later, in 1982, when I made my inaugural trip to the Oakland Coliseum as a major league announcer with the Blue Jays, the first person who came up to me to say hello was Hal Ramey. I knew that he felt badly for what he had done to me three years earlier. Hal knew he could have easily let me do those 40 games and still been very happy calling all the others. Without saying it, he was apologizing to me, and I accepted his apology. We'd see each other every time the Blue Jays were in Oakland. Hal Ramey is a good man.

Working for the Utah Jazz

Right after our Utah Pros season was over, Bill Maxwell came into my office and closed the door. "Jerry, we are out of business," he said. "Tomorrow, the New Orleans Jazz are announcing that they are moving here to Salt Lake City to become the Utah Jazz. Their general manager, Frank Layden, will be holding a news conference here tomorrow at the Salt Palace to make the announcement and answer any questions. I would like to have you there with me to take it all in." I was shocked and so disappointed. Yes, an NBA team was coming to our city. But we had our own team that was off to such a great start. Both Bill and I were new to professional basketball, but now it was over just as quickly as it had started.

I met Frank the next day and liked him immediately. Who didn't? Frank was as likeable as they came and blessed with a very keen insight into basketball. He was the head coach at Niagara University for years. Later, he was the Atlanta Hawks' assistant head coach. He had such a great sense of humour.

No one told stories like Frank Layden. For the next couple of months, Frank asked me to take him all around Salt Lake City to meet the people. He spoke in front of service groups and formal gatherings everywhere to introduce the city to its new team. Meanwhile, a whole new cast of young employees came in from out of town to run the team in its first season. I was not invited to join them in their front office.

Selfishly, I had visions of perhaps being the new Jazz radio announcer. I liked my chances, having just called an entire season with the Pros. When I asked Frank about that, he told me that Hot Rod Hundley, who had had a very good career in the NBA and was the Jazz radio announcer in New Orleans, was coming to Salt Lake with the team and would keep his old job. It was time once again for me to move on. Fred Ball was the director of the Salt Lake City Chamber of Commerce, and he knew me well. Fred invited me to have lunch with him to discuss the possibility of joining him to work for the Chamber in economic development. After meeting him and seeing both his enthusiasm to hire me and how good the job looked, I said yes. Thus began what I thought would be a career at the Salt Lake City Chamber of Commerce, meeting and helping new business leaders come to Salt Lake and become acquainted with the city and the state of Utah.

Six months later, I was enjoying my new job immensely when Fred came into my office and closed the door. I immediately thought of Bill Maxwell, who had just done that earlier in the year. *What now?* "Jerry, Frank Layden is in my office. He told me they made a mistake not hiring someone locally. He wants to speak to you about working for the Jazz. After you took him around town earlier this year, he thinks you would be perfect for their organization."

I was very firm in my reply. "No. I am happy here and love my job. I've been here for only six months, but I can easily see staying here with you for the rest of my career."

Fred was very understanding. "I think you should talk to him, then make your decision."

I said okay. We got up and went into Fred's office. Frank thanked me for considering his request and asked to have lunch with me and Jazz owner Sam Battistone to talk about my working for the Jazz. I was moved that the owner was going to be brought in to try to make this happen.

At our lunch, I found Sam to be very cordial. Frank told me my new job would be group sales director, and I would be the only local person hired. He knew how many contacts I had made over my years in Salt Lake City, and the Jazz needed that link to the community. I was still hesitant about moving from the Chamber to the Jazz and I told them I would think it over and get back to them.

Within the week Frank invited me over to his house to meet his family. In our conversation, he told me how much he loved baseball and that he had heard from so many people about my baseball broadcasts and the very real possibilities I had to call major league games. Frank then said something to me that turned my thinking completely around: "Jerry, I know you love your work at the Chamber. And I know being our group sales director isn't exactly the job you see as ideal for you. But remember this: if you take this job with us, you are back in the sports mainstream. The longer you stay out of sports, the less and less your chances are of reaching what you really want to do."

As I left his house, I realized he was right. By the time I drove back home, I had made the decision to leave the Chamber and work for the Jazz.

One of the real perks of being the group sales director that 1979–80 season was that I got to sit courtside right under the Jazz basket. I remember seeing Celtics rookie Larry Bird receive a pass in the corner. He quickly looked down at the brand new three-point arc, where his right foot was on the line. Bird paused, slid his right foot back a few inches, looked back up, and drained a three. Awesome. His teammate Chris Ford was credited with making the first-ever three in NBA history that season.

The Jazz had the great veteran Pistol Pete Maravich and Adrian Dantley, a young star out of Notre Dame. It was so interesting to speak with Pete. He would give me his undivided attention, talking about his views on nutrition and religion. His philosophy of life was unique and pretty esoteric. Adrian was quieter and worked hard each day to be able to compete. He was not the tallest or biggest player on the court by far, but he was strong and he was dedicated. After the season ended, I pursued something that I had never done before in my young career: I would be working for a radio station.

KWMS Radio

Dave Blackwell was a longtime sports writer for the *Deseret News* in Salt Lake. We had known each other for years as he covered all sports including the Gulls and the Jazz. He was very likeable and this came across on radio, where he hosted an hour-long sports talk show Monday through Friday from 6 p.m. to 7 p.m. on KWMS radio. But after a year, he told me he was leaving to go back to writing full time and asked if I would like to host that show. I quickly said yes. Dave introduced me to Tex Williams, a young man running his family-owned station that led to the call letters KWMS. Tex offered me a full-time job reporting on all sports during the newscasts in the city weekdays from 4 p.m. to 6 p.m. and then hosting the talk show right after that. I told him that I would love the job and asked if the call-in format for the talk show could be expanded so that I could interview guests each night and field the incoming calls for them. Tex liked the concept, and it wasn't long before the show went to 90 minutes. We had guests from the four universities in Utah: athletic directors, coaches from every sport, all kinds of players. As my own producer, I was also able to line up my own guests and interview the likes of Arnold Palmer, Ted Turner, boxer Gene Fullmer, and members of the Utah Jazz. I even had Caitlyn Jenner come into the studio for a full show, talking with our audience about her Olympic win in the decathlon.

That Sports Central show taught me how to interview people by simply listening to them. The better you are as a listener, the better your interview is going to be. Short, simple follow-up questions are the key to highlighting your guest. Sounds simple. But you have to do it. It was an important part of my career development. During my tenure, I also conducted a competition to recruit three young men for a Friday-night trivia panel. I wanted to connect more with our audience, so if you called in and stumped the panel, you were halfway to winning two tickets to see the Jazz. Then if the panel gave you a question and you answered it correctly, you won the tickets. After my final show, before my move to Toronto, I took all three out to dinner. It was bitterly cold outside as we walked across the street to the restaurant. One of the three had just a shirt on with no sweater or jacket. "You must be so cold," I said. "Where are you from?" The answer: "Winnipeg." I laughed out loud, not realizing just how apropos that answer was. Within a very short time, I would be Canada-bound and visiting Winnipeg with the Blue Jays caravan in January. I stood at the corner of Portage and Main. It was FREEZING!

First Major League Broadcast

In June 1980, I was doing some sound work in production at KWMS when the phone rang. I picked it up and heard a woman's voice say something that included the words: Baseball, Detroit, Early Wynn, and "Would you like to call three Blue Jays games over the upcoming July 4th weekend?" I honestly thought it was a joke.

"Who is this? What did you just say?"

"Jerry, my name is Sue Rayson with the HEWPEX Sports Network. We talked back in 1976. Tom Cheek's partner, Early Wynn, is going to an old-timers' game at Dodger Stadium next month. We would like to fly you to Detroit and have you join Tom at Tiger Stadium to broadcast the July 4th weekend games."

Sue took a few minutes to mention that she remembered when I'd first applied for the position back in 1976. She noted how much they'd enjoyed my tape and later my background information. Plus, as luck would have it, in 1980, the Blue Jays hired former Salt Lake Gulls manager Jimy Williams as their third-base coach. Sue and Len Bramson immediately reached out to Jimy to ask about me, and Jimy gave me a glowing recommendation, telling them how well he knew me as both a person and a broadcaster. Jimy helped me so much with the "break" that all young announcers in the minor leagues need to reach the next level.

Sure enough, a month later, on Friday, July 4, 1980, there I was on the field at Tiger Stadium meeting Tom Cheek, who promptly handed me a tape recorder. "Go find a pregame interview for our broadcast tonight." That was an easy call. I had just spent five years in the Pacific Coast League getting to know so many young players who, like me, all wanted to make it to the major leagues. My very first major league interview that night was with Roy Lee Howell. Roy had played third base for the Texas Rangers Triple-A Spokane club, where we first met in 1974. He was now the expansion Blue Jays third baseman. With that, my major league career began.

I was nervous that Friday night doing the play-by-play and am not embarrassed to admit it. Excitement and adrenaline were flowing. I got through my innings okay, but I was disappointed that it was not the real me. The next night I was much more comfortable doing the game and the play-by-play, but I still felt it was not the natural me at the microphone. I honestly began to wonder, if this was what it was going to be like at this level, perhaps I wasn't cut out for it.

But on Sunday afternoon — and for some reason, I have always enjoyed calling day games over night games, and don't ask me why — I broadcast that game with Tom like I had for five years in Triple-A. It came with my easy and natural flow. I was so happy. I knew then that I could broadcast major league games if given the chance. I did not need a plane to fly back home to Utah that night: I just sat in my seat, closed my eyes, and took off, reliving every moment of that wonderful weekend. All the work and preparation had paid off.

CHAPTER 7

TIME TO PINCH MYSELF

The 1982 season marked the beginning of my first full season as the Blue Jays radio broadcaster. I had broadcast the three games in Detroit in 1980, then 20 more games in 1981 with both Tom and Early. How things worked out at the end of the 1981 season couldn't have made me happier: the Blue Jays hired me full time and the Chicago White Sox offered Early a two-year radio broadcast contract. My transition into the Blue Jays job was a lot more gratifying knowing that Early was still going to call games on the radio. I first met him over dinner with my wife, Mary, Len Bramson, and Sue Rayson. We all got together at a downtown Toronto hotel before the 1981 season started. During the conversation, I asked Early how he got his name. He went on to talk about how his parents had met and fallen in love and had him out of wedlock and then married about a year later. Thus the name Early. I was touched by that story. Out of sheer curiosity, I wanted to know a little bit more. "What was your father's name?"

"Early."

Like father, like son.

My first spring training in 1982 was all brand new. I was just so happy to be a major league announcer. The first person I met was television broadcaster Tony Kubek. Tony was an outstanding baseball analyst working with Don Chevrier. Tony took me under his wing and shared so much of his baseball knowledge. He talked to me about a good work ethic and why it was so important to be prepared each and every day to inform and entertain the audience. Tony had fun every day, too, and that did not go unnoticed by me. He was a great mentor for a rookie broadcaster.

Bobby Cox

The next person I met that spring was new manager Bobby Cox, who made an immediate impression on me. It was no surprise later to see Bobby — who always deflected the credit to his players and protected them mightily from the media — ushered into the Hall of Fame at Cooperstown. For years I have enjoyed doing the manager's show. Bobby was the first. He couldn't have been nicer helping this young broadcaster get started. People would walk by before we did the show, teasing him.

"Hey, Bobby, how much are they paying you?"

His answer made me laugh: "Only twelve dollars a show. Jerry makes all the money!"

Bobby had a way of making you laugh and lightening the mood to get you to relax. But he also could be very firm with his players, demanding that they play hard and work hard at all times. Every player respected Bobby, and for good reason. He played everybody. He made everyone feel they were a significant part of the 25-man roster. He did that in great part by platooning players. He was one of the first managers in the game along with Orioles manager Earl Weaver to really take that to the next level. Right-handed hitting Garth Iorg and left-handed hitting Rance Mulliniks did so well platooning at third base over Bobby's years, they were dubbed "Mullinorg." Cox would use that platoon system as early as the 2nd or 3rd inning. If the other team switched pitchers from right to left or vice versa, Bobby made his move right then. Garth and Rance really appreciated that because they always knew they would be in the game and trusted Bobby's consistency throughout.

Buck Martinez (R) and Ernie Whitt (L) were the two catchers who platooned, and GM Pat Gillick agreed with Bobby's strategy, saying, "Buck and Ernie probably formed one of the best one-two combinations in baseball." Bobby not only maximized their abilities but kept the two veterans strong for the entire 162-game schedule working behind the plate. Another platoon tandem featured young right-handed hitting Jesse Barfield with the veteran left-handed hitting Hosken Powell. Bobby was so good for Jesse in his transition from a platoon player to one of the game's best right fielders.

For years, after calling the 7th and 8th innings, I would leave the radio booth and go down to our dugout to conduct the postgame show. Tom would throw it down to me for the interviews. This allowed me to be privy to some great insights. One cold night at Exhibition Stadium, the Blue Jays were in a very close game, down by a run in the bottom of the 9th inning. They had a runner called out at first base by veteran umpire Bill Kunkel. Bobby was furious. He immediately sprinted toward Kunkel from the third-base dugout, but as soon as Bobby got to first base, he quickly turned around and ran back across the field to the dugout. The next hitter flied out, and the Blue Jays lost.

As Bobby was leaving the field, I asked him why he returned to the dugout so quickly. "When I got to first base and before I could say a word he told me, 'Bobby, I'm sorry. I missed the call.' I said 'Thank you, Bill. I appreciate you saying that,' and I came back to the dugout. That's all I wanted to know."

Meeting Ernie Harwell

Another one of my lasting memories from that first spring training occurred before a game against the Detroit Tigers. The Tigers had bussed over from Lakeland to play that day in Dunedin at what was then called Grant Field. I was in the Tigers dugout taking down their lineup when I felt a tap on my shoulder and turned around.

"Hello, Jerry. I'm Ernie Harwell. Welcome to the major leagues and the Blue Jays." I can still hear his distinctive voice saying those words. From that day forward, this legendary and gentle Christian man shared his life with me. I saw the goodness in him, the ease he had around other people, and his love for what he did on the radio. He had no ego whatsoever. For all of his greatness and Hall of Fame career, he could also laugh at himself.

The following spring Ernie and his wife, Lulu, invited our family over to their house in Dunedin. Ben was six, and Joe was four. We were all sitting in the living room and as I was talking with Lulu, I looked over and saw little Joe with Mary at the sofa. He was crying.

"What's wrong, Joe? Why are you crying?"

Joe was very direct. "Where's Ernie?"

Mary said, "Right over there," as she pointed across the room.

Joe looked back at Ernie and started crying even more. "No. Where's Bert and Ernie?" All day Joe had thought he was going to meet Bert and Ernie from *Sesame Street*.

Ernie's immediate reply was priceless. "Miss Mary, Joe's not the first one disappointed upon meeting Ernie Harwell." That was classic Ernie. Years later, I was on my computer at my mother-in-law's place when Ernie's name popped up on my instant messages. "Betty, what would you like to say to Ernie?" She was quick to respond. "Hi, Ernie, this is Betty. I am Jerry's eighty-three-year-old mother-in-law." Ernie's answer was instantaneous. "Hi, Betty, this is Ernie. I always like playing with kids my own age."

That spring, I was in for another special treat when the Dodgers made the long drive across the Florida panhandle from their facility in Vero Beach for a game against the Blue Jays. As Tom and I were preparing for the broadcast in our tiny little radio booth, who should squeeze by us on his way to the Dodgers booth but legendary Vin Scully, calling the game back to Los Angeles. He nudged his way by us in his own inimitable way, saying, "I've never been in a confessional at a ballpark before."

Calling spring games with Tom was fun, and he made it very easy from the start. Tom told me to come into his innings whenever I wanted, and he would do the same in mine. Our boss, Len Bramson, decided that I would call the 3rd, 4th, 7th, and 8th innings, for which I was grateful. That opportunity allowed me to work not only four innings, but the 8th inning in particular. It so often dictates the outcome of the game. I was feeling more and more comfortable. "Tom and Jerry" had a nice ring to it.

The Coaches

There is a lot of work that goes on during spring training, especially by the coaches, but standing at the batting cage with the hitting coach can be very informal, and it's where I got to know Cito Gaston. Bobby Cox had come over from the Atlanta organization to manage the Blue Jays and brought Cito with him. Cito had been Atlanta's minor league hitting instructor. He played 11 years in the major leagues: six with the San Diego Padres and five with Atlanta. He was quiet and observant and a good communicator. For years, I would stand beside him and learn something new every day. Cito would wait for just the right time to reach out to teach or make a suggestion to a certain hitter or share a personal experience from his youth. It was always positive.

Early on, I asked Cito about his own philosophy on life. He had grown up in the South, where it wasn't at all easy being African-American. His playing career wasn't easy either. Yet throughout, he always stayed positive in good times and bad. He had a great outlook: "You are where you're supposed to be." That is my philosophy, too. It allows you to relax under trying circumstances and to find peace within yourself at that very moment. You can't change things that happen to you that are out of your control, but you can learn to deal with those changes in the most positive way. So simple and yet so powerful.

Jimy Williams capped off his minor league career in 1979 by managing Salt Lake to the Triple-A Pacific Coast League Championship. His overall success managing and coaching in the minor leagues led to his hiring as the Blue Jays' third-base coach the following season. Jimy "One M," as he was often called due to the unusual spelling of his first name, was an excellent manager. I saw that firsthand in Salt Lake. He was a knowledgeable instructor, a terrific in-game manager, and one of the best third-base coaches in the game. Jimy was light, had a great sense of humour, and had the ability to make it fun. In the heat of the moment, he might look a player right in the eye, take out his false teeth, leaving a big gap in his mouth, and then spin his cap around backwards before he delivered his message. He was able to defuse a tense situation with his antics to get a player's attention, so he could then impart his considerable baseball wisdom to make that player and the team better. As I watched Jimy in his three seasons in Salt Lake, I felt he would become one the game's best managers.

Al Widmar was the Blue Jays' pitching coach. He had been coaching for quite a while and had a wealth of baseball knowledge. Al could teach the game to any young pitching staff. Like Jimy, he also had a good sense of humour. You have to have that to be successful at the major league level as a player, a manager, and a coach. Al also was a presence on the Blue Jays winter caravan. He would continually have the entire room laughing with his oftentimes blue humour.

The last coach for me to meet was bullpen coach John Sullivan, from New York. Sully was all baseball. He had a no-nonsense approach and steadfast ways of competing both individually as well as on a team. Do it the right way or get out. John was a former catcher and a great instructor. It was all business for Sully, but that is what baseball is at the major league level. It's a business. The sense of humour is important, but it's a business first. Everyone quickly learns that. Some the hard way. John was the perfect complement to a coaching staff.

School Work First

During this 1982 season, I was very lucky to meet one of the kindest men in the game. Cleveland manager Dave Garcia. When I first met Dave at a game in Cleveland, I told him my wife and I had two young boys who were about to start their education. "My wife, Carmen, and I have five children. They are all university graduates," he said.

I said, "That is so good. You two must be so proud."

"We sure are, and here's why. No one in our two family histories had ever graduated from high school, let alone university. We had to leave school early to make ends meet. I told Carmen when we first got married, we would change that. Not only would we have high school graduates but college graduates, too. From the first grade on, we told our kids that when they got home from school and after a snack they had to go to their rooms for an hour to do their homework. After that, they could go out and play with their friends. Of course, we both laughed when the kids said, 'We don't have any homework.' And they were right. It was the first grade. So we said, 'Then you read for an hour in your room.' They did that from the first grade on and developed a love for reading. That one hour in first grade later led to two and three hours a day as their education continued. Studying became like breathing for them. It was all so natural once they developed the early discipline."

When I got home from that road trip, I told Mary about my conversation with Dave. "We are going to do that exact same thing in our house next year, when our boys start first grade." We did that for years. It worked out pretty well. Ben graduated from Purdue in 2000, and Joe from Notre Dame the following year.

CHAPTER 8

THE MAJOR LEAGUES

It was Friday, April 9, 1982, the home opener against the Milwaukee Brewers, managed by Buck Rodgers. Although Exhibition Stadium was frigid and windy that day, the Brewers' bats were as hot as a July day. They scored six runs in the very first inning, knocking out starter Mark Bomback, who could get only one out. Four relievers followed. The Brewers scored seven more runs in the 6th inning to seal the deal and close the fridge door. Final Score: Brewers 15, Blue Jays 4, in Bobby Cox's first game managing his new team. It is noteworthy that Bobby did not get ejected. He would finish his distinguished Hall of Fame career with a major league record 158 ejections plus three more in the postseason. He knew when to pick his battles, and this was not one of them.

In the Brewers' Opening Day lineup were three players of note: Paul Molitor, Robin Yount, and Jim Gantner. That trio played together in Milwaukee for a major league record 15 years before the Yankees trio of Derek Jeter, Jorge Posada and Mariano Rivera would pass them. Molitor would laugh and tell me about his days with Gantner and how funny he was without ever realizing it. Gantner was much like Yogi Berra, who would say the funniest things and then wonder why so many people were laughing.

Molitor told me about the time Gantner was warming up with Yount when all of a sudden Yount switched his glove from one hand to the other and began throwing left-handed. Gantner was so surprised: "Hey, Robin, I didn't know you were amphibious." Or the time Yount was at shortstop and Gantner at second when, with one out, a double-play ball was hit to Yount. He went to throw to second, but there was no Gantner, so he threw to first for the one out. The next hitter promptly grounded out to third to end the inning. "Jimmy, where were you on that double play ball?"

Gantner again answered like Yogi: "I'm sorry, Robin. I guess I got a case of ambrosia."

There was one more person who really stood out for me on the field that day. He had spent his formative years in the Pacific Coast League just like I had. That was first-base umpire Vic Voltaggio.

Over my five years in the Pacific Coast League, I had made a point of visiting all the umpires before games. I wanted to get to know them — talk with them about their families, find out where they grew up — and learn the rules from them. They turned out to be great teachers and friends. It was a terrific learning experience. It allowed me to understand the umpire's stance on many decisions, which, from the subjective and hostile perspective of the home crowd, were deemed to be missed calls when, in fact, the umpire got it right. Are umpires going to miss calls? Sure. But they are real people with real feelings. They work just as hard as the players and broadcasters do in order to maximize their abilities at the major league level. They deserve the benefit of the doubt. Vic and I were friends for years. It was good to see him rewarded with a major league job. Some minor league umpires made it, but most did not. Vic Voltaggio made it.

With that season opener in the books, I had launched my first full season as the Blue Jays' radio broadcaster. Of tremendous benefit to me were the five years I spent broadcasting Triple-A games in Tacoma and Salt Lake City. First, those years allowed me to become fundamentally sound calling games. It took me five seasons to achieve that. Second, and just as importantly, they afforded me invaluable opportunities to meet and get to know so many people, from players to coaches to umpires and other broadcasters. We were all driven with one goal in mind: to make it to the major leagues, no matter how long it took.

The Group of Eleven

There's an old saying: "It takes a lifetime to become an overnight success." That was certainly true for the 11 players on the 1982 Toronto Blue Jays who were also on the 1985 team that earned a franchise-record 99 wins and their first-ever American League Eastern Division Championship.

While I had met some of these players in 1980 and 1981 as a fill-in broadcaster, this was my first real opportunity to get to know them on a daily basis. I now had the benefit of unique access on the field, in the dugout, in the clubhouse, and on the road travelling with the team.

Dave Stieb

It all starts with pitching: Dave Stieb. Stieb was the rock in the rotation year after year. He was discovered by chance after a rain delay during a college game, where Pat Gillick's magic as general manager and scout came out front and centre.

Al LaMacchia and Bobby Mattick were two of Pat's best scouts and confidants. There they were on a wet and rainy night in Chicago, years ago, watching Southern Illinois University play a baseball game. As fate would have it, SIU ran out of pitchers as Al and Bobby watched. All of a sudden, the manager went out to the mound and pointed to the centre fielder to come in to pitch. From the moment he started warming up, the two Blue Jays scouts knew they had their man. Near perfect mechanics. Yes, he was an outfielder, but the effortless deliveries repeated time and time again led the Blue Jays to draft Stieb in the 5th round that June. From a college centre fielder, he developed into a franchise-record seven-time All-Star.

Scouting is the pure essence of the game: discovering raw talent with good makeup. After that, outstanding player development brings out the natural abilities. No team did that better than the Blue Jays during the Gillick years. As the 1983 season opened with Stieb — already a two-time All-Star — on the hill, the Blue Jays began a run of 11 straight winning seasons, culminating in back-to-back World Series Championships.

In looking back over my career, Dave taught me a lot about players — how to treat them as real people rather than who we think they should be. He was obviously very competitive. He also wanted no part of the media and interviews and all the demands that go with stardom. At first I thought, *why?* The answer came years later, when I got to know the real Stieb.

After retirement, Dave came back to spring training as a guest instructor. He was so good with everyone: he is relaxed and communicates his thoughts well. But Dave is also reserved and shy and likes his quiet time. Combining his natural desire for solitude with all the media demands that went with his perennial All-Star seasons made him uncomfortable, as it would anyone. Dave is a very friendly person when you get to know him, but he was definitely not very friendly to the opposition when he was on the mound. His goal was to get you out — pure and simple. It's the old cliche: "Don't judge a book by its cover" (including this one).

There are two other Blue Jays who were this exact same way: Jack Morris and Duane Ward. During their playing careers, you had best not get in their way. Yet after their retirement, I saw how helpful they were to all those around them. Both joined me on the radio and did outstanding jobs as analysts, adding valuable insights for our audience. Duane became a mainstay for the many amateur clinics the Blue Jays put on every summer across Canada. He teaches youngsters not only how to play the game the right way, but how to conduct themselves on and off the field.

On September 24, 1988, Stieb had a no-hitter with two outs and two strikes in the bottom of the 9th inning in Cleveland. Julio Franco then hit a routine ground ball to second baseman Manuel Lee. When Lee came in to field it, the ball inexplicably took a five-foot-high bad hop right over his head and bounced into right field for Cleveland's only hit. Everyone was stunned. Six days later, in his next start pitching at Exhibition Stadium against the Orioles, Dave had another no-hitter in the top of the 9th inning. Again with two outs and two strikes on the hitter, Stieb jammed left-handed pinch hitter Jim Traber with a great pitch in on his hands. Traber fisted it just fair over the first base bag and just out of the reach of tall first baseman Fred McGriff for the Orioles' lone hit.

That is how close Dave Stieb came to tying Johnny Vander Meer, who is the only pitcher in major league history to pitch back-to-back no-hitters, which he did in 1938 with the Cincinnati Reds. Dave later threw his one and only no hitter September 2, 1990, in Cleveland. There were no bad-hop hits or bloop singles in that one to break his heart. When he retired the last batter, he embraced his catcher Pat Borders. At the same time, he looked up into the press box and smiled at author and friend Kevin Boland, who had written Dave's 1986 biography, entitled *Tomorrow I'll Be Perfect*.

Stieb had a slider second to none. It would buckle a hitter's knees, it could fool you that badly. Dave continually stood up Hall of Famer Jim Rice for called strikes that had Rice talking to himself. After his long and distinguished career with the Blue Jays in their infancy, Dave deservedly won a World Series ring in 1992, adding four wins to the cause. He came back as a Blue Jay in 1998, winning a game and saving two others out of the bullpen before officially retiring.

Jim Clancy

Jim Clancy was known as "Big Clance." He won 128 games as a Blue Jay and was the franchise's winningest pitcher until Stieb passed him on his way to a still franchise-best 175 victories. Jim was one of the early mainstays on the mound in Blue Jays history.

One of my first and most vivid memories of Jim happened in my first year, in 1982. I walked into the clubhouse at Exhibition

Stadium and saw him across the room at his locker playing his guitar and smoking. That's when smoking was allowed in the clubhouses, and Jim definitely wasn't the only one doing it. In 1972, Chicago White Sox All-Star Dick Allen appeared on the cover of *Sports Illustrated* juggling baseballs while smoking in the dugout.

Clancy was even quieter than Stieb. Neither said much when interviewed by the media. Jim was six-foot-four and weighed 220 pounds. That was big then, but not so big today, when seemingly all starting pitchers are at least six-foot-six. One memorable windy day at Exhibition Stadium, Clancy got a start he never envisioned against the Texas Rangers. In the 2nd inning, he went into his windup and was blown off the mound! He started another windup and again got knocked off the hill, with severe gusts of wind coming in off Lake Ontario that were unbelievable. It got to be pretty funny until it happened a third time. That's when the plate umpire suddenly threw up his hands and called time, waving the players off the field until the wind subsided. It was the only game in Blue Jays history briefly suspended because of wind. No rain. Just winds strong enough to knock your socks off . . . the mound. Jim quietly went about pitching 15 years in the major leagues, the first 12 with the Blue Jays. He never said much, but he laughed a lot and was a good teammate.

Stieb and Clancy call to mind a valuable lesson I learned from Carl Yastrzemski. The first time I visited Fenway Park as the Blue Jays radio broadcaster, I went up to Yaz, as he was affectionately known, and asked to interview him. Afterwards, I was disappointed and felt let down. He was bland and showed very little personality — this was the iconic Carl Yastrzemski? I'd expected him to be outgoing and witty while also funny and entertaining. But in our interview, he showed none of those qualities. He told me how when he went to the plate, he wanted it quiet. He did not want catchers like Yogi Berra yapping at him while he was trying to concentrate on each pitch. He would tell Yogi to shut up, and Yogi would, for a pitch or two. But then he'd be right back at it. "Hey, Yaz, are there any good restaurants here in Boston?" Carl would once again have to step out of the box. He said this went on his whole career with Yogi. Yastrzemski also said that he made it very clear to his teammates they were not to run if they were on base when he was batting. It was too distracting.

Later, when I began to think about it, I realized that Carl Yastrzemski was very real with me. I had mistakenly put this star on a pedestal and imagined how he should be. However, his honesty came through loud and clear, and I learned a lot from that simple five-minute interview.

These early experiences quickly broadened my outlook as a major league broadcaster. It was up to me to find and appreciate the real person in that uniform. On one occasion I asked Jim Clancy, "What do you remember most about high school at St. Rita's in Chicago?" His answer said it all. "Friday night football games and the fights in the stands." It doesn't get more real than that.

Luis Leal

Quiet and appreciated by his team, his manager, and his coaches, Venezuelan Luis Leal pitched six years with the Blue Jays. Every staff needs a pitcher or two in the starting rotation who can give you a lot of quality innings to keep you in games, and Leal proved he could be this guy during his 1982 season, with 38 starts and 249 innings pitched. Those days are gone now with five-man rotations. Leal provided manager Bobby Cox with quality innings and a chance to develop a young team into a winner. Luis would help the Blue Jays win 99 games and a division title in 1985.

Leal was the starter and tough-luck loser in Cleveland on May 15, 1981, when Len Barker pitched his perfect game. Later, in May 1983, Luis became a different part of Blue Jays history: after Stieb and Clancy had thrown back-to-back shut-outs against the Orioles, Leal made it a franchise-record three straight shutouts, defeating the Detroit Tigers, 4–0, the next night. Those three shutouts were all at the old Ex and remain unequaled. Clancy's shutout took just 1:48 to play. It's safe to say that will never be equaled, let alone the team's all-time record of 1:33, which was set on September 28, 1982, also by Clancy, who pitched a complete game shutout defeating the Minnesota Twins and Frank Viola, 3–0. After Luis Leal retired, he was named the pitching coach for his native Venezuelan team in the World Baseball Classic; he was now helping others as he had helped the Blue Jays.

Catchers: Buck and Ernie

Complementing that trio of pitchers in 1982 were the veteran catchers Buck Martinez and Ernie Whitt. Buck and Ernie skillfully handled a young pitching staff. They also helped to break in a young catcher, Geno Petralli, drafted by the Blue Jays in the third round of the now defunct 1978 MLB January Draft-Regular Phase. One of the best trades that Pat Gillick ever made was on May 10, 1981, when he dealt minor league outfielder Gil Kubski to Milwaukee for Buck, who went on to catch six seasons with the Blue Jays. Buck was part of a litany of future stars that Pat Gillick found and stole from other organizations. Many of those players came in the Rule 5 Draft: George Bell, 1987 AL MVP; Kelly Gruber and Manuel Lee, star third baseman and shortstop during the 1992 World Series Championship season; and pitcher Jim Gott, to name a few. If a player was left off the 40-man roster and unprotected at that time after three years, he was fair game for all the other teams to draft in December for a paltry $50,000; Gillick became famous for acquiring a lot of something while not giving up a lot of something. Pat's list of successful trades like these is endless, and it's one of the reasons why he is enshrined at Cooperstown; it is not just the big splash trades that are important, but also the ones that oftentimes go unnoticed.

John Albert "Buck" Martinez is from Sacramento, California. We had a lot in common from the start, which has led to a life-long friendship. For catchers, it's all about handling the pitching staff. Then you try maximizing other parts of your game. The best catchers are the most unselfish. Buck was one of the best that way. Only one player in Blue Jays history has been a part of a double play that resulted in a broken leg. On July 9, 1985, Buck's season came to an abrupt end against the Mariners in Seattle. Mariner Phil Bradley tried to score from second on a base hit to right, and slid hard at the plate. Here's how Buck tells it: "Bradley came around third and bowled me over at home. I tagged him out but broke my leg and dislocated my ankle in the collision. But his ass was out! As I am sitting there at the plate, I threw to third to try and get Gorman Thomas, a former teammate of mine in Milwaukee. The throw went into left field.

George Bell got it and threw back to me on a bounce. I tagged Gorman, who tried to tiptoe around me. It is the only time in the history of the game that a 9-2-7-2 double play has ever been recorded. Not to mention a broken leg and a dislocated ankle. George then wanted to help by carrying me off on the stretcher. When he picked up his end, he jammed my foot into his back, and it shot pain up to my eyeballs!"

It wasn't often that I mentioned a player's full name on the broadcast, but in Ernie Whitt's case I probably did once a season. When I first arrived in Toronto, I remember the crowds at the old Ex chanting, "Otto! Otto!" for Otto Velez. In 1982, Otto played his sixth and final year as a Blue Jay. His home runs and big hits brought a smile to my face when I heard how the crowd expressed their gratitude for him. His nickname was "Otto the Swatto," and appropriately so. Then, in a game a year later at Exhibition Stadium, I heard: "Ernie! Ernie!" after one of his home runs sailed over the right-field fence. "Listen to this crowd chanting, 'Ernie! Ernie!' as Leo Ernest Whitt circles the bases. How Ernie must love hearing this." Turned out Ernie did. "Jerry, when I hear the fans chant, 'Ernie, Ernie, Ernie,' as I come to the plate, it's great. I guess it means that they have seen me come through before, and they like seeing me up in situations where the game is on the line."

Ernie played 12 seasons with the Blue Jays and, along with Buck, was integral in celebrating a division-winning season in 1985. When Ernie left the team at the end of 1989, he was the last original Blue Jay from their inaugural 1977 season. In his own quiet way, Ernie was a leader among the pitchers. When Cox started to platoon Ernie and Buck in 1985, he prolonged both of their careers and made them both better. That's what great managing can do not only for teams but for individuals, and Ernie recognized this, offering high praise for his manager Bobby Cox: "He'd go to war for you if you didn't dog it on the field."

When I first moved to Canada, I remember someone telling me that Toronto was Detroit's playground. No Blue Jay ever fit that description more perfectly than Detroit native Ernie Whitt. Ernie's participation in the 1985 All-Star Game was all the more noteworthy when he caught his teammate Dave Stieb. When Whitt's playing career was over, he began a whole new career as a successful manager and coach for the Canadian National teams under the direction of Greg Hamilton. Ernie was Canada's manager at the 2004 Olympics in Athens and later managed Team Canada in both the World Baseball Classic and the Pan American Games. His team won the gold medal at the 2011 Pan Am Games in Guadalajara with a thrilling 2–1 win over the United States.

On September 14, 1987, at Exhibition Stadium, the Blue Jays routed the Baltimore Orioles, hitting a still major league record 10 home runs. The old record was eight. When rookie Rob Ducey homered into the left-field bleacher seats for his first major league home run, it was the team's eighth of the night, tying the record. Ernie then came up and hit his third home run of the game to break the record with nine. He was then lifted from the game. Back in the clubhouse, a number of his teammates were praising him for his record-breaking historic home run. As he was showering, someone came in from the dugout. "Ernie! You aren't the record holder anymore. Fred McGriff just hit one for number ten."

Whitt could hit home runs. Two of his biggest and best were momentous grand slams. The first took place at Exhibition Stadium on Sunday, June 23, 1985. Red Sox pitcher Bruce Kison had drilled George Bell in the 4th inning. Bell charged the mound and proceeded to deliver the most famous karate kick in major league history. Tempers flared and fights broke out. In the 6th inning, up stepped Whitt against Kison with the bases loaded. Ernie belted a grand slam to right that ignited both the crowd and the Blue Jays bench. As Whitt circled the bases he yelled at Kison the entire time until he finally stepped on home plate with total retribution.

In 1989, the Blue Jays did the unthinkable, placing Ernie and his bat front and centre once again. Trailing the Red Sox 10–0 at the end of six innings at Fenway Park, the Blue Jays rallied and came up in the 9th inning, trailing 10–6. After the team had already scored one run, Whitt stepped into a pitch and hit a grand slam to deep right for an 11–10 lead. The Red Sox tied it in the bottom of the 9th. Junior Felix later homered in the 12th inning for one of baseball's most memorable come-from-behind wins, 13–11. It was part of the Blue Jays winning a record 15-straight games at venerable Fenway.

Outfielders: Lloyd and Jesse

Next up on that 1982 roster were two amazingly young and talented outfielders in Lloyd Moseby and Jesse Barfield. The two would team with George Bell to form one of the best and most formidable outfields in the 1980s. Bell, Moseby, and Barfield: what a trio. Years later there would be a Bell, Moseby, Barfield bobblehead day at the Rogers Centre to honour the three of them. It's interesting to note, Bell was not on the 1982 team; due to injuries, George played only 37 games, all in Triple-A Syracuse. It wasn't until 1984 that he began to leave his mark, swatting 26 home runs and driving in 87.

When I had the pleasure of calling my first-ever major league game on July 4, 1980, at Tiger Stadium, the Blue Jays had a 20-year-old DH in their lineup that night. Lloyd Moseby and I were both rookies, starting our career together in Toronto. Growing up in Oakland, California, "The Shaker" was a great basketball player in high school, where he got his nickname. He had the uncanny ability to shake his defender and get free for the open shot, which he made most of the time.

Baseball, however, was this great athlete's true love. Breaking into the big leagues at the tender age of 20 was a testament to that. His outgoing personality was second to none. Lloyd always gives back, appearing at numerous Blue Jays functions year after year, amusing fans and players alike with his infectious smile and joy. Years ago, I was driving north along Alt. 19 in Dunedin, Florida, after a Blue Jays spring training game, when I burst out laughing. There, on the marquis of the hotel where Lloyd and his wife were staying and expecting their first child, it read: "IT'S A MOSE-BOY!"

Lloyd might be the only person in the history of major league baseball to steal first. Or so it seemed anyway. On a bright sunny day at Exhibition Stadium against the White Sox, Moseby, with head down, took off for second and easily stole the base. But the throw skipped into centre field. Lloyd never saw the flight of the ball. After his slide into second, he popped up and saw the centre fielder holding the ball. Moseby immediately thought his teammate had flied out, so he raced back to first to avoid being doubled up. He slid into first, beating the centre fielder's throw. We're not finished.

That throw got away from the first baseman. Moseby saw this and again took off for second base. He slid and once again beat the throw. His teammates were laughing so hard in the third-base dugout, they were literally falling on the ground. The next day the headlines blared: "Moseby steals second base twice, having run 270 feet to go 90."

That White Sox centre fielder was Kenny Williams, who later became a Blue Jay. Kenny was the starting centre fielder when Dave Stieb threw his no-hitter in Cleveland. The same Kenny Williams who, as a Blue Jay in 1990, rounded third base and bowled over his third-base coach, John McLaren, knocking him to the ground. While winded and dazed, Kenny still managed to score, making the blooper reels for years to come. Williams was the general manager in Chicago when the White Sox won the 2005 World Series. Welcome to the wild and wacky world of baseball.

Before a hometown crowd on September 19, 1983, Lloyd Moseby became the first Blue Jay to score 100 runs. The next night, his close friend Willie Upshaw became the first Blue Jay to drive in 100 runs. Two of the most significant days in Blue Jays history. That and February 1, 2018, when Moseby was inducted into the Canadian Baseball Hall of Fame.

In September 1981, a young Jesse Barfield, who was all of 21 years of age, made his major league debut. Five years later, he became the first Blue Jay ever to hit 40 home runs. Those 40 homers in 1986 led the major leagues. Three more than Hall of Famer Mike Schmidt that season. You ran at your own risk and peril against Barfield, and most of those times you were thrown out — his arm from right field was like that of the great Roberto Clemente, who was one of the greatest stars of his era. But as good as Barfield was on the field, he was even better off it. Friendly to all, he quickly became a crowd favourite and was a great teammate who never put himself first.

Jesse proved to general manager Pat Gillick and his teammates over the years that you could be a devout Christian in
baseball without proselytizing in the clubhouse. Barfield represented everything good in the game as a great teammate. My
admiration for him grew with each day.

Jesse was the first Blue Jay ever to hit a pinch-hit grand
slam. As an aside here, the first grand slam in Blue Jays history
was pretty memorable, too. It was hit at Exhibition Stadium
in June 1977 by shortstop Hector Torres off a young Yankees
left-hander named Ron Guidry. Gillick had the line of the day
after the game. "I'm not sure who was more surprised: Hector
or Guidry."

Barfield owes a lot to Bill Gullickson for becoming a Blue Jay.
In 1977, Bill was recognized as one of the best high school pitchers in the states, pitching for Joliet Catholic High School near
Chicago. In a game against Joliet Central, played before a dozen
scouts, Bill's blazing fastball was dominant. That is, except for one
batter, who twice took Gullickson's fastballs deep for loud doubles
off the fence. That was Jesse. From that point on, scouts began
to look at two stars in that area. The Montreal Expos drafted
Gullickson in the first round that June while the Blue Jays took
Barfield in the ninth. *Call it two!* What a baseball tandem they
were for years in Canada.

Jesse finished his professional career in 1993, playing baseball in Japan for the Yomiuri Giants. His teammate was Lloyd
Moseby. Barfield was well spoken and thoughtful, which led him
to the Blue Jays CBC TV booth as an analyst in 2007 and 2008.

That young and talented 1980s Blue Jays outfield, with Bell
in left, Moseby in centre, and Barfield in right, helped take
the Blue Jays to their 99-win 1985 season, and with it a first-
ever American League Eastern Division Championship. On

October 5 of that year, it all came down to the next-to-last day of the season at Exhibition Stadium against the intimidating New York Yankees. When Ron Hassey hit a fly ball to left field, Bell fittingly caught that last out and dropped to his knees to celebrate with Tony Fernandez and his teammates.

Bell, Moseby, and Barfield became synonymous with excellence.

Infielders: Damo, Willie, and "Mullinorg"

Rounding out the 11 players on the 1982 team who were there for the 1985 championship season were four infielders. They were all key players. Their successful growth and development were essential towards winning and establishing the Blue Jays as one of the best franchises in the game.

DOM-ah-so Garcia . . . not Da-MOSS-oh. That was one of my most difficult challenges in correctly pronouncing a player's name, let alone a first name, that I can recall in my years with the Blue Jays. His nickname was Damo (DOM-OH), which did make it much easier over time to say his first name correctly, although I had to pause each time to make sure I got it right.

Damaso was fiery and outspoken. He had a temper that led to some fisticuffs with teammates. That anger also saw a displeased Garcia burn his uniform in the clubhouse after a game in Oakland. But the Blue Jays would not have developed over four years to win 99 games in 1985 without him. He played the game hard and expected everyone else to do the same. He got the most out of his abilities both at the plate and playing second base. Garcia was durable and exciting to watch.

His banner season was in 1982, Bobby Cox's first year as manager. Damo hit .310 in the leadoff spot. He stole 54 bases and won the Silver Slugger award for his offensive production at second base. In 1985, he led off again, stealing 28 bases. He was a force to be reckoned with on the base paths. When he finished his career with the Expos, he became one of only 56 players to appear with both the Blue Jays and the Expos. Garcia was not only part of that unique Canadian baseball history but was also a two-time All-Star, in 1984 and 1985.

I will never forget my first Blue Jays road trip to Arlington, Texas, to play the Rangers. One morning, I looked down at the hotel swimming pool from my room and was so surprised. The pool was completely full of kids splashing around and having a ball. I said to a player, "Did you see all those kids today in the hotel swimming pool?"

"Those are the Upshaws. When Willie comes in to play, they all drive over from Blanco, and the fun starts in the pool. For Willie, it's all about his family."

Willie Upshaw was a Blue Jay from 1978, when he took over at first base for veteran John Mayberry, through the 1987 season. Then Willie handed over the reins to Fred McGriff. Upshaw is gentle and soft-spoken, but one of the toughest and most determined competitors ever on the diamond. GM Pat Gillick used three words when I asked him about Willie. "Class, class, class."

When you think of Blue Jays first basemen, you think of great ones — John Mayberry, Fred McGriff, John Olerud, and Carlos Delgado — and Willie is a part of that legacy that quickly comes to mind. Upshaw was taken in the December 1977 Rule 5 Draft from the New York Yankees, the team that originally signed him.

It is very easy to put Californians Garth Iorg and Rance Mulliniks together. Two outstanding people and players, they were the platoon tandem at third base under manager Bobby Cox from 1982 to 1985. Look no further than the 1985 division-winning season as a testament to their unique abilities. The right-handed hitting Iorg batted .313 with 22 doubles, 7 home runs, and 37 RBIs against lefties on the hill. The left-handed hitting Mulliniks batted .295 with 26 doubles, 10 home runs, and 57 RBIs. They combined to hit .303, using their 198 hits to rack up 48 doubles, 17 home runs, and 94 RBIs. What a year for any third baseman, let alone these two playing that one position. It showed the genius of Bobby Cox. It also reflected two players who, when they came to the ballpark each and every day, were mentally and physically ready to play.

Early in my career, Blue Jays general manager Pat Gillick pulled me aside to offer some heartfelt constructive criticism that was gentle but effective. It had to do with Garth and his older brother, Dane. I had noted on the radio that the Blue Jays had taken Garth in the expansion draft from the New York Yankees after the Yankees had drafted Garth out of a northern California high school in 1973. I then mentioned that I had also met his older brother, Dane, who was drafted by the Phillies in 1971 out of Brigham Young University in Provo, Utah. As Garth's at-bat went on, I said that for me as a parent, it was so nice to see Dane go to college at BYU, so that if baseball didn't work out he would have something valuable to fall back upon. I said I felt that was better than being drafted right out of high school. If you had the chance to go to college, take it and you would be better off. A couple of days later on the field, Pat stopped me and said that he had heard my comments about the Iorg brothers.

"Jerry, I know how you feel as a parent, and there is a lot of merit to what you said. However, for me as a general manager, I would prefer to sign kids out of high school, so we can develop them our own way in our minor league system. For a player, I feel those three years are better spent with us than in college. So when you are on the radio, if you could remember that is our philosophy here with the Blue Jays, I would appreciate it." It was as nice as anyone has ever asked me to do something differently. It showed again why Pat is a Hall of Famer both in Cooperstown and in life. I heard his message and never forgot it.

Garth is a member of the Church of Jesus Christ of Latter-day Saints. I was very familiar with that church, having lived in Utah for six years. Like his Blue Jays teammate Barry Bonnell, who was also a member of the Mormon Church, along with Jesse Barfield and other Christians in the clubhouse, Iorg never wore his religion on his sleeve. Players like these stood out as witnesses to their faith in major league clubhouses. Garth and his wife, Patti, have three sons and they all play professional baseball. Isaac, the oldest, would have everyone in stitches in the dugout before games, imitating his father's very unorthodox batting stance.

Garth would stand bent over at the plate on the toes of his front foot but would also lean back toward the catcher as the pitch was thrown. This unique stance led to a lot of laughs with Isaac and so many opposite-field hits down the right-field line that the right-field corner became known as "Iorg's Corner."

In my second year broadcasting Triple-A games in Salt Lake for the Gulls back in 1977, I met Rance Mulliniks for the first time. He had been in Double-A during the previous season in El Paso, Texas, and now he was the Gulls' shortstop. In just 58 games with Salt Lake he drove in 51 runs with 11 home runs and 17 doubles. It didn't take him long to earn his first promotion to the major leagues; he was smart and a good player. So smart, in fact, that during his time with the Blue Jays, I often asked him about his first-pitch off-speed base hits. He told me many times he would look for changeups on a first pitch that often led to doubles hit up the gaps. He had studied pitchers enough to know that an off-speed pitch was likely on that first delivery. He did his homework. Not too many hitters are that adept sitting on first-pitch changeups. Rance was, and he took full advantage. He was a keen student of the game and helped teammates whenever he could. Mulliniks would save his best teaching for when it counted the most, in Game 2 of the 1992 World Series in Atlanta. But that's a story for later.

One of the joys for me growing up in the San Francisco Bay Area was to hear Bill King on the radio broadcasting Golden State Warriors games. Then, for 25 years, he called Oakland A's games. Bill was great with people and loved what he did, and he was honoured with the 2017 Ford Frick Award. When he passed away after the 2005 season at the age of 78, after undergoing hip surgery, I was sad to say goodbye to a loyal friend who always made time for me. But whenever the Blue Jays were in Oakland, I took great pleasure in sharing a special moment with other Californians who had also listened to Bill in their youth. Back in 1982, Garth and Rance were two of those. I loved watching the expressions on their faces when they met King for the first time and shared their stories with him. We were those kids lying in bed at night with the lights out, listening to Bill King on our radios. Rance would later broadcast Blue Jays games as an analyst on CBC TV with Jim Hughson and Jesse Barfield during the 2007 and 2008 seasons. Mulliniks returns every year to Toronto to join in club activities and promotions and is a welcome addition.

CHAPTER 9

DOING WHAT I LOVE TO DO

As the 1982 season began with the cast of 11 players leading the way toward the 1985 season, it was a pleasure to settle into the radio booth each day with my new partner, Tom Cheek. Tom was from Pensacola, Florida. He had worked some Montreal Expos games with Dave Van Horn just prior to coming to the expansion Blue Jays as their lead announcer, working with Hall of Fame pitcher Early Wynn. One of the things I loved most that first season was going down to the dugout after the 8th inning to interview the postgame guest.

Those interviews led to some wonderful stories, but none more meaningful than one in 1996 from a young Blue Jays catcher named Angel Martinez. Or at least we thought that was his name. Angel had been to a few spring trainings, where I had first met him. He was quiet and did not speak much English at first, which is common for a lot of young players from the Dominican Republic. Veterans, too, for that matter. He broke in as a rookie in 1995, playing in 62 games.

A year later in his second season, we were sitting in the third-base dugout at the then SkyDome after he had collected the game-winning hit. As I was waiting for Tom to finish with the totals and then send it down to me, I casually asked Angel how he was doing.

"Good and especially after my game-winning hit."

Then I happened to notice his catcher's mitt lying right beside him, and I looked at the open pocket. The name Sandy was written on the edge of the pocket.

"Is that your girlfriend's name?"

His answer caught me totally off guard. "No, that's my name. Ever since I was a baby, my mother has called me Sandy. Angel is my first name, but no one in my family or my friends ever calls me that. Only here. I just haven't mentioned it to anyone."

"Sandy, thank you for sharing that with me. No longer are you Angel Martinez. From now on you are Sandy Martinez. Are you okay if I tell everyone what you just shared with me right here for our interview?" He said that would be fine. Tom threw it down to me in the dugout and I opened up that postgame interview with the new Sandy Martinez story. I am proud to say that from that point on in his eight-year major league career, he was called Sandy.

Another memorable interview occurred after a Blue Jays game at Yankee Stadium in the early '80s. The Yankees won it on a big home run by Dave Winfield. As soon as the Blue Jays were retired in the top of the 9th inning, I asked the Blue Jays bat boy if he would go across the field and ask Winfield to come over to be on our postgame show. I honestly didn't think I had a chance of having him on. First of all, he was one of the biggest stars in the game, and I had never met him. Second, he was in a very public and ugly feud with his owner, George Steinbrenner.

Here was the gist of what was going on at that time: Steinbrenner had made Winfield the highest-paid player in the game when he signed him to a 10-year contract as a free agent in 1980. But the Yankees owner never forgave Winfield or his agent after misunderstanding a "cost of living" increase in the terms of the contract, raising its cost from $15 million to $23 million. Steinbrenner disparaged Winfield in the press in 1985: "I let Mr. October get away, and I got Mr. May, Dave Winfield, instead. He gets his numbers when it doesn't count."

As I looked up from the dugout, who did I see coming over but Dave Winfield. He stepped into our dugout and sat down. I introduced myself and told him we would be on in just a minute. "Jerry, it's a pleasure to meet you. I know that my name has been in the news a lot lately with George Steinbrenner. We are having our differences, and the lawyers are now a part of it. You ask me anything you want during this interview, and I will be happy to answer your questions." I was so taken aback by this man who made me, a perfect stranger, feel so comfortable and relaxed. It was one of the most interesting interviews we had for our audience that year, and it was all because of Dave, who openly and insightfully talked about his confrontation with his owner.

Years later, in 1992, when he became a Blue Jay for his one and only season, the team was in Seattle playing the Mariners in early May. As I was walking around Seattle, I found a small bookstore. Browsing through the sports section, I noticed a book entitled *Winfield: A Player's Life*. It was his autobiography that had come out in 1988. I bought it.

On our many flights that season, Dave proceeded to sit down to share his life's stories with me. He was busy, but he always made time for me and gave me his undivided attention. Although he couldn't seem to escape controversy — including an incident at old Exhibition Stadium in 1983 that resulted in a dead seagull and dropped animal cruelty charges — he was one of the classiest people I have ever met.

A third postgame interview stands out for all the right reasons, too. On September 6, 1995, the numbers on the Orioles warehouse out in right-centre field changed from 2,130 to 2,131, as shortstop Cal Ripken passed the immortal Lou Gehrig in consecutive games played. It was a record many thought would never be broken. Now his 2,632 consecutive games played record is the one that may never be broken. At the end of the month, the Blue Jays finally played Baltimore in Toronto after that "Orioles Magic" Ripken moment. Before the game, I went into the Orioles clubhouse and saw Cal sitting at his locker. We had known each other for a number of years. He was always polite and friendly.

"Cal, win or lose tonight, will you please come over to our dugout for a postgame interview with me to talk about passing Lou Gehrig earlier this month. I know you have had all kinds of media attention, but if you could do this for our audience, I would love to have them hear you talk about that special moment for you."

"Jerry, I would be happy to do that. I'll see you after the game in your dugout."

The Orioles won that game, 5–0, but our audience won even more. Cal came over and sat down with me for a good six or seven minutes. He openly shared what had happened on that night of September 6. It is still one of my favourite interviews, and I took it all in just like our audience did.

Daily Routine

From day one in my broadcasting career, I have been able to stick pretty closely to a good daily routine. It is something that works for me, but everybody in our profession is different. I always tell young sportscasters: "You be you and do what makes you comfortable. Don't copy anyone. Try to get the most out of your own talent with a good work ethic, and make it your goal to improve each and every broadcast during your entire career. A good daily routine, especially in baseball with its 162 games, is essential."

I would get up around 8 a.m., do 20 minutes of back exercises — which I have done each day for more than 50 years to avoid spine surgery, going back to an old high school baseball injury — then go out and get a Starbucks. I'd then spend a couple of hours reading player bios of the opponents, and have lunch around 11:30 a.m. while reading the local newspapers for quotes and interesting storylines, plus things I missed from the game the night before. After a 30-minute nap, I'd leave for the game around 3 p.m. and would arrive and lay out all my paperwork, then go down to the field and visit with the coaches, players, and managers during batting practice to gain information to use for the audience. After eating dinner in the press box, I'd take an hour before the game to put it all together while also visiting with other broadcasters or friends at the game. I'd broadcast the game, then head home or back to the hotel and get online to see other scores and interesting developing stories. Then I'd read in bed for about 10 minutes, with lights out around 12 a.m. Repeat for six months while also finding quality time to spend with my family.

Tom and Jerry

The 1982 season began a wonderful run for Tom and Jerry on the radio, and we broadcast Blue Jays games for the next 22 seasons. That included the amazing back-to-back World Series Championships in 1992 and 1993. We had a lot of fun being compared to the famous cartoon duo. Tom, with his build, was definitely the big cat. He rose above most everyone in a room, while I physically fit the part of the little mouse at his side. They say opposites attract. I have felt the best teams on radio are opposites. Different voices are so good for the listening audience, so you know who is talking. That was very true for us. Tom had the big baritone voice, while I had the higher and thinner voice with a lot of inflection.

We also had different styles in how we approached the game. I loved that Tom was a Blue Jays fan who just happened to be sitting behind the team's radio microphone. His emotions could be heard by all: if the Blue Jays scored and won, he was so happy on the air, as you would expect. But if they hit into double plays and made errors and lost games they should have won, his voice dropped an octave. You could hear the disappointment — which was okay. That was Tom and the reason why fans loved him.

My style was just the opposite. I love the game of baseball. There are 162 games played each season. There is a reason why you win and a reason why you lose. As I have said on numerous occasions on the air after certain games: "The Blue Jays didn't lose this game tonight. The (opponent) won it." There is a difference. I feel great pride in being the Blue Jays announcer while still maintaining my objectivity in highlighting the game itself. That means calling spectacular plays made by both teams that really, in many ways, determine who wins and loses — along with a well-pitched game by either starter. I see and call the game to the best of my ability without being biased, which includes being impartial when it comes to umpires and their calls. It's all a matter of subjectivity and what side you sit on, but I have managed to sit right in the middle without partiality. The majority of the fans know I am definitely the Blue Jays radio broadcaster by the pride I have in my voice when I talk about Canada's team. That's good enough for me.

When I look back at the 36 years I spent with my first and only major league team, I consider myself blessed. There are only a handful of broadcasters in the history of the game who are in that select company. I am very grateful to be one of them. But I would be remiss here if I didn't tell you I am just as proud of my five formative years broadcasting in the Triple-A Pacific Coast League with the Tacoma Twins and the Salt Lake City Gulls. I learned so much, not only on how to call the games but also how to prepare for those games. Back then there were no media guides or computers or stats anywhere; you prepared by talking with everybody in the game. I was just the middleman taking all the great information I gathered on the field up to the radio booth and then passing it on to our audience, informing and entertaining.

I enjoyed when people came into the booth before the game and saw all my handwritten notes spread around my scorebook. Also note: there was no laptop. When I say to people, "I read all my ad-libs," they laugh. But it's true. All that began in Triple-A, and it still works today.

While preparation is essential to every broadcast, there is another dimension that is paramount for the radio audience: can you paint a picture with your words each night, so that your audience can *see* the game in their own mind and *feel* like they are right there at the ballpark, just by listening?

CHAPTER 10

OFFSEASON TO REMEMBER

When the 1982 season was over, my boss Len Bramson asked me if I would like to work over the winter with our flagship station, CJCL 1430. I said, "Sure." Friends of mine laugh when I tell them I taught my boys to say, "Sure," when asked to do something and work out the details afterwards. For the next three winters, I had so much fun immersing myself in all things blue and white — on the ice, that is. The Toronto Maple Leafs were my new beat! I went on the air each night at 6 p.m., Monday through Friday right after the news, with a ten-minute sports wrap-up show. It led to many interesting interviews. I had the time and turned these features into a five-part series used all week. The first one was memorable.

Gus Badali was Wayne Gretzky's agent. I met him one day at Maple Leaf Gardens after a Leafs practice. We talked about how much he liked baseball. "Gus, could I please get a phone number from you?"

"Sure. I'll be happy to give you Wayne's number out in Edmonton."

"No. I don't want Wayne's phone number. I would like to

have his parents' number." I had heard so many nice things about Walter and Phyllis Gretzky but had never met them. Wayne got all the headlines, but the way he conducted himself off the ice spoke volumes to me. As a young parent myself, I wanted to know who the two people were behind this wonderful hockey player and person.

I gave Walter a call. "Jerry, we would love to meet you. Come on out to our house in Brantford one evening next week so we can talk." It turned out to be one of the most enjoyable and informative evenings I have ever spent.

Walter was very outgoing and friendly while Phyllis was quiet and shy, but both were so nice. As we were talking, I noticed three large black garbage bags that were tied at the top and tucked into corners of the living room. "What are those garbage bags doing in your living room?" I asked. Walter laughed. "Those are fan letters that are simply addressed 'Wayne Gretzky: Brantford Ontario.' We keep them here for Wayne, in case he wants to sort through them when he comes home."

The second thing that caught my attention was the famous ice rink in their backyard, complete with lights and nets at each end. By the time I met him, Walter had been putting together his homemade rink, a.k.a. "Wally Coliseum," for nearly 20 years, so that Wayne and his sister and three brothers could skate and hone their hockey skills. Sure enough, as I looked out the window, there were youngsters Glen and Brent skating away, firing pucks at the nets under the lights. Our conversation later took us to the basement, where I saw a pool table that was stacked two feet high with plaques and pictures and various awards that Wayne had already received. There was no more room on the walls; gold medals were hanging everywhere. It was an awesome display.

Walter then took me to Wayne's bedroom, where up on the wall near the bed hung a handmade faded brown sheet of paper with a grid on it all marked in pencil. There were lines drawn straight across the sheet with more lines coming down it. In the lower right-hand corner was the number 378. "When he was 10 years old in our Brantford Atom league, Wayne kept track of the number of goals he scored during the season. These are those games and the 378 goals he scored. He also had 120 assists. This has been in his bedroom ever since." Walter had given Wayne some great advice when he first started to skate. "Go to where the puck is going. Not where it has been." His gifted son took that to heart and did the rest. Wayne left home at the tender age of 14 to begin his journey toward a storied NHL career for all of us to enjoy.

When the visiting was over and I had met Glen and Brent (Wayne's sister, Kim, and third brother, Keith, were not home), Walter, Phyllis, and I adjourned to their kitchen, where I interviewed the two of them. Even though Phyllis was shy, she contributed beautifully to our taped conversation. It ran as a five-part series the following week on CJCL. Phyllis had made a delicious pie, and we all had a piece at the end of the night. Then, before I could catch myself, I asked for a second slice. Phyllis laughed as she cut it for me. My wife, Mary, thought that I had been a bit bold in making the request, but it was worth it!

Fred McGriff

During the 1982 offseason, the Blue Jays made a trade with the New York Yankees, who were looking for a veteran closer. The Blue Jays had one in Dale Murray. GM Pat Gillick knew he had value in Murray, but he also knew he had to continue to build his young team for the present and the future. With that December 9 trade, Gillick showed his true genius and his ability to surround himself with knowledgeable scouts who recognized talent whenever and wherever they saw it. Epy Guerrero (no relation to Vladimir or Vlad Jr.) was one of Pat's best scouts — he helped bring so many talented players from his native Dominican Republic to the Blue Jays and combed innumerable ballparks outside the Dominican on the lookout for young players who could make a difference.

Guerrero was sitting in the stands at McKechnie Field in Bradenton, Florida, one day in the summer of 1982, watching the Yankees' young Gulf Coast League team play a game against the Pirates' Gulf Coast team. In centre field, 400 feet away from home plate, there is a 25-foot-high green wall atop the fence that forms a hitter's backdrop. Here is how the conversation went that day when Epy called Pat after the game.

"Pat, I just saw something I have never seen before here in Bradenton. A young first baseman with the Yankees hit a ball not only over the centre-field fence, but over that green hitter's backdrop wall, too! He has some awesome power. If you ever get an opportunity to trade for this player, do it. His name is Fred McGriff."

Sure enough, when Pat engineered the deal with the Yankees, it was initially Dale Murray and young outfielder Todd Dodd going to the Yankees for veteran outfielder Dave Collins and pitcher Mike Morgan. Then Pat threw in: "What about Fred McGriff in the low minors? Can we include him, too?" Fred played 19 years, hitting 493 home runs. That is scouting at its best.

CHAPTER 11

VETERANS AND ROOKIES ALIKE

Fresh off their trade with the Yankees, in addition to several other newcomers to the 1983 roster, the Blue Jays were ready to roll into the new season and reach that first milestone. Dave Collins was the catalyst at the top of the order.

Dave and I had been together in Salt Lake City, where he was a young star in the Angels organization. You'd hear, "Collie! Collie! Collie!" a lot during his Blue Jays tenure. He was so fast and could steal a base for you at any time.

Dave stole 60 bases in the 1984 season, setting a record that still stands in Blue Jays history. He had stolen 79 with the 1980 Cincinnati Reds, making it very fitting that he was born in Rapid City, South Dakota. The left fielder used his speed to make up for an average arm by charging ground-ball base hits and stopping base runners from taking the extra base. Collins was one of the best hitters against the knuckleball that I have ever seen. I asked him what he did to be so successful against the likes of Charlie Hough and the Niekro brothers, Phil and Joe. "I get right up on top of the plate. Then I try and hit everything right back through the middle. See ball. Hit ball."

There was big Cliff Johnson from San Antonio, Texas, who was another veteran Gillick brought in to help the cause. Bobby Cox showed his magic again, platooning at the DH spot with Cliff and another veteran left-handed hitter, Jorge Orta. They combined in 1983 for 34 home runs and 113 RBIs. My happiest memory of Cliff goes back to August 5, 1984, in Baltimore. It was a day game against the Orioles. For two years I had anxiously awaited for Cliff to collect his 19th pinch-hit home run. He had been tied for the longest time with the Cincinnati Reds Jerry Lynch, at 18, for the major league record.

That day, in the 8th inning, Cliff came to the plate as a pinch hitter against veteran lefty Tippy Martinez. At the microphone, I had completely forgotten about Cliff's record-making possibility, proving once again that the best calls on radio are the most spontaneous. As an aside, this is why before the game I never told my on-air partners who were former players (Joe Siddall, Jack Morris, Alan Ashby, and Warren Sawkiw) what I was going to talk to them about. I wanted their answers to be spontaneous and unrehearsed because I felt that worked best for our audience.

When Cliff drilled Tippy's pitch to very deep left-centre field at Baltimore's old Memorial Stadium, I watched the ball like everyone else. That is until I noticed Cliff smiling and waving to his teammates in the first-base dugout well before he had reached first base. That's when the light went on. I took Cliff around the bases, highlighting what he had just done: passing Jerry Lynch's mark and setting a new major league record with his 19th career pinch-hit home run. It was so much fun for me and all of Johnson's teammates after he had waited so long to set the new mark.

That moment also taught me a valuable lesson as a broadcaster: do not start speculating in the late innings of a game about what you think is going to happen. Don't say, "If the Blue Jays can hang on to win this game tonight," or "If this pitcher can save this game here with two outs." Best to save it. What I found works best for me is simply to let it happen, then use all of my prepared material and interesting facts that go with the accomplishment. It's a win-win for you and for your audience. I don't believe in "jinxing it," but fans sure do. Cliff would hit his 20th pinch-hit homer with the Blue Jays in 1986. That major league record stood until 2010, when Canada's own Matt Stairs hit No. 21 on his way to 23 pinch-hit home runs, which is still the major league record.

In the early days of my Blue Jays career, there was only one team bus for the road, and Tom and I got to ride on it. What a hoot! One time, I asked big Cliff, "You've been around a long time. Who are some of your former teammates?" Before Cliff could answer, Buck Martinez shouted from the back of the bus, "Babe Ruth. Lou Gehrig," and the bus erupted with laughter. And woe to the bus driver who missed a turn or got lost on the way. They would hear from Rick Leach. "Hey, Bussy! I just saw a sign that said, 'Thunder Bay, five miles!' What the hell?"

There were two young emerging stars on that 1983 team: shortstop Tony Fernandez and left fielder George Bell. Tony played in his first 15 games that season, collecting nine hits toward 2,276 in his illustrious 17-year career. That included four different stints with the Blue Jays, four Gold Gloves, five All-Star selections, a postseason batting average of .327 in 43 games, and a World Series ring with the 1993 club. And talk about devices before there were devices: Tony was often injured in his long career as a Blue Jay, and with each different injury he would come into the clubhouse with some kind of exercise device that he had either made or found somewhere. He used them constantly, leading to his nickname, "Mr. Gadget."

As a young broadcaster, I had heard that the city of San Pedro de Macoris in the Dominican Republic was often referred to as the "shortstop capital of the world." So many shortstops in the major leagues came from that city, but Tony was the marquee player. He was one of the first to patent the long, arching throw from the hole at shortstop to get his man by a half stride most every time. Tony was a remarkable defender and, in my opinion, a Hall of Fame shortstop. The Blue Jays would not have won the 1993 World Series without him.

George Bell, like Fernandez, was another Epy Guerrero find in the Dominican. Bell came via Philadelphia and the Rule 5 Draft. The Phillies tried to hide him after his first three years with them in the minor leagues, but you didn't hide anything from Pat Gillick. Bell had his good moments and his not-so-good moments as a Blue Jay, to be sure. One interesting story that features both of them occurred over the first two regular season games of 1988. After Bell's 1987 AL MVP season, Gillick and manager Jimy Williams paid a visit to George in the off-season. Bell's defensive skills were diminishing, and they wanted him to consider becoming the team's full-time designated hitter. After putting up a bit of a fight, with hopes of staying in left field, he reluctantly agreed. Opening Day in Kansas City saw the Blue Jays face Cy Young Award winner Bret Saberhagen. That afternoon, as the designated hitter, Bell became the first player in major league history to hit three home runs on Opening Day. They were all off Saberhagen. Postgame, when asked about his heroics as the new DH, George didn't offer much. After a day off, Jimy started Bell in left field in the second game. George went 5 for 5. Afterwards in the clubhouse, George was loud. "See! Five for five! I should be in left field!" He didn't mention the three home runs he had hit in the opener as the DH.

Bell would play the majority of his games that season in left field, but he would hear it from the fans in Toronto, who booed him for his poor defence.

"The fans can kiss my purple butt."

I liked George a lot. He played hard and was a no-nonsense competitor who gave it his all. He mellowed as his career went on. Years later, I appreciated Bell even more after talking one day in the clubhouse with young Blue Jays infielder Domingo Cedeno. Domingo was signed by the club in 1989 as an amateur free agent out of a high school in La Romana in the Dominican Republic. He played in just 15 games in 1993, hitting only .174 and then just .196 the next season. However, in 1996, Cedeno hit a solid .280. I praised him during that season both in private and on the radio.

"Domingo, is there any one particular reason why you are hitting so well this season? You have so many hits with two strikes." It didn't take him long to highlight his mentor. "This past winter I played ball in the Dominican and my hitting coach was George Bell. He is the best hitting coach I have ever had. He taught me patience and how to hit a baseball with two strikes. Now I am so confident at the plate and know I can do it thanks to George." I had no idea that Bell was a hitting instructor in winter ball, let alone teaching this effectively to others who wanted to learn. George was one of the best two-strike hitters in Blue Jays history. Now he was giving back in his home and native land to other young players. Domingo would go to the Texas Rangers the next season. He continued to excel at the plate, hitting .282 to again reward his hitting guru.

Alfredo Griffin started all 162 games at shortstop in 1982 and then did that again in 1983. Steady and reliable, quiet and understated, friendly yet shy, soft spoken and a great teammate.

All the ingredients needed to become a winner who earned four World Series rings — his first with the 1988 Los Angeles Dodgers, two more with the Blue Jays in 1992 and 1993, and a fourth as the Angels' first-base coach when they won the 2002 World Series against the Giants — and a Gold Glove in 1985 with Oakland, for good measure.

At the end of September 1983, a glossy 89-73 record marked the first winning season in the Blue Jays' young history and started their 11-year streak of playing better than .500 baseball.

CHAPTER 12

KEY MOMENT

The 1984 season once again saw the Blue Jays win 89 games, but this time it was different. The club finished second behind the front-running Detroit Tigers, who won 104 games. The Yankees dropped to third, a game ahead of the Red Sox, while the Orioles tumbled from 98 wins to 85, finishing fifth. The Tigers started off an unprecedented 35-5. Yet on June 4, when the Blue Jays arrived at Tiger Stadium, they trailed Detroit by only five games and split the four-game series.

A few reinforcements had been brought in prior to spring training to boost the pitching staff. One of these was relief pitcher Dennis Lamp, signed in January as a free agent. Not only was Dennis a real character who had fun with everyone, he could pitch. He certainly showed that in 1985, going 11-0 and helping the Blue Jays to a 99-win season.

As I parked my car at Exhibition Stadium one day, I happened to notice Dennis getting out of his car and being mobbed by fans as he walked to the players' entrance. The fans were hooting and hollering and having a ball, which piqued my curiosity. Someone explained, "He was imitating you on the radio!" Dennis was a great voice impersonator who did a perfect Muhammad Ali as well as capturing the essence of radio broadcasters he had heard during his career with the Cubs and the White Sox. That included the iconic voice of Harry Caray.

Dennis told me, "When I was with the White Sox in the early 1980s, before Harry went to the Cubs, the pitchers would sit down in the bullpen when at home and listen to him on the radio. We laughed at so many things he said. 'Here come the White Sox leading off the 7th inning: Oscar Gamble, Claudell Washington, and Ralph Garr — The Venus de Milo outfield. No arms.'"

Only Harry could turn a 2,000-year-old marble sculpture into a baseball metaphor.

I had heard many stories about Harry, who was idolized by Chicago fans for his passion, rooting for his team during broadcasts. His legion of fans felt exactly the same way Harry felt. One day I got a glimpse of what it was like to be a fan of Harry Caray. The Blue Jays had a night game in Chicago against the White Sox while the Cubs had a day game at Wrigley Field. I made a point of staying in my hotel room all afternoon to hear Harry call the game on TV. I was not disappointed.

Cubs second baseman Ryne Sandberg had just signed a seven-year, $49 million contract with the Cubs in the offseason. The Cubs were trailing by a run when Sandberg came up to the plate in the bottom of the 8th inning. "Here's Ryne Sandberg with a chance to tie it up or give the Cubs the lead. Two men on and two men out. Here's the pitch to Sandberg. Popped up! He's making seven million dollars a year, and he just popped up."

I would often have lunch at the restaurant he opened in downtown Chicago in 1987. Many times, I saw Harry eating with friends at a table right in the middle of the room, among all of us. There was no private back-room dining for Harry. He was happy when people came over to say hello and shake his hand. At Harry Caray's, the length of the bar is exactly 60 feet, six inches, for all those baseball diehards there to soak up the ambiance while enjoying a beverage.

That season, Dave Stieb went 16-8 with a 2.83 ERA. He continued to amaze with his effortless delivery and durability, pitching 267 innings. Newcomer Doyle Alexander pitched 261 innings. Doyle was a perfect fit in the four-man rotation, going 17-6. He was very quiet and very workmanlike. He went about his business with a purpose and did not let media or small talk get in the way of his focus and concentration. I remember Doyle as someone who seemingly had two men on base every inning he pitched and yet left them on base time and time again. A true veteran who put the game of baseball first, respecting the fact that major league baseball is a business where winning is paramount. Jim Clancy and Luis Leal each won 13 games. Jim Gott was a key swing man in the pen, pitching in 35 games, 12 as a starter.

Another new pitcher in 1984 was left-hander and reliever Bryan Clark, who was traded to the Blue Jays from Seattle for outfielder Barry Bonnell. Bryan had a very difficult 1984 season in his one-and-only year in Toronto. He went 1-2 with an ERA of nearly six at 5.91. He pitched out of the bullpen 45 innings, allowing an alarmingly high 66 base hits, and his 22 walks exceeded his 21 strikeouts. It just wasn't his year.

One story that went around at the time reflected the kind of season it had been for Clark. Luis Leal had started against the Tigers at Exhibition Stadium. He got knocked out after three innings, trailing 6–0. Bobby Cox then went to his bullpen for Bryan, who gave up six more in two-plus innings. Now it was 12–0. Bobby came to the mound again. "Bryan, give me the ball. It's 12–0, and the Tigers have the bases loaded with Alan Trammell up. We're going to the bullpen and Roy Lee Jackson."

"No, Bobby. I'm not giving you the ball."

"Bryan, there are 35,000 people here today. Don't embarrass yourself and don't embarrass me. Give me the ball."

"Bobby, you can't take me out now. I struck this guy out the last time."

"I know, Bryan. It was in this same inning. Give me the ball."

That year, the Blue Jays also drafted a young right-hander, Dane Johnson, out of St. Thomas University in Miami, Florida, in the second round of the 1984 amateur draft. He later pitched for the Blue Jays in 1996. The quiet and much-appreciated Johnson was named bullpen coach in 2015, after serving as a roving minor league pitching instructor in the Blue Jays organization since 2004. Dane is one of the very few who can actually say he pitched for the Brother Elephants of the Chinese Professional Baseball League. He has had quite the baseball journey, to say the least. And no one is better out in the bullpen.

When You Least Expect It

One of the best among many traits Bobby Cox had as a manager was his ability to quickly see when he had made a mistake in judgement and change his decision. That happened at the end of spring training with rookie pitcher Jimmy Key. As the Blue Jays broke camp and departed Dunedin, Florida, to begin the season in Seattle, Bobby had put together his 25-man roster. It did not include Key. Cox had told Key he had had an impressive camp but would begin the season in Triple-A Syracuse, but after sleeping on that decision for just one night, he called Florida and told them to put Key on the next flight to Seattle. Bobby knew in his heart that Jimmy should be on the Opening Day roster. Bobby's insight and feel for the game and his players combined with the ability to adjust quickly and move forward is what made him special. Key pitched out of the bullpen all season long that year, collecting a rookie club record 10 saves. His 15-year career included 116 wins as a Blue Jay of his total 186 victories, and a 1992 World Series ring.

Just after he moved to the starting rotation in 1985, Jimmy shared something with me that made me a much better broadcaster. The day before his start, a pitcher would chart that day's game live, directly off the clubhouse TV. They would write down every pitch for the pitching coach and that day's starter to later review. One day as I was walking by the clubhouse, Jimmy got my attention in his very soft-spoken and honest way. "Jerry, are you guessing up there in the radio booth on the pitches thrown? I had the radio on, listening to you as I was watching the television. You missed a number of pitches and what they were. Why don't you call the pitches off the TV monitor like we do?" Those few words turned my career completely around. I told Jimmy I was guessing whether it was a curve or slider or something else, watching with my naked eye from upstairs.

When I went up to our booth at Exhibition Stadium, I looked for a TV monitor. Sure enough, there was a small one anchored up on the wall off to our right. It had been attached there since 1977. Neither Tom nor Early ever used it. That day I asked our engineer to please take it off the wall. I put it in front of me, just off to my left. I started to "practice" taking pitches off the centre-field camera to see what that was like. My one fear, of course, was to call the pitch off the monitor and then lose sight of the ball when it was put into play. Not good for a play-by-play announcer. This was all new for me. I was getting more comfortable but I still wasn't doing it full-time.

Then the Blue Jays went into Baltimore to play the Orioles. Their radio announcer, Jon Miller, was a good one. I had known for years. Jon was in the early stages of making a name for himself on TV as the voice of Sunday Night Baseball, with Hall of Fame second baseman Joe Morgan. Miller won the Ford Frick Award in 2010. After I called my 3rd and 4th innings and Tom took over for the next two, I purposely leaned back in my chair and saw Miller at the microphone two booths to my left. He was calling every pitch off the monitor. Right then and there I said to myself: "If Jon Miller can do that, then so can I."

I began calling every pitch off the monitor and I quickly found that it was fairly easy to move my eyes from the TV to the field when the ball was put in play. On those rare occasions when I did not immediately pick up the ball, player movement would tell me where the ball was. The quality of the broadcast was so much better, and it took my play-by-play to another level. The body language of the hitter, the catcher, and the umpire told its own unique story with each pitch. It proved so essential to making the most accurate calls without guessing. I have Jimmy Key to thank for that.

One postscript to this story involves my radio partner Joe Siddall, who started with me back in 2014. Joe caught 13 professional seasons. I could tell from our first broadcast, Joe had very insightful comments to share with our audience. To help him get started, I purposely stopped using the monitor to call pitches. Rather, I let Joe elaborate on them. Sliders and curves became "breaking balls" from me, so Joe could define those pitches with greater detail and insight as to their effectiveness. It was clearly his strength and a tremendous benefit for our listeners.

After the 1984 season ended, the Blue Jays traded veterans Alfredo Griffin and Dave Collins to the Oakland A's for their closer Bill Caudill. Bill saved 36 games for the A's in 1984, and he was one of the premier closers in the game at the time. In January, GM Pat Gillick chose an unknown right-hander from the Texas Rangers organization as a free agent compensation pick for losing free agent Cliff Johnson. His name was Tom Henke, and he would figure very prominently in the upcoming season. A day after Henke's acquisition, Gillick traded pitcher Jim Gott and two minor leaguers to the San Francisco Giants for veteran left-handed reliever Gary LaVelle, who would prove to be very valuable during the regular season but a major disappointment in the postseason.

CHAPTER 13

WATCH OUT, AMERICAN LEAGUE

The 1985 campaign began with a 13-7 April that quickly led to a 30-15 mark by May 31. This was a team to be reckoned with. Gillick knew it, and so did everyone else in the Blue Jays clubhouse.

By midseason, Pat continued to add one veteran after another in his quest to reach the playoffs. On July 9, Al Oliver came from the Dodgers for Len Matuszek. Oliver was in his 18th season. Al had worn No. 0 when he was a Montreal Expo in 1982 and 1983. He had originally taken that number when he was traded from the Pirates to the Rangers after the 1977 season, and for good reason. "Zero is a starting point for me, and I wanted to start all over again." His presence was just what the Blue Jays were looking for on their way to 99 wins. Oliver hit five home runs and drove in 23 runs, many of them in key late-game situations, over his 61 games. Al's nickname was "Scoop." I asked Lloyd Moseby what he thought of his new teammate at the time. "Scoop was a philosopher. He broke the game down into its most simplistic form. If he went zero for four, he would tell you that he really didn't go zero for four and explain why. You never really understood Scoop."

On August 28, just before the playoff rosters had to be set, the club reacquired Cliff Johnson from the Texas Rangers for three minor leaguers. When Cliff was a Blue Jay in 1984 he wore No. 44. Now he wanted to wear No. 0 but was told Oliver had it. So Cliff asked for and received No. 00. You don't often see 0 and 00 on the same 25-man roster. In Cliff's 24 games, he made the most of his 20 hits, driving in 10 runs. With Johnson and Oliver at the plate and Lavelle on the mound saving eight games and winning five others, the Blue Jays took off. And then along came an unknown out of nowhere.

The Terminator

On July 29, at old Memorial Stadium in Baltimore, the Blue Jays defeated the Orioles, 4–3, in 10 innings. A newcomer just summoned from Triple-A Syracuse got the win, pitching two scoreless innings for starter Jimmy Key. It marked the beginning of a truly remarkable career for Tom Henke, the pride of Taos, Missouri, population 780. People ask me all the time, "Who is your all-time favourite Blue Jay?" My answer: "Tom Henke." And there are many reasons why.

Tom was a bricklayer in Taos. He was humbly and modestly raising his family with his wife, Kathy, when he started his professional baseball career. He made it to the Texas Rangers, pitching in a handful of games in the early 1980s under manager Doug Rader, an original Blue Jay back in 1977. Rader had some issues managing his temper at the time, which included yelling at his players and demeaning them right there in the dugout when things weren't going well, and then sending those players directly to Triple-A the next day.

Rader did that with Henke in Texas. Then, as the manager of the Angels, he did it to a young centre fielder named Devon White, who was unceremoniously sent to Triple-A armed with Rader's words that he wasn't good enough to hit at the major league level, let alone lead off to utilize his speed. Gillick acquired both of them for next to nothing. Much to Doug's credit, he later opened up to *Sports Illustrated* about his personal battles to control his temper as a manager. I thoroughly enjoyed the article. He began keeping a daily journal, realizing how self-destructive he was, as well as hurtful to others. The journal was a source of cleansing. He wrote in it daily for a couple of years and said it helped him considerably.

When Henke was picked up by Toronto in January, the team already had a newly acquired closer from Oakland in Bill Caudill, who was one of the best closers in the game at the time. Henke began the 1985 season in Triple-A Syracuse. Tom never lashed out or held court with the media about how he was treated in Texas. Instead, his class and character pointed him in the direction of simply pitching his best and patiently waiting for his opportunity. That opportunity came at the end of July. Caudill was struggling while Henke, in Syracuse, had off-the-chart numbers: 51 innings, only 13 hits allowed, 60 strikeouts, only 18 walks, and 18 saves in 39 games. He was ready. After his debut in Baltimore, Henke never looked back. He was instrumental in saving 13 games down the stretch and saving the season for the AL East champions.

One night at Exhibition Stadium, Henke came in for a save opportunity against Cleveland in the top of the 9th inning. Joe Carter was still with Cleveland at the time. Carter came up with two men on and two outs, and he hit a pitch deep to left field but just foul. He was retired on the next pitch, and the

Blue Jays won. After the game, I went into the clubhouse and saw Henke surrounded by members of the media. I listened from outside the media circle as they asked him about Carter's near home run. "As soon as Joe hit that ball down the left-field line, I quickly said to myself, 'I sure hope Jerry is up there in the radio booth saying, *hooking, hooking . . . foul!*' And he did."

On a bright Sunday afternoon on September 1, a month after Henke's debut, the Blue Jays were playing the Chicago White Sox at Exhibition Stadium. Landing at the Toronto airport with the game in progress was John Cerutti, a September call-up and Henke's former teammate in Syracuse, who was about to make his major league debut. In the 7th inning with the bases loaded, one out and the dangerous veteran and left-handed hitting Harold Baines at the plate, Bobby Cox summoned the lefty Cerutti from the bullpen. As Bobby left the mound, a classic meeting took place between catcher and pitcher, the kind that you sometimes see in the movies but rarely in real life.

"Hi, John, I'm Steve Nicosia. I was just signed by the Blue Jays a few days ago."

"Hi, Steve. I'm John Cerutti. I've been pitching in Syracuse this season and just arrived in Toronto a couple of hours ago. Nice to meet you."

"John, what do you throw?"

"All four pitches . . . fastball, curve, slider, and change."

"Great. Let's get Baines." And with that, Nicosia went back behind the plate.

To begin his major league career, Cerutti proceeded to strike out Baines with the bases loaded. Later John laughed and said he'd thought there would be more. "After I struck out Baines, I saw Bobby come out of the dugout to the mound. I thought 'Wow. This is great. Now he's going to tell me how to pitch to

Carlton Fisk.' Instead Bobby reached for the ball and said 'Nice job. We're going to the bullpen for Roy Lee Jackson.'" A couple of weeks later on the road Henke and Cerutti went to see *The Terminator* in the theatre. As they left the show, Cerutti said, "From now on, Tom, I'm calling you 'The Terminator.'" For the rest of Henke's outstanding career, that's what he was called.

Henke pitched 14 years in the major leagues, eight of those with the Blue Jays. He capped his years in Toronto as the closer for the 1992 World Series Champions. Tom pitched three more seasons after that with the Texas Rangers and the St. Louis Cardinals. Not many players go out at the top of their game. In fact, very few do. Henke was one of the rare exceptions. In 1995, Tom went back "home," so to speak, pitching for the St. Louis Cardinals before family and friends. Many would come over from Taos to see him. He saved 36 of 38 games that season to surpass 300 saves, reaching a total of 311. After that season, he retired. His manager Tony LaRussa pleaded with him in the offseason to reconsider, but Henke was adamant about wanting to spend all of his time with wife, Kathy, and their four children.

One of those four children, Amanda, was born with Down syndrome. Since 1995, Tom has hosted the annual Tom Henke Charity Golf Classic to raise money for the Special Learning Centre, a school for children with special needs. I have had the pleasure of flying over to emcee one of those events for Tom. Henke also volunteers with Down syndrome charities, the Special Olympics, and the Cancer Society. Rex Hudler, a long-time friend and Kansas City Royals TV announcer, has a child born with Down syndrome, but for the Hudler family their son, Cade, has "Up syndrome." I like that.

No Right Hand: Pitcher Jim Abbott

During the early part of the 1985 season, Blue Jays TV broadcaster Tony Kubek waved me over to watch some early batting practice with him. There were two pitchers who had been invited by Pat Gillick to throw from the mound just before the upcoming June Draft. One was right-handed and the other left-handed. The right-hander was young Todd Stottlemyre. You could tell he came from good baseball bloodlines. His dad, Mel, was a long-time pitcher with the New York Yankees and later an excellent major league pitching coach. Pat worked with the Yankees before being hired by the Blue Jays, and he knew Mel real well. Todd was good; he threw with conviction. You could tell he had learned a lot from his dad. A month later, the Blue Jays drafted him in the first round (third overall), and he started 16 games that season.

Then Tony asked, "Do you notice anything different about the left-hander?"

"No. He looks pretty smooth out there, has good mechanics and rhythm."

Tony said, "Take a closer look and tell me what you see."

What I then saw amazed me. I had never seen or heard anything about Jim Abbott until that very moment. Abbott was finishing up his last year of high school in Flint, Michigan, where he grew up. Born without a right hand, Jim passed on signing that June with the Blue Jays, who selected him in the 39th round. He instead opted to go to the University of Michigan, where he starred for the Wolverines the next three seasons. In 1988, the Angels made him a first-round pick. He went on to pitch 10 seasons in the major leagues. At Yankee Stadium in 1993, he pitched a no-hitter against Cleveland. He was near flawless, pitching without a right hand.

When preparing to pitch, Abbott would rest his mitt on the end of his right forearm. After releasing the ball, he would quickly slip his hand into the mitt, usually in time to field any balls that a two-handed pitcher would be able to field. Then he would secure the mitt between his right forearm and torso, slip his hand out of the mitt, and remove the ball from the mitt, usually in time to throw out the runner at first or sometimes even start a double play. At all levels, teams tried to exploit his fielding disadvantage by repeatedly bunting against him. That tactic was never effective.

Jim was a remarkable young man. I was always so inspired when we talked. Every season when Abbott's team would come to play the Blue Jays, he would invite a group of seven or eight kids with physical disabilities from the Toronto area, many without arms or hands like himself, to sit in the dugout with him before the game. Those kids loved taking it all in, and Jim did it in every city. When he was 10 years old in Little League in Flint, the opposing manager had his first eight kids in the lineup try to bunt their way on base against him. When he retired the eighth hitter in a row, the other coach stopped. Not once did Jim complain; he just pitched. He was that close to becoming a Blue Jay — Gillick once again showed his eye for talent and the character you need to succeed in the show.

Expansion Ecstasy

History was made at the Ex on Saturday, October 5, 1985, in the next-to-last game of the season. The Blue Jays defeated the New York Yankees, 5–1, to win the American League Eastern Division title and advance to the playoffs for the first time in their history. Doyle Alexander pitched a complete-game five-hitter before 44,608 fans. Most fans will recall the final out, when Ron Hassey flied out to shallow left field as George Bell came in to make the catch.

One of my most cherished moments as a Blue Jays radio broadcaster took place in the clubhouse after the game, with champagne sprayed everywhere and beer poured on everyone, including myself. I got the chance to hug and congratulate every player in that room, and to tell each one what I thought he meant to the team and contributed for the win. The players glowed with smiles of pure joy. The looks on their faces said it all. Especially those 11 players who'd begun the journey back in 1982.

Saturday's victory over the Yankees was a historic moment in another way as well. The home plate umpire was veteran Jerry Neudecker. Jerry used the outside balloon chest protector behind home plate his entire career, as did the other American League umpires. National League umpires all used an inside chest protector. Neudecker retired two days later, after a long and distinguished career, and his balloon chest protector went straight to Cooperstown, where it is on display as the last of its kind ever used in a major league game.

Sunday was pretty historic, too. Yankee pitcher Phil Niekro went the distance to win his 300th game, beating the Blue Jays and John Cerutti, who was making his first major league start. Niekro won it, 8–0, pitching a complete-game shutout.

Noteworthy for the veteran knuckleballer, who pitched 21 years, was that he did not throw a knuckleball the entire game until Tony Fernandez doubled with two outs in the 9th inning. Instead, Niekro had used sinking fastballs, curveballs, screwballs, and "blooper" pitches as he called them.

"I always wanted to pitch a whole game without throwing knuckleballs because people think I couldn't get people out without throwing them." Niekro ended the game with a flourish. He struck out veteran Jeff Burroughs on three pitches — all knuckleballs — to win his 300th. "I decided if I was going to win the three hundredth," Niekro explained, "I should finish it with a knuckleball. That was the pitch that got me there."

The regular season ended with Blue Jays right fielder Jesse Barfield leading all American League outfielders with 22 assists, Bobby Cox being named AL Manager of the Year, and Dave Stieb winning the AL ERA title at 2.48. Quite a season.

Expansion Agony

In the American League Championship Series, the Kansas City Royals overcame a three-games-to-one deficit and rallied to defeat the Blue Jays in seven games. Their veteran catcher John Wathan told me something in the KC dugout before Game 5 in Kansas City that continues to influence my broadcasts, including both of the Blue Jays playoff series in 2015 and 2016. "Jerry, in baseball, a three-game winning streak is nothing." How right he was. Not only did the Royals win three in a row to defeat the Blue Jays in the ALCS, they won the World Series over the St. Louis Cardinals the exact same way. Thirty years later, the Blue Jays won three in a row against the Texas Rangers to come from behind and win the 2015 American League Division Series.

I mentioned earlier that pitcher Gary LaVelle helped the Blue Jays considerably during the regular season after coming over from the San Francisco Giants, but then was a major disappointment in the playoffs. Gary had complained of soreness in his left elbow at the end of the regular season. Yet when the playoff roster was put together, he insisted he was healthy enough to pitch. The Blue Jays weren't sure. LaVelle was the only lefty in the bullpen to counter the Royals' great left-handed hitter and future Hall of Famer George Brett. But LaVelle continued to insist he was fine, and he won out. In his first appearance in Game 2 of the playoffs, Gary came out of the bullpen to start the 8th inning. He walked Brett on four pitches. He left the mound with a sore elbow. LaVelle never pitched again in that playoff series. That infuriated many, including bullpen coach John Sullivan. Brett batted .348 in the series. The Blue Jays did not have a left-handed answer against him late in those games.

Popeye, Nitwits, and Big Daddy

After the disappointment of losing to the Royals in the 1985 American League Championship Series, the Blue Jays and their fans received some more disheartening news. Manager Bobby Cox announced he was going back to Atlanta to become their general manager. The job had a lot of benefits, and Bobby couldn't turn it down. The Blue Jays quickly named third-base coach Jimy Williams as their new manager. Having watched him manage in Salt Lake City for three years, I felt he was going to be one of the game's best managers. His 1986 team finished fourth with a record of 86-76, trailing Boston by nine and a half games. That included a 9-11 April, followed by a 14-15 May. Then the club got hot and had three straight winning months before a disappointing 13-18 finish in September/October to fall out of the race.

One of the real pleasant surprises that year turned out to be a rookie right-handed pitcher who was in the Blue Jays organization for a number of years. Mark Eichhorn had worked his way up the organization ladder and was called up to pitch in 1982. But then a severe shoulder injury at the end of the season nearly ended his career. Mark bottomed out in Double-A with continuing arm issues. It was then that the very likeable Eichhorn started to drop down with his sidearm delivery, going submarine style and throwing what became known as a "frisbee slider." With that pitch, he remarkably worked his way all the way back to the major leagues, winning the *Sporting News* American League Rookie Pitcher of the Year Award in 1986. Later, he would slip on two World Series rings with the Blue Jays as well.

Mark was one of the happiest and most outgoing Blue Jays I ever met. He still has that same disposition to this day. His joy was there for everyone to see and hear, especially when he did his perfect Popeye impersonations. Off the field, he took his joyful heart to churches with his girlfriend and future wife, Mariann Goodnight — a beautiful last name — where I remember Mark pitching spiritual hymns pretty well there, too.

Eichhorn left the Blue Jays after the 1988 season to pitch for Atlanta and the Angels. He returned to Toronto for both the 1992 and 1993 World Series Championship seasons, capping his tremendous professional career when it seemed for a moment like it was over. A testament to the strength of character "Popeye" showed throughout.

There was another unique story on the 1986 team, and it had to do with a star quarterback who started all four years he was at the University of Michigan under legendary head coach Bo Schembechler from 1975 to 1978. Rick Leach was now a Blue Jay after leading the Wolverines to three Rose Bowls. When the Detroit Tigers made him a first-round draft pick in June 1979 (13th overall), he chose baseball over football. Rick was always upbeat and fun to be around. His close friend and fellow Michigander, Ernie Whitt, was his teammate. They always poked fun at one another.

Leach would see Whitt coming his way with his three young kids and yell out, "Here comes Ernie and the nitwits." Everyone burst out laughing. It went back and forth between the two of them for years. Leach had his best season in 1986, batting .309 with five home runs and 39 RBIs over 110 games.

There was also a 21-year-old on the team who came over from the Kansas City Royals as a teenager in another classic Pat Gillick trade. His name was Cecil Fielder, or "Big Daddy," as he would later be known. He was just starting an excellent career. As it turned out, so was his young son Prince. Cecil played just a handful of games over the four years he was with the Blue Jays, which included hitting only 31 of his eventual 319 home runs. One of the funniest memories I have of Cecil was seeing four-year-old Prince on the team bus standing on his seat right next to his daddy and scowling at me. There was no smile. The kid was ferocious looking. But you knew he was going to be a serious competitor even with the opposite personality of his dad. The irony is Prince finished his career hitting exactly the same number of home runs as big Cecil.

After the 1988 season was over, Cecil's contract was purchased by the Hanshin Tigers in Japan, where he starred with them in 1989. It turned his career around and was the best thing that ever happened to him. It was there where he learned to hit the curveball and play first base. He hit 38 home runs. The next season, he returned with the Detroit Tigers, and on the last day of the season at Yankee Stadium, he hit home runs 50 and 51 to cap a brilliant return to the major leagues as an everyday player. Fielder opened a lot of eyes regarding the value of playing in Japan, as many players would later attest.

Tough Pill to Swallow

In 1987, the Blue Jays had a strong nucleus of players under Jimy Williams, who was now entering his second season as manager. The overall 96-66 record reflected that. But the season will always be remembered, sadly enough, for the seven-game losing streak at the very end as the Tigers swept the final three games at Tiger Stadium, winning the division by two games. Seven of the last 10 games were against the Tigers. Had it been a World Series, it would have been one of the best and most memorable ever played. Every game went down to the last pitch, decided by one run. Two of the games went to extra innings, both of those won by Detroit.

The first of those took place at Exhibition Stadium on a Sunday afternoon to cap a four-game series. The Blue Jays had won the first three games and were looking for a sweep to push the Tigers out of the race. But Kirk Gibson homered in the top of the 9th inning off ace closer Tom Henke, dramatically tying the game. The Tigers won it in 13 innings by a score of 3–2. Sometimes you have to tip your cap, and this was one of those losses. The sad part was the Blue Jays did not win another game the rest of the season — the Milwaukee Brewers came in and swept the three-game series by scores of 6–4, 5–3 and 5–2. Then it was off to Detroit for the weekend and the last three games.

The Blue Jays needed one win to force a playoff game on Monday. You could feel the tension in the air. And in the Blue

Jays clubhouse. Friday night saw another one-run game as the Tigers prevailed, 4–3. Saturday night was another heartbreaker with Sparky Anderson's Tigers winning in 12 innings, 3–2. On Sunday in the 2nd inning, Tigers outfielder Larry Herndon hit a fly ball to deep left field. George Bell climbed the fence and reached out as the ball went just over his glove into the seats for a home run. It was the game's only run. Both Jimmy Key and Frank Tanana went the distance in a masterpiece.

You could hear a pin drop in the clubhouse afterwards. So disappointing. So close and yet so far. There was Jimy standing in front of the media, answering questions. In anything, and especially in professional sports, I have always felt it is good to be intense. But the key is to be intense without being tense. There is a difference. I saw tension welling inside of Williams over his couple of seasons as manager. That levity and good sense of humour and smile and laughter that I saw in him as a Triple-A manager and later a major league coach had disappeared.

Even as we did the manager's show each day, Jimy would start out by saying, "I'm not talking about that," or "Don't ask me any questions about yesterday." I would have to stop him before we went on the air. "Jimy, I have to ask you the question. It's part of my job. You answer it any way you want, but give me an answer."

In baseball, you hear a lot about a team reflecting its manager's personality. That is so true. I saw that firsthand with Williams, who just couldn't seem to relax, especially when he had to deal with the media. It was downright hard for him. Jimy was let go by the Blue Jays after a 12-24 start in 1989. He would later manage the Boston Red Sox for five seasons and then the Houston Astros for three. In his 12-year managerial career, his teams would finish second seven times without ever finishing first.

The 1987 season had its bright moments. There was the record-setting 10–home run game on the night of September 14. Veteran knuckleball pitcher Phil Niekro was a Blue Jay for three weeks. He was 48 years old in the last year of his 24-year Hall of Fame career. He was in the whirlpool tub so often over just three weeks, his teammates put a flag on it that read *U.S.S. Niekro.*

Veteran pitcher Mike Flanagan was acquired from the Orioles on August 31. He was an excellent addition with his pitching skills, quick wit, and great sense of humour. Mike had players, fans, and this broadcaster laughing incessantly. The players in 1987 were given Hondas to drive all season long in Toronto with the team logo on the side of the door. After Mike's 1987 season, he came back the next year and told everyone that he was driving Phil Niekro's car. How did he know?

"Because I found his teeth in the glove compartment."

Flanagan also used to say that he'd heard Nolan Ryan grunt on every pitch on his way to tossing seven no-hitters and making the Hall of Fame. Mike said he tried it. "I couldn't get anybody out, and I hurt my vocal cords."

Flanagan won 23 games with the Orioles and the Cy Young Award in 1979. Later, he called himself "Cy Young" having won it as a young Oriole; Steve Stone was "Cy Present," as he had won it as an Oriole the following season; Jim Palmer was "Cy Old" poking fun at the veteran; young left-hander Scott McGregor was "Cy Future"; and Oriole pitchers who were no longer effective were "Cy-onara."

Sadly, with all of his humour and creative abilities on the field and later as an Orioles television broadcaster and eventually their general manager, Mike took his own life in August of 2011. He was 59.

One of the heroes during a record-setting 10–home run game on September 14 was homegrown talent Rob Ducey. It was his first-ever home run in the majors. A rookie on the 1987 team, Rob was born in Toronto and raised in nearby Cambridge. He played with the Blue Jays and the Montreal Expos over his 13-year career. He also competed on the Canadian Olympic team, making him the first Canadian to play for all three of those teams. Matt Stairs, Denis Boucher, and Shawn Hill would follow. Rob also went on to coach Team Canada at the Word Baseball Classic and the Olympics in 2006 and 2008, respectively. Rob's dad, Ed Heather, began scouting for the Blue Jays in 1992 and was named the *Toronto Sun*'s Scout of the Year in 1997. Ed was a big reason for the development of Rob's major league–calibre abilities.

It All Starts behind the Plate

Exhibition Stadium hosted its last full season of Major League Baseball in 1988, in which the Blue Jays finished 87-75, tied for third place with Milwaukee. A few lucky newcomers got the chance to play at the team's first home before moving three kilometres east the following year.

Sal Butera, a catcher, signed as a free agent in March and is still with the organization today, both in the front office and in uniform at season's end, instructing and throwing batting practice. His son, Drew, who is also a catcher, owns a World Series ring with the 2015 Kansas City Royals. Sal has a World Series ring, too, that he won when he was with the 1987 Minnesota Twins. They both found themselves pitching in major league games, too. Sal worked twice in blowout games, logging two scoreless innings with the Twins in 1985 and the next season with the Reds. His career ERA is 0.00. Drew pitched in three games and a total of four innings. He allowed two runs and has an ERA of 4.50. Dad will remind Drew of this every now and then.

By the way, that 4.50 ERA is a "quality start" by Major League Baseball standards. Allowing three earned runs or fewer over six innings qualifies, although a true quality start, in my opinion, is pitching seven innings allowing no more than three earned runs, which computes to a much more respectable 3.86 ERA. It allows your set-up man to pitch the 8th inning and your closer the 9th.

Pat Borders

The last young notable on the 1988 team was Pat Borders. From Lake Wales, Florida, Pat spent six years in the Blue Jays' minor league system. He played third base his first two years, and in one of those years committed 41 errors. The next two seasons he tried his hand at first base, where in one season alone he made 20 more errors. Finally, venerable Bobby Mattick, who was then the Blue Jays' vice president of baseball operations, asked Pat if he would consider catching. Borders said, "Yes," and, as they say, the rest is history.

Pat went on to catch for 17 years in the major leagues, the first eight of those with the Blue Jays. He was the 1992 World Series MVP. On the team's charter flight from Atlanta back to Toronto after the Blue Jays had won it all, my family was on the flight with me. Our son Joe went up to where Pat was seated and asked him if he would please sign his World Series cap.

Pat said, "Sure," and signed it for Joe.

"Could you please put MVP under your name?" Pat replied, "Joe, I can't do that. There are so many others on this team who could have won that award."

When Joe came back to our seats and told me that, I just smiled. "Joe, that is what makes Pat a leader on this team in his own quiet way. He never takes any credit but instead gives it to all of his pitchers and then to everyone else. He is the ultimate unselfish teammate and as modest as they come. We should all try to be like that."

Borders chewed tobacco his entire career. Not a good habit, for sure, but many a ball player in those days did it. One day I walked into the Blue Jays clubhouse and went over to mention something to him. What I saw right next to him made me laugh out loud. "Pat, look at you! Look at all these cards and letters from your fans stacked almost to the ceiling. You are so popular."

"Jerry, they all say the same thing. I'm not sure I'm that popular. Pick out any letter in the stack and you'll see what I mean."

So at random I picked one out from the pile. *"Pat, we love you. Our whole family loves you. And we want to keep you around for years and years well after your career is over. So could you please stop chewing tobacco? It can lead to cancer and all kinds of health issues. We only want the best for you as a person. Our prayers are with you to please stop chewing tobacco for your family's sake and ours. Thank you!"*

Pat looked at me and smiled. "Every offseason I stop chewing tobacco because of all these wonderful letters from the fans. Then two weeks into spring training I realize that I just can't play without it. Maybe someday when I retire I can stop altogether." Here's hoping, for Pat's many fans who loved him, he was able to do that.

CHAPTER 14

CHANGING OF THE GUARD

The Blue Jays began April of 1989 losing six of their first eight games. It got worse. The club ended the month losing seven of eight to finish 9-16. May wasn't much better as the team headed to Minnesota on May 12 for a weekend series at the Metrodome against the Twins. The Blue Jays were reeling with a mark of 12-21.

Friday night saw a tough 6–5 loss. Then, on Saturday, two things happened. First, there was another loss, this time by a score of 10–8. Second, and far more significant, Jimy brought in closer Tom Henke to pitch in the 6th inning with two on and a run in. The Twins were already leading 7–1. Henke would pitch the last three innings, giving up one of Tony Castillo's runs and one of his own. He was not a happy camper. When I reached the field, the Blue Jays were batting in the 9th. When the game ended, Tom was visibly angry. He stormed by me and threw his glove halfway up the stairs on his way to the clubhouse, yelling and screaming.

In a postgame interview, Jimy was asked why he brought his closer into the game in the 6th inning down by that score of

7–1 and then used him for three innings. He tersely replied in a silent clubhouse, "We're trying to win a ballgame." There were a few thoughts I had at that very moment that have stayed with me my entire career. Yes, a manager tries to win a ballgame. Every game for that matter. But he also has to manage all 162 games during a long regular season. Not just one game, and especially not just one game in May. There has to be a certain mindset looking at the finish line rather than what is directly in front of you, and that includes resting players and pitchers in many circumstances and having them stay in their roles. This is why Henke was so upset. His role was the closer, except for an occasional appearance in the 8th inning to close out a game with a four- or five-out save. Right or wrong, it was easy for me to see where Tom was coming from.

To be fair to Williams, I could see where he was coming from, too. His mindset was centred on that one game. The losses were piling up; Jimy's job was on the line. His tenseness was on clear display in the dugout and in front of the media. In the long run, it cost him not just a game but the clubhouse. Three of the best managers I have ever seen excel at managing gruelling 162-game seasons and getting the most out of their players under often trying circumstances were Bobby Cox, Cito Gaston, and John Gibbons. Bobby won 14 straight division titles with Atlanta, Cito won two World Series, and John took his teams to two straight American League Championship Series in 2015 and 2016. These teams were a direct reflection of their managers, who had easygoing personalities but demanded from their players the competitive edge necessary to win over a long season.

For a fan, the season is that one game they are watching. That is what a fan is: a fanatic for his or her team. But that fandom can also result in a lot of negativity that can be heard from every quarter outside the clubhouse. If a manager can keep things relaxed in the clubhouse, the team's chances of winning are far greater over the long haul. The following day, the Blue Jays lost to Minnesota, 13–1. After that game, the organization did something it had never done before in its history: fire a manager during the season.

Enter Cito Gaston Stage Left

When the Blue Jays returned home, GM Pat Gillick announced that hitting coach Cito Gaston would take over the club as the interim manager. When asked about that, Cito said that was very much okay with him. He loved being a hitting coach and was willing to fill in until a new manager was found. The team quickly went 5-1. That often happens when a tense team suddenly relaxes and begins to have fun again, playing under someone else. Meanwhile, Pat was talking to the New York Yankees and owner George Steinbrenner negotiating for a new manager. Gillick was very much interested in having Lou Pinella manage his team. Lou had managed the Yankees in 1986 and 1987 and then again for a fired Billy Martin in 1988 when he was in the Yanks' front office. However, to part with Pinella, Steinbrenner wanted some compensation and asked for young pitcher Todd Stottlemyre. Gillick said no and settled on keeping Cito. Turned out to be the perfect call for all three.

The 1989 team went 77-49 under Cito's leadership and won the American League Eastern Division. Gaston was on his way to becoming the first African-American manager ever to win a World Series. He did not stop at winning just one. Stottlemyre remained a Blue Jay and was a key starter to help Cito win those two World Series in 1992 and 1993. Pinella left the Yankees front office after the 1989 season to manage the Cincinnati Reds. His Reds led wire-to-wire and won the 1990 World Series.

End of an Era

The brand new SkyDome was ready for business, and on May 28, 1989, the Blue Jays played their final game at Exhibition Stadium against the Chicago White Sox — but not before making some history during those last few months.

On a bright and sunny April 16, Kelly Gruber blooped a single to centre field in the bottom of the 8th inning against the Kansas City Royals to become the first Blue Jay ever to hit for the cycle. Some suggested Kelly should have tried to go to second for a double, but I disagree. It was already 12–8 Blue Jays. There were two on with only one out as the team was looking to add on, and they did so with Gruber's hit. I thought it was the right call to stop and go back as the ball fell in front of a charging Willie Wilson. Final score: 15-8.

Then on May 4, rookie Junior Felix entered the history books when he homered to right field at the Ex on his very first major league pitch, against Angels right-hander Kirk McCaskill. Felix became just the 60th player in major league history at that time to hit a home run in his first at-bat, and only the 13th to do it on the first pitch. But Junior was not the first Blue Jay to do this.

On April 7, 1977, Opening Day, pinch hitter Al Woods came up in the bottom of the 5th inning. He hit the first pitch he saw in the majors, deep to right for a home run. Years later at the

Rogers Centre in 2010, catcher J.P. Arencibia became the third Blue Jay to homer on the first pitch he saw. Then, just when I thought I'd seen it all, a month after Arencibia's debut, Daniel Nava, the pride of my alma mater, Santa Clara University, was called up by the Boston Red Sox to Fenway Park. He came up in the second inning for his first major league at-bat. The bases were loaded. You guessed it. On the first pitch, Nava hit a grand slam to right field, becoming only the second player in history, with Cleveland's Kevin Kouzmanoff in 2006, to do that. After his heroics, in the postgame scrum with all the media surrounding him, Daniel said that he'd taken some pre-game advice from Red Sox radio broadcaster Joe Castiglione to heart. "Before the game, Joe told me to swing as hard as I could on the first pitch because that is the only 'first pitch in the majors' I am ever going to see."

George Bell would hit the last home run at the Ex, in the bottom of the 10th inning of the final game ever played there, to beat the Chicago White Sox, 7–5. A "ballpark walk-off home run."

Beginning a New Era

On the evening of June 5, 1989, more history was made as the Blue Jays hosted the Milwaukee Brewers in the first stadium to have a fully retractable motorized roof. A crowd of 48,378 took in the game, as did many others in the 348-room hotel attached to it, with 70 of those rooms overlooking the field.

Left-hander Jimmy Key dropped in a first-pitch curveball to future Blue Jay and Hall of Famer Paul Molitor that was taken for a strike. Speculation was that Molitor was asked to take that special first pitch. After all, he was rightfully known as "The Ignitor," who loved to jump on first pitches, but not here. Home plate umpire Rocky Roe quickly called time and tossed the ball to the Blue Jays' third-base dugout for posterity's sake. The baseball was sent to Cooperstown to celebrate the occasion. Molitor then doubled and later scored the game and building's first run. So much for first-pitch base hits for someone who collected 3,319 hits on any count over his 21-year Hall of Fame career.

The Brewers won the game, 5–3, as Milwaukee outfielder Glenn Braggs hit the first-ever home run at the SkyDome. Afterwards in the Blue Jays clubhouse, I remember seeing Fred McGriff surrounded by members of the media, who were inquisitive about the new facility. One of the reporters asked Fred if he would have liked hitting the first home run. With that megawatt smile of his, McGriff laughed and said, "I didn't hit the first home run, but I stole the first base!" which he did in the 7th inning. The Blue Jays would have to wait one more game before registering their first win at the SkyDome, when John Cerutti defeated the Brew Crew, 4–2. John got a lot of help from his catcher Ernie Whitt, who went 3 for 3 and drove in three runs. The team continued to win in June and July.

August would impact the club then and in the future. On the 1st, newly acquired outfielder and veteran Mookie Wilson made his Blue Jays debut, having just been obtained at the July 31 trade deadline from the New York Mets. Mookie was outgoing and friendly, and it was obvious he loved playing the game. Two things stood out for me that I asked him about. First, he always hustled out of the batter's box. "Jerry, I have done that since I was a kid. I think 'double' when I put the ball in play, and until the defence stops me from doing that, second base or even third is where I want to end up. Running hard is something that has helped me so much in my game." The second thing intrigued me as a basketball coach. It was the way he ran. He said something to me I never forgot and used with my players after that. "I run with my elbows. I know it sounds funny to say, but by thrusting my elbows back and forth as hard as I can it keeps my momentum moving forward and makes me quicker with the natural speed I have."

On August 26, the Blue Jays signed a young left-handed pitcher from Kelowna, British Columbia, Paul Spoljaric. As nice as they come, Paul put together a yeoman-like six-year major league career that included two stints with the Blue Jays, from 1994 through 1997 then later in 1999.

When Paul and his wife, Lisa, got married, I was at their wedding reception. The emcee that Saturday night was John Shannon, who produced *Hockey Night in Canada* every Saturday, and who would later win a Sports Emmy Award for his coverage of the XIX Winter Olympics in Salt Lake City, Utah, in 2003. Lisa's dad, John Wells, who was a sportscaster on TSN, and John Shannon were longtime friends.

"Many people have come up to me tonight asking me why I am not producing the *Hockey Night in Canada* game in Montreal. Here's the reason: when Lisa was five years old, she came up to me and said, 'Uncle John, when I get married someday, will you be my emcee?'

"'Sweetheart, the day you get married, I will be there as your emcee no matter what my schedule is and that is a promise.' And ladies and gentlemen, that is why I am so happy to be here tonight for Lisa and Paul. Lisa, I love you." That was the first time I had met John Shannon. Talk about first impressions. Paul and Lisa have five beautiful children. One of the most loving families you would ever want to meet.

John Olerud

On August 26, another young man signed a Blue Jays contract. His name was John Olerud. It took him only eight days to arrive in Toronto. Fresh off the campus of Washington State University, where the Blue Jays had made him a third-round draft pick in June, John made his major league debut September 3rd at the SkyDome. He was a late-game replacement at first base for Fred McGriff against the Minnesota Twins. In his first major league at-bat, against pitcher German Gonzalez, I was at the microphone to call his single on the ground to right field. He never looked back, playing 17 remarkable seasons in the major leagues without ever playing in a minor league game until he was on a rehab assignment for three games in 2005 with the Red Sox Triple-A team. He put up one of the most famous numbers in Blue Jays history when he hit .363 to win the American League batting title in 1993.

While playing baseball one afternoon in February 1989 at Washington State, John collapsed on the field. When he was revived, the doctors took x-rays but could find no cause for the episode. Fortunately for John, his father, also named John, was a doctor and the head of dermatology at the University of Washington hospital in Seattle. John Sr. was not satisfied, so he called a friend and fellow doctor to ask for a second opinion. That doctor took another x-ray and immediately called in John's dad. "Here it is, John. The first x-ray missed your son's aneurysm, which you can see right here. It's tucked in the middle, just below the base of his nose. We have to go in right now and perform surgery."

The next day, Olerud underwent a six-hour surgery to repair the aneurysm. It is worth mentioning here that John's dad had asked the surgeon if he could go in from the left side. He knew his son was left handed and thus all his activities were dominated by the right side of his brain. This way, if there was a problem of any kind with the surgery, going in on the left side might help minimize the damage to the right side of his brain. That is why when you meet John for the first time or see pictures of him, you notice the indentation over his left eye. It is his forever reminder about how lucky and blessed he is. He wears his scar proudly.

On the evening of August 4, Dave Stieb took the mound at the SkyDome against the New York Yankees. Remember, he had just missed pitching back-to-back no hitters in 1988 against Cleveland and Baltimore with two outs in the 9th inning. Once again, Dave had two outs in the 9th inning, only this time he had a perfect game going. Twenty-six up and 26 down. Roberto Kelly came to the plate. I was watching down on the field near the Blue Jays third-base dugout, getting ready for the postgame show. When Stieb fell behind 2-0 on the count, my heart slumped. A great count for a hitter. On the next pitch, Dave threw a slider that flattened out over the plate. Kelly ripped a double down into the left field corner, spoiling Stieb's bid for some major league history. He would hang on to win the game, 2-1. Only the Tigers' Jack Morris won more games in the American League in the 1980s than Stieb. They would become teammates in 1992, helping the Blue Jays win their first World Series Championship.

On September 30, 1989, closer Tom Henke struck out the Orioles' Larry Sheets, and, with a fist pump and hug from his catcher Ernie Whitt, the Blue Jays had rallied from a 12-24 start to the season to win their second American League Eastern Division Championship. In the American League Championship Series, the Oakland A's prevailed, winning four of five games to advance to the 1989 World Series. A perennial thorn in the Blue Jays' side, Rickey Henderson led the way for the A's with two home runs, a double, a triple, and seven walks without a strikeout. He was named the series MVP. Rickey would later come to the Blue Jays in August 1993 to help them win a second straight World Series, joining former Oakland teammate and starter Dave Stewart, who beat the Blue Jays twice in the 1989 ALCS.

In Game 4 of the ALCS at the SkyDome, the A's Jose Canseco launched a mammoth home run down the left field line that went two rows into the fifth deck. Canseco became the first batter ever to reach the fifth deck at the Blue Jays' new facility, hitting that home run off veteran lefty Mike Flanagan. As Flanagan left the SkyDome later that sunny afternoon, he handed his sunglasses to his wife, Kathy. "Here. Put these on. I don't want anyone to know that you're my wife." Flanny always had a great sense of humour no matter the situation.

Even though the Blue Jays 1989 season fell just short of the mark, it stood tall after the 12-24 start. The Cito Gaston era had begun. The popular hitting coach soon became an even more popular manager.

A postscript to the 1989 season. A magnitude 6.9 earthquake struck the Bay Area on October 17, just before Game 3 of the "Bay Bridge World Series" between the Giants and the A's. Tom Cheek and I were in the radio booth on the upper deck about to broadcast the game across Canada. I had experienced many earthquakes growing up but nothing like those 15 seconds. I looked down from our booth and thought, *We're going to be down there in the lower seats any second.* Five years earlier, the San Francisco city counsellors had passed a bill to remove the rigid joints at Candlestick Park and replace them with flexible ones. That decision saved thousands of lives that day, including ours.

CHAPTER 15

CONTINUING TO REFINE

The 1990 season saw the Blue Jays go 86-76 and finish in second place in the tough American League East. There was sizzle and steak that year, and the Blue Jays' attendance showed it, drawing a major league record 3,885,284 fans. The Blue Jays led Boston by a game and a half with one week left to play but lost six of their last eight games, finishing two games back. I have always felt the best teams get to the playoffs after a long and arduous 162-game schedule. It's a marathon, and this once again proved that. Fans want it right now, but baseball is like no other when it comes to a six-month grind, plus another month for the playoffs.

Young third baseman Kelly Gruber owned it. He hit 31 home runs and drove in 118, won a Gold Glove, stole two bases in the All-Star Game at Wrigley Field, and topped off his baseball season with an incredible victory off the field. In 1991, ABC-TV Sport had an open competition among all athletes in all sports, called *The Superstars*. Winners included O.J. Simpson, Herschel Walker, Decathlete Dave Johnson, and Kelly Gruber. Kelly became the first and only baseball player to win the Superstars title. In my opinion, Kelly Gruber was the best athlete who ever put on a Blue Jays uniform. He had it all, and I believe he could have been a Hall of Fame third baseman with a career much like the great Mike Schmidt, but the likeable Gruber lacked one vital element to his game: a strong work ethic.

It was one of the aspects of his game that truly disappointed manager Cito Gaston. Kelly was continually late, and he lacked a discipline that you must have in any walk of life to be a success, but especially in the demanding game of baseball. This is why, after the 1992 season, the Blue Jays traded him to the Angels. Cito later noted the Blue Jays would not have won it all in 1992 without Gruber, but it was time for Kelly to move on for the good of the team.

As my years as a broadcaster went on, I saw how two key factors — talent and dedication — help to define a player's career. I then saw a third component that separated the stars from the superstars and Hall of Famers. That was having a sixth sense for the game and how to play it. Roberto Alomar had that. Not only could he beat you with his five Hall of Fame tools — the ability to hit, hit with power, run, field, and throw — but he had a sixth tool as well: an awareness of what was always going on around him on the field and at the plate. He was able to maximize his abilities to the fullest to beat you. Paul Molitor clearly had that as well, as I observed him during his years in Toronto. That is why they are Hall of Famers.

On September 24, the Blue Jays quietly signed Toronto-born brothers Rob and Rich Butler as amateur free agents. Rob debuted with the Blue Jays in 1993. That October, he collected a pinch-hit single off the Phillies' Curt Shilling at Philadelphia in Game 5 of the World Series. Rob went on to win that World Series with his hometown team, making him the only

Canadian to win a World Series with the Blue Jays. Rich would make his major league debut with the Blue Jays in September 1997. After their careers ended, they started their own Butler Baseball Academy, located in Ajax, Ontario, teaching the game to youngsters of all ages.

Coaches

The Blue Jays added three new coaches to the 1990 team, and all of them were instrumental in helping the club win their two championships a short time later. There is a moment from a bus trip with new pitching coach Galen Cisco that I still think about. We were talking about our families, and he began telling me about his grandmother, who had just celebrated her 105th birthday. He reached into his wallet and pulled out a picture for me to see. "This is how special my family is to me and my wife, Martha. Here is a picture taken recently of our family. Six generations. Some people have five generations that they can point to, but because my grandmother is still with us, we have six." It was family first for Galen.

Hitting coach Gene Tenace was added in 1990. He figured in significantly, helping the Blue Jays to victory. The two World Series rings he won in Toronto gave him a total of six with his four as a player. Gene had a nice easy way about him and connected well with players, but he could also be firm when he needed to be. He had just the right combination to teach and reach rookies and veterans alike in a tough business.

Lastly, there was new first-base coach Mike Squires from Kalamazoo, Michigan. Mike was a great teacher of the game and especially at first base, where the slick-fielding left-hander had won a Gold Glove with the White Sox in 1981. The year before, he made some history as a lefty catching in two games for two innings. There are a lot of theories as to why there aren't any left-handed catchers. Suffice to say, there have been only three in the last 100 years, with Dale Long in 1958 and the Pirates' Benny Distefano, who was the last to do it, in 1989.

As 1990 came to a close, there was emerging in the bullpen a force to be reckoned with, complementing closer Tom Henke. That was Duane Ward, a huge part of the two World Series Championship years.

CHAPTER 16

SPECIAL YEAR FOR ALL

Before the 1991 season even started, GM Pat Gillick engineered the best trade in his Hall of Fame career, helping to propel his team from pretenders to contenders to World Series extenders.

On December 4, 1990, the Blue Jays traded first baseman Fred McGriff and shortstop Tony Fernandez to the San Diego Padres for outfielder Joe Carter and a young second baseman named Roberto Alomar. Pat was in conversation with the Padres GM Joe McIlvaine with a deal already in place: McGriff for Carter. Then Gillick asked about Alomar. When McIlvaine asked about Fernandez, the deal was struck. Pat was able to make trades like this because he had players like John Olerud and Manuel Lee ready to replace veterans. This depth was critical. It reflected a farm system rich with talented and potential impact players at the major league level, who could also be traded for experienced impact players. "A good trade is a good trade for both teams," as the old saying goes in baseball. This was a good trade for both teams. But especially the Blue Jays — as the next three years would attest.

On the day the trade was announced, Carter was playing

golf in San Diego. When he reached the clubhouse, one of the attendants saw his bag with his name on it. "Are you Joe Carter with the Padres?"

"Yes, I am," Joe smiled.

"Not anymore," the kid responded. "You've just been traded to the Toronto Blue Jays. I heard it on the radio a few minutes ago."

Two days earlier, Gillick had traded Junior Felix and Luis Sojo to the Angels for Devon White, a young and graceful centre fielder who had fallen out of favour in Anaheim. At the end of that first week in December, the Blue Jays signed a veteran free agent who was not only a role model in the clubhouse and on the field but also a key contributor over the next two years. That was Pat Tabler, who retired at the end of the 1992 season with a coveted World Series ring, richly deserved. It was amazing what had happened in one week in the offseason to bring so much ability and talent to the city of Toronto. The impact was felt immediately.

Hosting the All-Star Game

Fans were treated to an exciting 1991 season as the team went 91-71 to win the American League Eastern Division convincingly, seven games over the Boston Red Sox. In addition, the Blue Jays not only led the major leagues in attendance but became the first team in history to draw 4 million fans: 4,001,527, to be exact. The team would draw 4 million fans for three straight years.

Toronto hosted the 1991 All-Star Game, which always includes the Home Run Derby the day before. On that day in the brilliant Toronto sunshine, 50,000 fans were all wearing colourful Gatorade hats. Your favourite-flavoured sherbet was everywhere. It was spectacular to see, but the Home Run Derby was even more spectacular.

The Orioles' Cal Ripken stood at home plate and had the crowd applauding with each of his swings. He launched one home run after another and sat down to a thunderous ovation after hitting his 15th home run and taking a commanding lead. It appeared as if Cal had stolen the show. Cecil Fielder came out of the third-base dugout representing the Detroit Tigers. The former Blue Jay stepped in and promptly fouled off a couple of pitches with big swings, almost falling down as a result. His teammates roared with laughter. And then big Cecil did something that had never happened at the new SkyDome.

He smashed a high majestic drive to straightaway centre field. The ball sailed over everything and landed in the Sightlines restaurant. The crowd looked on in disbelief, then, realizing they had just seen a first, roared. Cecil smiled and looked back at his teammates, who looked on in stunned disbelief, too. He wasn't finished. Three pitches later, Big Daddy did it again, dropping another baseball into the exact same place where people were both watching and eating. There was a very appropriate headline in the newspaper the next day: "There's a fly in my soup." Now when the broadly smiling Fielder looked back, there was Kirby Puckett and many others on their knees, bowing to him in front of the dugout. Cal Ripken may have won the Home Run Derby that day, but it was Cecil Fielder who won the hearts of the fans. And the heart of the man who first brought Cecil to Toronto.

Sitting in the press box, I looked back at Pat Gillick, who is very emotional. As he watched Cecil and heard the crowd's reaction, I could see Pat's eyes welling up. That's who Pat is. He had seen something that nobody else saw in this 18-year-old kid in the Royals organization back in 1982. Nine years later, here he was crying tears of joy for someone who had turned into one of the most feared hitters in the game. The Home Run Derby added an exclamation point. It would take a number of years after Cecil's All-Star Home Run Derby feat for Cleveland's Jim Thome to finally reach Sightlines restaurant in a regular season game. Big Jim would hit 612 home runs in his 22-year career. In his first year of eligibility in 2018, Thome was inducted into the Hall of Fame in Cooperstown, New York.

The American League defeated the National League in the All-Star game, 4–2. Blue Jays lefty Jimmy Key was the winning pitcher while the loss was pinned on "El Presidente," Dennis Martinez, of the Expos. It was just the second major league All-Star Game to take place outside the United States. In 1982, the Montreal Expos had hosted the game at Olympic Stadium.

The Blue Jays continued to play well in the second half, finishing strong with a September/October record of 18-13 and winning the division handily, only to lose in the playoffs to the Minnesota Twins in four games.

The season included a fun personal family note. Left-handed reliever Ken Dayley joined the team that year as a free agent, signing a three-year contract. My two sons, Ben and Joe, were bat boys on a road trip that summer. Joe had pretty good-sized feet and got a pair of spikes to wear from one of the players. Ben did not; his feet were too small, so he wore tennis shoes with some bright lime-green shoelaces. The players razzed Ben about his shoes and, in particular, the lime laces. That is, until the team promptly went on a five-game winning streak. "Ben, you keep those shoes on! And do NOT change those laces." Ah, baseball superstition. You gotta love it. After the winning streak ended, I talked to Ben in the clubhouse. "No one in here wears a size seven shoe like you do. That's just too small. You are going to have to stick with your tennis shoes." Suddenly, I heard a voice from a corner in the clubhouse say, "Jerry, I wear size sevens. Your son can have a pair of my shoes." It was six-foot, 170-pound left-hander Ken Dayley. Not many major leaguers wear size seven shoes. Only fitting.

Coaching Basketball

People always asked me: "What did you do in the offseason?"

At the end of the 1991 baseball season, I began my avocation coaching basketball for 25 years. It all started in November, coaching the team at Islington Middle School, where my son Joe played. Believe it or not, when I drove to the school to conduct practice for the very first time, I sat there in the car and froze, thinking, *Can I really do this?* A couple of reflective minutes went by.

Jerry, get out of the car. These are sixth, seventh, and eighth graders! Run your practice.

I never looked back. Five years at Islington ended with a 19-4 team. My two best players, Tim Platt and Hiwa Barnes, ran the pick and roll to perfection, like John Stockton and Karl Malone of the Utah Jazz. Both Tim and Hiwa went across the street to Etobicoke Collegiate to begin their high school careers. Looking for more of a challenge, I went over there with them as the new Rams Bantam Coach. That eventually led to being the longtime junior boys' coach and finally the senior coach, where in my final year our team went 18-9 and played for the Etobicoke City Championship for a second time in my coaching career, each time losing to a very good Martingrove team. I retired from coaching at the end of that 2015–16 season.

One of the best teams I ever coached at Etobicoke was the 2007–08 team that went 0-19. By mid-October, we had our 15 players. In our first game, we trailed 22–4 at the end of the first quarter. For five months, we worked hard every day in practice and in the classroom, too, where I always insisted on academics first and basketball second. If you weren't going to listen to your teacher in the classroom, I knew you weren't going to listen to your coach in the gym. In our last game in mid-February, and with the same 15 players, we went into Richview Collegiate to face the number-one-ranked and only undefeated team in our league. We had the ball and trailed by just six points with 2:54 to play, eventually losing by nine. That is how far that close-knit group came in one season.

As a footnote, on that 0-19 team was a great athlete and baseball player, who was a ninth grader just beginning to learn the game of basketball. Connor Panas went on to star on the diamond at Canisius College in Buffalo, New York, with his teammate Brett Siddall, Joe's son. Connor was also drafted in the 9th round by the Blue Jays in 2015, while Brett was chosen in the 13th round by the Oakland A's. Panas helped the Dunedin Blue Jays win the 2017 Florida State League Championship with those athletic skills and the next season helped the Double-A New Hampshire Fisher Cats win the Eastern League Championship. From winless teams to championship teams, it's all about how you compete.

CHAPTER 17

REACHING THE PROMISED LAND

As the Blue Jays moved into the 1992 season still nursing their wounds from a devastating playoff loss to the Minnesota Twins, two significant additions were made: Jack Morris and Dave Winfield. It didn't take long for the two of them to make an impact. Morris was just coming off perhaps one of the greatest World Series games ever pitched: he went the distance — 10 innings — in Game 7, enabling the Twins to beat Atlanta, 1–0, to win it all.

One of my most vivid memories of Jack occurred during that spring training. I happened to casually ask one of the pitchers how things were going. He was very firm and direct with his answer: "On day one, Jack Morris showed up in the clubhouse at the crack of dawn well before anyone else. We all knew immediately that he meant business. He was here to do one thing: to win another World Series. It was an early wake up call for all of us."

Jack Morris

Jack and I appreciated each other as competitors — Jack on the mound and me up in the booth. It takes a certain discipline and routine to do your best each and every day, and I had a close-up look at Jack's work ethic when he became my broadcast partner for the 2012 season.

About two months into that 2012 season, I noticed that when the Blue Jays were getting badly beaten, Jack disappeared on the air from about the 7th inning onward, and he would pack it in for the rest of that game. When I'd finally had enough of this, I confronted him after a game. "How many games did you complete in your career?"

He quickly answered: "One hundred seventy-five."

"Jack, what I want you to do for the rest of your broadcasting career is to pitch complete games for our audience. And when the Blue Jays are losing by a lopsided margin, find a way to finish strong and complete that game."

He said: "Thank you, Jerry. I appreciate you telling me this. From now on I will complete every game we broadcast, regardless of the score." He did from that day onward. Jack was born with the "competitive gene," as I like to call it, and it applies in everything you do in life. I was so proud of Jack, who finished the last four months of that season with true professionalism on the radio, pitching one complete game after another.

During that season I met his wife, Jennifer, and their eight-year-old son. Miles adored his dad. The very few times during the season when he came to Toronto for a visit, he would come into the booth and just sit on Jack's lap, taking it all in. His body language told me how much he loved his dad. At the end of that season, I talked to Jack: "You have grown so much as a broadcaster this season. Let me make a suggestion to you: First, think about the possibility of moving your family from St. Paul to Toronto, where the weather is very similar all year round, and be my radio partner for the next ten years. You can do this and do it well. I would love to have you work with me for those broadcasts.

"But, secondly, I also want you to think about another possibility for your family. Stay in St. Paul and find some part-time work with the Twins, so you can be with Miles during his formative years, from eight to eighteen. Otherwise, you will be spending the next ten summers away from him. I don't want you to have any regrets." Jack thanked me and said he would talk about this with his wife and get back to me. A month later, he called to thank me. He had agreed with Jennifer that staying in St. Paul was best for his family and, in particular, for Miles. He was going to ask out of his contract with Sportsnet and wanted me to know first. Sportsnet then graciously allowed that to happen. It was the right thing to do.

In 1992, Morris led the way, becoming the first ever Blue Jays pitcher to win 20 games, going 21-6. He would celebrate on the field in Atlanta, his unbridled enthusiasm captured on the cover of *Sports Illustrated* with his teammates. It was the first World Series Championship ever won outside the United States, enjoyed by all of Canada. On December 11, 2017, Jack would have one more celebration, which was richly deserved and long overdue, when he was inducted into the Hall of Fame in Cooperstown.

Dave Winfield

Dave Winfield was beloved by all in Toronto during his one and only season as a Blue Jay. His "Winfield wants noise!" became a rallying cry for everyone who came to the SkyDome to watch him and the team play. He had a pulse on what was happening around him, both on the field and in the clubhouse, and this innate ability helped the Blue Jays immensely in 1992.

At the end of April at Detroit's Tiger Stadium, rookie left fielder Derek Bell took a swing and fouled a ball straight back. He immediately grabbed his wrist. He had broken his hamate bone and would be out for six weeks. Manager Cito Gaston inserted veteran Candy Maldonado into the lineup to replace Derek. Six weeks later, Maldonado was hitting well below .200, and Bell was ready to return. I remember sitting quietly in the dugout with Winfield around that time and asking him about this situation. "Jerry, we cannot win a World Series with rookie mistakes. We are a team capable of winning it all. You have probably read a lot recently about Cito lobbying Pat Gillick to leave Candy in the lineup, despite what he is hitting. I am one hundred percent in agreement with Cito. We need Maldonado's veteran presence in the lineup, and he will hit. I am very confident of that." Sure enough, Cito won out with management, and Candy went on to hit .360 over the next couple of months, solidifying his spot in left field for the rest of the season. The Blue Jays took off. Dave had seen it coming, and he backed his manager all the way. Winning that coveted World Series ring is something he will cherish forever.

Dave continued to play after his one and only year in Toronto. He collected his 3,000th hit with the Minnesota Twins. Quite a moment for one of the three mega-star Hall of Famers born in St. Paul, Minnesota. Paul Molitor also collected his 3,000th hit with the Twins, and Jack Morris won four World Series Championships, including one in Minnesota.

Late in the 1992 season, against the Chicago White Sox

at U.S. Cellular Field, Winfield blasted a long home run deep to left field. As he stepped on home plate, there were my sons, who were bat boys that night. Joe was at the plate picking up Winfield's bat while Ben stood in front of the first-base dugout, waiting to shake his hand at that very special moment. The 40-year-old Winfield had just become the oldest player ever in major league history to collect his 1,000th extra base hit.

Juan Guzman

With Morris and Winfield setting the tone, the Blue Jays quickly jumped to a 6-0 start on their way to a 16-7 April. It was the first of five winning months for the World Series Champions. Their only losing month came in August, when they slipped to 14-16. Joining Morris in the starting rotation was No. 66, Juan Guzman. He became a vital cog in helping the Blue Jays win not only the 1992 World Series but the next year's as well.

Juan was a gentle soul and as likeable as they come — but what a fierce competitor he was on the hill. Guzman was originally signed by the Dodgers, and he laboured for a number of years in the minor leagues with control problems. Then one winter in the Dominican, it all came together for him. General manager Pat Gillick saw Juan emerging, too, as did Pat's ever-present scouts. Pat quickly scooped up Guzman in a trade with the Dodgers, who never knew what hit them.

All of this tied into Juan's jersey number. Numbers have always fascinated me; I am sure it goes all the way back to my days as a kid watching my San Francisco Giants. When I think of a player, his number automatically pops into my head. I asked Juan how he came to be wearing such a high number.

"When I pitched in winter ball that one season, I had a pitching coach named Ralph Avila. He was so good and took me under his wing. He taught me how to control all my pitches and have the confidence to throw them on any count. He not only taught me the mechanics of how to pitch but also the mental approach to pull it off. That winter ball season, I was wearing 66. Later I was traded to the Blue Jays, and I told Ralph that I would wear No. 66 with my new team, to honour him for all that he did for me as a coach and as a friend."

Guzman went 16-5 in 1992, with an ERA of 2.64, earning him an All-Star berth. The following season, number 66 would go 14-3, pitching 221 innings and slipping on another World Series ring.

The Golfer

Another valued starter in 1992 was the low-key Jimmy Key, no pun intended. Jimmy had a wonderful career as a Blue Jay.

In 1984, Key collected 10 saves, a rookie record for the Blue Jays. In that role, he showed he could pitch under pressure. His calm and unflappable personality combined with his ability to pitch set him apart from his peers. It was the only year he pitched out of the pen. His true value was pitching deep into games as a starter and saving the bullpen from excess innings. In 1992, Jimmy went 13-13, pitching 217 innings and allowing only 205 hits. He had great control, walking only 59. He pitched to contact, very effectively, with excellent command of all of his pitches, including an outstanding curveball. As a left-hander, he had an outstanding pickoff move that fooled one baserunner after another.

People often ask me which Blue Jays players were the best golfers. The two best I ever saw were starters Jimmy Key and the late John Cerutti, which makes sense, since starting pitchers have four days off between starts and more time to hit the links. Sadly, when John passed away in 2004 from a heart condition, he was the reigning club champion at the East Lake Woodlands Golf and Country Club in Oldsmar, Florida.

Todd Stottlemyre and the Mayor

Most people in baseball are very familiar with the name Stottlemyre. I grew up watching Mel pitch on TV during his 11-year career, all with the Yankees, in the 1960s. He then went on to coach in the major leagues for 25 more seasons, where I had the pleasure of becoming friends with him. His two sons, Mel Jr. and Todd, went on to pitch in the major leagues, too. Todd was a very important part of the Blue Jays winning the World Series in back-to-back seasons. In 1992, he went 12-11 with an ERA of 4.50, pitching 174 innings. The following season he won 11 more games, adding another significant 177 innings pitched.

"Stott," as he was known by his teammates, always wanted to get better. An admirable trait, but sometimes his competitive juices got in the way on the mound. That is, until veteran pitcher Dave Stewart joined the team for the 1993 season. Dave noticed a couple of things right off the top. First, Todd was getting two quick outs and then letting the inning unravel, which frustrated Todd to no end. And second, these situations led to Todd allowing his emotions to get the best of him while on the mound.

Dave pulled Todd aside early in that 1993 season with his arms completely outstretched. "Todd, when you aren't focused and you show your emotions on the mound to everyone in that other dugout, you are giving them the advantage and hurting yourself." Then Dave brought his hands in inches apart. "The next time you are on the mound I want you to concentrate completely on that catcher's glove and nothing else. Make that one pitch your priority and narrow everything down to that. Don't give those other guys any advantage." Much to his credit, Todd did that in 1993, helping the Blue Jays win their second World Series Championship on his way to a 14-year major league career. Dave Stewart was that kind of special teammate and mentor.

Another memorable Stottlemyre story revolves around one of those rare moments when brothers on opposing teams go head to head. That happened at the SkyDome one July night in 1990, when Todd started against the Kansas City Royals. His older brother, Mel Jr., was out in the Royals bullpen. Before the game I had visited with their mom, Jean, who was in town specifically for that game. She was very excited to see them pitch against one another, as she had not seen them do that in their careers. The game was not kind to Todd or, as it turned out, to his mother. He lasted only three innings, giving up four runs on seven hits before Cito had to take him out of the game. Meanwhile, Mel came into the game in the 6th inning and blanked the Blue Jays over two innings, allowing only two hits. The Royals won the game, 6–1. After the game, I saw Jean standing outside the Blue Jays clubhouse and asked her what she'd thought of the night. "This is the first time and the last time I will ever see my boys pitch against one another. It was so hard for me to watch!"

Todd had a playful personality. He would kid and tease, and he could take it as well as he could dish it out. His baseball pedigree turned out to be a plus for him and for his brother, too, who became a major league pitching coach like his dad. On many occasions, I have seen how hard it is to follow in a father's foot-steps, especially when those steps happen to be from a father who excelled at the game like Todd and Mel Jr.'s. You have to be yourself.

The best example of that came for Todd at the SkyDome in the victory parade after the Blue Jays had defeated the Philadelphia Phillies to win their second straight World Series in 1993. The mayor of Philadelphia, Ed Rendell, had called out the Blue Jays in no uncertain terms. He had guaranteed that the Phillies would win the World Series, and there would be no celebration north of the border. Well, as I was the emcee on the stage that day, I brought up Todd to speak. He quickly grabbed the microphone from me and in his "no uncertain terms," he bellowed out to the crowd of more than 50,000 fans: "I got one message to the mayor of Philly, and I hope you're lookin': you can KISS MY ASS!"

Boomer and Coney

Another very valuable starter was the "Boomer" David Wells. The six-foot-three, 190-pound lefty pitched in 44 games, including 14 starts. He was the proverbial swing man and fit the role perfectly. He won seven games and saved two others. David pitched 21 years in the major leagues, with the will to compete and the discipline to work at his craft twelve months a year.

One of the best moments in Wells's career as a Blue Jay occurred in Game 6 of the 1992 World Series. It turned out to be the clinching game, in which Cito Gaston used four — count 'em, four — starters to beat Atlanta and bring home to Canada a first World Series Championship. "Boomer" was one of those starters.

David Cone began with the ball and pitched six masterful innings, allowing Atlanta only one run. Then starter Todd Stottlemyre came in to pitch the 7th. He retired the first two batters he faced, but he couldn't retire speed merchant Otis Nixon, who reached first base. That's when Cito went to his next starter: the lefty Wells. Wells promptly threw in behind Nixon as he broke for second. Otis was thrown out at second trying to steal to end the inning. A great move by Cito and an even greater move by Wells. Later, a fourth starter, Jimmy Key, pitched in the 10th and 11th innings. It was the classy Key who — with Nixon at the plate in the bottom of the 11th with two outs and the Blue Jays ahead, 4–3 — told Cito at the mound: "Go to the pen for Timlin; he'll have a better shot at throwing out Nixon if he tries to bunt."

Key proved to be prophetic. Nixon tried to bunt his way on up along the first-base line and was thrown out by Timlin, leading to my partner Tom Cheek's great call: "Timlin to Carter, and the Blue Jays are World Series Champions! The Blue Jays are World Series Champions!" It took that kind of depth and some very shrewd managing by Cito to win the 1992 World Series in dramatic fashion. And no one was more instrumental in making that all happen than pitcher David Cone.

In late August of that season, the Blue Jays called a press conference at the SkyDome. Pat Gillick stunned everyone by announcing the acquisition of right-hander David Cone from the New York Mets for second baseman Jeff Kent, who had hit eight home runs as a backup infielder, and young outfielder Ryan Thompson. Gillick was thrilled. "Getting David Cone in 1992 put us over the hump and got us to where we had to go. Once in a while a guy will slip through waivers, and he slipped through." Cone was leading the major leagues in strikeouts. Now, all of a sudden, he was a Blue Jay. He let his pitching do the talking for him. After those outstanding starts, he would just quietly blend in to his surroundings, letting others take the credit while he simply took it all in.

In late August, my dad flew in from the West Coast for a visit. I had told him all about the Blue Jays and their tremendous team and how they were even better with David Cone now coming aboard from the Mets. He landed that afternoon and came right to the SkyDome to see the Blue Jays play the Milwaukee Brewers. Final Score: Brewers 22, Blue Jays 2. Milwaukee set a new club record with 31 hits. On the drive home after the game, my dad was laughing. "So this is the team you said was so good?"

This game happened just two days after Cone had been acquired from the National League. It was Cone's turn that night to chart the game, getting ready for his first start as a Blue Jay the following day. "I guess he's thinking, *tough league*. We'll have to ice his wrist down after that one," remarked Key, the starting pitcher who got knocked out of the game very early. David, in his own quiet way, was a winner and was vital to helping the Blue Jays win the ultimate prize that season. He would later parlay all that he learned on the mound into becoming an excellent TV analyst both for the New York Yankees — a team for which he pitched a perfect game — and for the MLB Network.

Jeff Kent went on to hit more home runs than any second baseman in major league history. Someday, he could find himself in the Hall of Fame in Cooperstown. That is just fine. When you trade someone of that calibre to acquire a player who helps you not only get to the World Series but also win it, you make that trade every day.

The Emergence of Duane Ward

The Blue Jays bullpen in 1992 was headed up by closer Tom Henke. The 8th inning set-up man was Duane Ward. When you included a very strong supporting cast pitching in the 7th inning, the games were pretty much over when the Blue Jays had the lead after six innings. It was an ideal situation.

Tom became the mainstay in the bullpen from 1985 right on through the 1992 season, collecting 217 saves of his overall total of 311. Just as effective out of the bullpen was Ward, who pitched the 8th innings. He often came in to retire the 3-4-5 hitters.

Duane was so focused and so competitive, no one wanted to mess with him. He had one goal in mind, and that was to win it all. He was one of the most valuable of all Blue Jays. The set-up man in 1992 was one of the best closers in the game in 1993, with a club-record 45 saves, winning another World Series ring. In my opinion, one of the most devastating injuries in Blue Jays history happened after that 1993 season: Duane came down with a sore right shoulder that never healed from all the wear and tear he had put his arm through. He pitched for nine seasons with the Blue Jays. In five of those years, he came out of the bullpen to pitch more than 100 innings, including 127 in 1990. Had those innings not finally taken their toll, there might have been another ring or two for Ward and the Blue Jays after 1993.

One other interesting footnote to Duane's career has to do with his own baseball superstition. He wore the same long-sleeved blue-and-white sweatshirt every day for well over a thousand straight games before it was somehow lost in the clubhouse in Milwaukee. Ward had sewed it up over the years to repair holes and tears and rips that crept into it, so that he could continue to wear that shirt over his long career. He was the best seamstress in baseball.

After retirement, "Wardo," as his teammates called him, went on to give back for years, bringing baseball to kids across Canada through the Honda Super Camps program. Duane loved teaching baseball to kids of all ages; he was so positive with smiles and laughs for all. He also was my partner on radio for a few years, and he provided great analysis for our fans on what he was seeing both on the field and, in particular, on the mound.

Pat Hentgen and Danny Cox

Oftentimes, when you look back at a starting pitcher who has had success in the major leagues, that pitcher started in the bull-pen his first season. Key was like that back in 1984, saving 10 games pitching exclusively out of the pen. In 1992, that pitcher was Pat Hentgen. Pat pitched in 28 games but only two as a starter, winning five important games and getting comfortable at the major league level. You could immediately see that he belonged. It wouldn't take long for him to blossom as a starter. The following season, Pat won 19 games. I would always remind him that he was really a 20-game winner, the 20th win coming in Game 3 of the World Series in Philadelphia. He won 131 games over 14 seasons, 10 of those with the Blue Jays, including the 20-win season in 1996 that earned for him the A.L.'s Cy Young Award. For me, he was a better person than he was a pitcher.

In talking about his career, Pat was really as surprised as anyone. "Jerry, when I was pitching early on at Fraser High School just outside of Detroit, where I grew up a Tigers fan, I was five-foot-eight and not that strong. Then between my sophomore and junior years, I grew six inches. All of a sudden I was pitching the same way I had done before but now with a much stronger body and leverage to make me that much more effective."

I got to know his dad and mom, Pat and Marcia, very well over the years. Their son is a direct reflection of his caring parents. Now Pat and his wife, Darlene, are that same way with their three daughters. In Pat's formative years, Marcia could not watch her son pitch; she was just flat out too nervous. Pat was scheduled to start Game 7 of the 1993 World Series, which never took place thanks to Joe Carter's dramatic walk-off home run off the Phillies' Mitch Williams in Game 6. Marcia couldn't even watch that moment in her seat. She got up before the last inning started and was pacing back and forth on the 100-level concourse behind home plate, when all of a sudden she heard the roar of the crowd. She knew the Blue Jays had won it all. Everyone was hugging everyone in the bedlam, including Marcia, who was hugged by a gentleman who said to her, "You look so happy!" to which Marcia replied: "I couldn't watch because my son is Pat Hentgen, and he was supposed to start tomorrow night's game, and now he doesn't have to!"

The gentleman lit up with a huge smile of his own. "I'm Bud Molitor, Paul's dad. I couldn't watch either because he was on base." The two had never met before until that very moment.

Years later, Pat's dad died of cancer. It broke my heart along with so many others. I was fortunate to be calling a game on TV that spring in Dunedin the year he passed away. From the TV booth I saw Pat's father in a wheelchair, watching from above the upper stands tucked under the roof along the first-base line. The TV crew got a great shot of Pat and Marcia taking in the game that they loved so much. I had the chance right then to speak glowingly on TV about the Hentgen family. A moment to remember.

Another stalwart in the bullpen was the reliable six-foot-four, 235-pound right-hander Danny Cox. When the starters did not go seven innings to turn the ball over to Ward in the 8th and Henke in the 9th, it was Danny who bridged the gap in the 6th and 7th innings with yeoman work. Those two innings are vital to a team's success, and Cox provided that. Danny would later work with youngsters in addition to spending time with his wife and three children in Illinois. He spent many hours organizing fundraisers for the Armed Forces and the Make-A-Wish Foundation. Danny was bigger than life on and off the diamond.

Get Ready for "Timlin to Carter!"

Another key member of the Blue Jays bullpen was six-foot-four right-hander Mike Timlin, who was called up in 1991. Timlin settled into the pen nicely over the next two years, surrounded by veterans from whom he learned a lot. This helped Mike to pitch 18 years in the major leagues, seven of those with the Blue Jays.

Timlin is class through and through, and one of the most positive people I have ever met. He goes with the flow and, as a result, got the very most out of his abilities. After rising from the role of set-up man to closer, he struggled and then fell back to the position of set-up man. That happens. But in Mike's case — unlike many others — his intestinal fortitude and ability to accept sliding back into the set-up role helped him later to dominate hitters as an 8th-inning pitcher with the Boston Red Sox, winning two more World Series rings with Boston in 2004 and 2007.

Not many are on the mound to end a World Series as Mike was in Game 6 of the 1992 World Series in Atlanta. There he was fielding Otis Nixon's two-out bunt bid for a base hit and tossing the ball to Joe Carter at first base to end it. In a game that is incredibly fast to play, Mike noted afterwards: "I thought that ball would take forever to get to Joe." I'm sure many Blue Jays fans watching on TV felt exactly the same way.

One day, Timlin and I were talking about Atlanta's left-handed relief pitcher Mike Stanton in the 1992 World Series, and Timlin told me that they had been teammates in high school in Midland, Texas. He pulled out an old black-and-white picture of his Midland High School baseball team. Again baseball continues to amaze me over the years. What are the odds that one high school baseball team would produce not one but two major league pitchers of renown, who would combine to pitch for a total of 37 years? Not only were they adversaries in the 1992 World Series, but they would later be teammates with the Boston Red Sox in 2005. Stanton just missed by a year celebrating the 2004 World Series Championship won by Timlin in Boston.

Devon White

As much as the 1992 team dominated the opposition with its outstanding pitching and defence, the offence was not to be overlooked either. From Devon White at the top of the order right on down to Kelly Gruber, Pat Borders, and Manuel Lee at the bottom, the Blue Jays could score their share of runs. "Devo," as he was called, is a special person. He represented yet another steal for Pat Gillick, taken from right under the noses of the California Angels. White had been sent down to the Angels' Triple-A team after being told he wasn't a very good hitter — in particular, a leadoff hitter. In December 1990, in a six-player deal, the Blue Jays acquired Devon along with pitcher Willie Fraser and sent Junior Felix, infielder Luis Sojo and two other minor leaguers the other way.

White turned out to be yet another testament to Cito Gaston's leadership and uncanny ability to instill confidence in his players. He looked at Devon's career numbers over six seasons with the Angels, which showed a batting average of .247, an on-base percentage of just .295, a slugging percentage of .389, and two Gold Gloves won in centre field, and he called Devon into his office. "I know what these numbers say. I also know that you were told by the Angels that you are not a leadoff hitter. I disagree. Here, I want you to play every day in centre field, and I am going to have you hit leadoff. Don't look over your shoulder. You are my leadoff man. I will take everything you give us. Now go out and have fun."

In his five seasons with the Blue Jays, Devon hit .270 with a .327 on-base and a .432 slugging percentage. He chipped in with 126 stolen bases and was caught only 23 times, scoring 452 runs in 656 games and winning two World Series rings. He later became the Blue Jays' Triple-A hitting coach, teaching others how to play the game with the same confidence he was taught by Cito and his coaching staff.

With Devon continually reaching base in the leadoff spot, he was a perfect addition to the offence, with second baseman Roberto Alomar hitting right behind him. What an awesome twosome they formed in front of Joe Carter, Dave Winfield, and John Olerud.

Hall of Famer Roberto Alomar

Willie Mays and Roberto Alomar are the two best players I have ever seen. Mays played for the Giants from 1952 to 1972, and I grew up watching him. I then covered Roberto's five years in Toronto, which allows me to make that statement. Both were gifted, both worked hard, both had a sixth sense for the game, both had a very high baseball IQ, and both could beat you in any and all ways. From a bunt to a home run to a stolen base to a marvellous defensive gem at any time in the game, Willie and Roberto were simply the best. This is also why, in my opinion, there is no such thing as a clutch hitter. Clutch situations come up the 1st inning and continue throughout — games can be won or lost early, not just over the last few innings.

Alomar played his first three seasons in the major leagues at second base with the San Diego Padres. Over those years, he committed a total of 61 errors, with 28 of them coming in his second season in 1989. He wasn't even making the routine plays. Yet, here he was with a pedigree that included his dad, Sandy Alomar Sr., who played for years in the majors. Roberto's faulty fielding opened up the door for Pat Gillick to neatly acquire him and all his talent from the Padres. With a change of scenery coming to a winning team and a renewed commitment to working on his defence, Roberto was on his way to stardom.

Alomar was such a presence in both the 1992 and 1993 seasons, helping the Blue Jays win two World Series rings. As a final testament to his ability to reach the greatest of heights, you just have to go back to the last day of the 1993 season, when Roberto made something happen that had not been achieved in 100 years. John Olerud led the league in hitting that 1993 season. He became the first Blue Jay ever to win a batting title, hitting a robust .363. Paul Molitor hit .332 to finish second. On the final day, Cleveland's Kenny Lofton was third in the league in hitting, with Alomar fourth. Roberto went 3-4, finishing with a batting average of .326, just narrowly easing by Lofton, who finished at .325. It marked the first time in a century that teammates finished 1, 2, 3 for the batting title.

I am happy to see Roberto on a daily basis at Blue Jays games. He works in the front office, lending his baseball expertise to the team, as well as giving back to the community that embraced him over his years with the Blue Jays. He has time for everybody.

I would be remiss if I didn't talk about the incident that occurred in 1996, in Toronto, which later led to a lifetime friendship between two highly competitive and outstanding human beings. Roberto had left the Blue Jays the year before and was returning to the Rogers Centre with the Baltimore Orioles. After being called out on strikes by home-plate umpire John Hirshbeck, Alomar spit in Hirshbeck's face. It got even uglier after that, with name calling and accusations. Point being: it did not look good on Roberto. There remained a strained relationship between the two over the next two seasons as that black cloud continued to hang over Roberto.

And then it happened. Roberto left the Orioles after playing with them for three seasons under the guidance of former Blue Jays GM Pat Gillick and went to play in Cleveland. Why is this significant? Because the Hirshbeck family lives just outside of Cleveland, and John's three children were devoted Cleveland baseball fans. Keep in mind that John's eight-year-old son, John, had died in 1993 from Adrenoleukodystrophy, or ALD. This rare genetic condition causes inflammation of the brain, affecting one in 18,000 people. Sadly, 21 years later, in 2014, another son, Michael, would die of the same ALD condition.

With Roberto now playing for Cleveland, John's kids had a dilemma. "What do we do, Dad? We love Roberto playing second base for our team. We want to root for him." The word got back to the Cleveland clubhouse. The person in charge of the umpires' quarters arranged a meeting between John and Roberto the next time Hirshbeck's crew worked a series in Cleveland. At that meeting, the two openly came together and talked about the situation. Roberto sincerely apologized to John and arranged to meet his kids at a game, starting a life-long friendship for the two families. The Hirshbeck children had their new hero both on the field and off, as their dad took Roberto into his family. In life we all make mistakes. Here were two outstanding human beings, and it took a while, but they got it right. I couldn't have been happier for the both of them. We are only as good as the adversity we are able to come back from; this was a perfect example of that.

Joe Carter

Another Blue Jays great who comes back to Toronto on a yearly basis is Joe Carter. His annual golf tournament has raised thousands of dollars for his charities, helping kids in Toronto achieve their dreams. Joe has always been bigger than life, as they say, both on the field and off it.

He played seven years in Toronto from 1991 through the 1997 campaign. He had remarkable stamina over his 16-year career: four times he played in all 162 games, and five other times, played between 155 and 158 games. He was also a model of consistency, with remarkable numbers at the plate in the 1992 and 1993 seasons. In 1992, he hit 34 home runs with 119 RBIs and 30 doubles. The very next year, he hit 33 home runs with 121 RBIs and 33 doubles. Joe will always be known for his 1993 walk-off World Series home run against Philadelphia Phillies closer Mitch Williams in Game 6, winning it, 8–6. There are a couple of other things people might not be aware of that makes that one swing so special.

My late partner, Tom Cheek, was at the microphone when Carter lined his walk-off home run down the left-field line and into the Blue Jays bullpen. Joe was watching it all the way as he ran down the first base line. He knew it was fair and was just waiting for the baseball to disappear into the bullpen. When it did, he began jumping up and down in pure joy as he approached the first base bag, paving the way for Tom's iconic and beautiful in the-moment call: "Touch 'em all, Joe! You'll never hit a bigger home run in your life." The best calls are spontaneous: if you try to rehearse them, as some broadcasters do, you lose the effect that has your heart jump during the moment. Tom made this call looking at Joe jumping up and down on his way to first. Tom did not want Joe to miss first base in all the excitement and later be called out for doing so. His call was perfect and came at just the right moment.

After the game, my wife, Mary, was visiting with Joe's mom and asked, "What were you thinking when you saw your son hit the home run and jump up and down with such excitement?" With a big bright smile on her face, she said, "My son, the kangaroo!" She captured the moment for all of us.

When people ask me why I love baseball so much, I tell them because of the rich history. It's a game that features twice the number of games of any other sport and has such amazing and unique trivia that you can only marvel in looking back. Joe's home run was a part of that.

Only twice in major league history has a World Series ended with a walk-off home run. In 1960, the Pittsburgh Pirates' Bill Mazeroski homered off the Yankees' Ralph Terry in Game 7 at Forbes Field in Pittsburgh. Then Joe did it 33 years later at the SkyDome. In the bedlam and celebration at home plate in Pittsburgh, veteran Pirates shortstop Dick Schofield was there with his teammates to pummel and congratulate Mazeroski. When Joe hit his walk-off home run, there to greet him at home plate in the mob scene was shortstop Dick Schofield Jr. — injured in May — celebrating with high fives. What are the odds that a father and son would both be at home plate for the only two walk-off home-run celebrations in World Series history, 33 years apart?

Hazards of Signing Autographs

In Cito Gaston's 1992 Opening Day lineup, a young first baseman named John Olerud followed cleanup hitter Dave Winfield. John was drafted out of Washington State in Pullman, Washington, at the end of his junior year in 1989. That season, he not only won the Pac 10's Triple Crown, leading the league in average, home runs, and RBIs, but he also went 15-0 *on the mound*. John was as quiet as they come; his 2,239 career hits, two World Series rings, and overall play spoke loudly enough. I remember standing right next to Olerud's father in the jubilant clubhouse after Joe's walk-off home run. He looked at his son and said to me, "He is a better person than he is a baseball player. We are so proud of him."

There was one funny story about John that you had to see to believe — luckily, I saw it. It occurred when John and I took a cab together out to the Kingdome in Seattle on August 1, 1993. John was the talk of baseball at that time, hitting better than .400. As we got out of the cab and began walking only about 100 feet to the gate, there was a mob waiting to get his autograph — and why not? In addition to his batting average, John was born in Seattle and raised in nearby Bellevue.

As the crowd started to swallow up Olerud, I went through the turnstile that separated the fans from inside the Kingdome and waited for John on the other side. It took a while as John was always very gracious in signing autographs. When he finally spun through the turnstile, his light blue shirt was covered with black and blue sharpie markings, from dots to swipes. The autograph hounds were all trying to get their pens into his hand. I had heard stories about this and will never forget actually seeing a shirt that was pretty much finished after a mere 10 minutes. John took it all in stride with that gentle smile on his face.

Father of All Those Ls

To win a World Series, it all starts behind the plate. You need a quality person who is unselfish and a true mentor, who helps and guides his pitchers through each game and each season, making them the story. That person was Pat Borders, who always gave the credit to everyone else. Borders is such an interesting person. Born in Columbus, Ohio, he was raised in Lake Wales, Florida, where he still lives with his wife, Kathy, and their nine children, all of whom have first names beginning with an L: Levi, Luke, Lance, Lindsay, Laura-Beth,

Leah, Lily, Livia, and Landry Kate. I would say that is just plain Lovely.

From humble beginnings on the diamond, Pat rose from a six-year minor leaguer playing three different positions in the Blue Jays system to the height of two straight World Series wins. He capped it by being named the 1992 World Series MVP. Borders's presence was typical of the great ones behind the plate who rise to prominence because of their desire to make everybody around them better.

A perfect example of this happened in 1992. The team, with family members, including mine, was making its way to the bus parked at the SkyDome, which would take them to the airport. Mary was walking to the bus with our sons, Ben and Joe, who were out in front of her, when she heard Pat: "Hey, guys, carry your mom's bags for her." The boys immediately stopped and went back to get those bags. That was the dad in Borders, the man with the good heart.

One day in spring training in 2016, after watching a game in Sarasota, I was driving back to Dunedin, listening to a University of South Florida Bulls baseball game on the radio. I always like to listen to young broadcasters, and the Bulls' broadcaster was pretty good. All of a sudden, I was surprised to hear: "And now to the plate here in the seventh inning is catcher Levi Borders, who is two for three today." I smiled big time because this could only be Pat's son. Levi got a base hit. "Now batting is third baseman Luke Borders, who is one for three this afternoon." It was one of the best innings I ever heard on radio.

On August 7, 2009, Borders, along with many of his 1992 and 1993 World Series alumni, came back to the Rogers Centre to be honoured in a pregame ceremony before a game against the Baltimore Orioles. It was Pat who received the honour of catching the ceremonial first pitch from then Blue Jays manager Cito Gaston. He also caught a ceremonial first pitch — a wicked cut fastball on the outside corner — from yours truly on August 11, 2018, celebrating the 25th anniversary of the back-to-back World Series wins. A pleasure for both of us. In June 2015, Borders began his first season as manager of the Williamsport Crosscutters, the Philadelphia Phillies' short-season Single-A affiliate. Don't be surprised if you see not only Pat return to the major leagues someday, but maybe another Borders or two as well.

Ike, Tabby, and Leiter

On July 30, 1992, just before the trade deadline, the Blue Jays traded outfielder Rob Ducey and catcher Greg Myers to the California Angels for relief pitcher Mark Eichhorn. Mark had made his major league debut in 1982 with the Blue Jays, where I first met him. "Ike," as he was known, was beloved in the clubhouse and became a key member of the bullpen for both the 1992 and 1993 seasons.

Pat Tabler was another important figure in 1992, finishing his 12-year major league career in Toronto. The next season he moved into broadcasting. Tabler will always be remembered in his career for hitting with the bases loaded, going a spectacular 43 for 88 in those situations, batting .489. He was one career hit away from batting .500 with the bases loaded. Pat was an outstanding teammate and is still working on TV with Buck Martinez. In his role as a broadcaster, he does his homework: he is down on the field daily, communicating with players, coaches, and managers, and he gathers all kinds of information in other

1956 — Choking up on the bat, at the age of 10.
Little League, here I come!

1958 — Joining
the Boy Scouts as
a 12-year-old.

1959 — Here I am at age 13, with Pony League teammate Kenny Marder (L) and my sister, Anita.

1966 — KSCU Radio goes on the air for the first time, and so do I as a 20-year-old sophomore at Santa Clara University.

Summer of 1966 — Riding up Grouse Mountain in British Columbia — saddle shoes and all — with my dad.

June 1968 — Graduating from Santa Clara University with cap and gown in hand while wearing my U.S. Army ROTC uniform.

December 27, 1971 — Heading down the aisle in Kalamazoo, Michigan, with my loving wife, Mary.

1972 — That's me on top of the hill, sitting on a folding chair while taping a Santa Clara Broncos football game against the University of Nevada, Reno Wolf Pack.

1976 — Moving to Salt Lake City, Utah, at the age of 30, with lots of hair and lots of glasses.

1976 — My first year calling Triple-A games in Salt Lake City, Utah, began with a billboard!

1985 — In the radio booth at the Metrodome in Minnesota, with Tom Cheek and our engineer, Bruce Brenner.

1985 — In a joyous clubhouse with Tom Cheek, celebrating the Blue Jays' first-ever American League Eastern Division Championship.

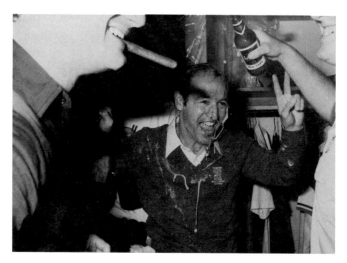

1985 — Doused with Labatt beer in the Blue Jays clubhouse after clinching the American League Eastern Division Championship.

1985 — In California with my family (L–R): brother-in-law Jim Madsen; mom, June; me; my sister, Anita; mom's husband, Walt Madsen; niece Traci.

1986 — Decked
out in my Telemedia
Broadcasting Systems
coat and tie, ready to
go to work.

1986 — Pitcher
Dennis Lamp catching
both the baseball
thrown by Tom Henke
and the one-dollar bill
I held out for Tom to try
to hit. Which he did!

1986 — Enjoying my office, which includes the Slippery Rock pennant representing the team that Puget Sound defeated in my first-ever play-by-play radio broadcast.

1987 — In a visiting radio booth in chilly April, preparing for a game with jacket and hat at the ready.

1987 — Interviewing Hall of Fame pitcher Phil Niekro, who was a Blue Jay for all of three weeks.

1991 — On the Blue Jays Winter Caravan, meeting Prime Minister Brian Mulroney in Ottawa! (L–R) Paul Beeston, Pat Gillick, Denis Boucher, me, Len Bramson, Jimmy Key, PM Brian Mulroney, Chris Speyer, Gord Ash, Herb Solway.

1992 — At spring training with Blue Jays bat boys, and sons, Joe (L) and Ben (R).

1993 — At the batting cage while on the road, with John Olerud (#9), Joe Carter (#29), and Devon White, with my trusty notebook in hand.

1996 — Interviewing one of my best friends in baseball,
Paul Molitor, on his return to Toronto with the Minnesota Twins.

Opening Day 2005 — With Tom Cheek and Warren Sawkiw in
St. Petersburg, Florida, against the Tampa Bay Rays, as Tom called
the last inning of his remarkable career.

2010–11 season — At Etobicoke Collegiate, where we won the Junior Boys Western Division and got to play for the Etobicoke City Championship.

2012 — Receiving the Jack Graney Award from Scott Crawford of the Canadian Baseball Hall of Fame, with (L–R) Mary, Ben, Joe, and his wife, Kathy.

2015 — Having fun at the batting cage at the Rogers Centre, with Blue Jays manager John Gibbons.

2015 — In the home radio booth at the Rogers Centre, preparing for the game.

March 2017 — My last spring training in Dunedin, with my outstanding partner, Joe Siddall, before I retired at the end of that season.

2018 — Proud parents Ben and Megan holding our grandsons Coleson (L) and Emmett (R).

August 11, 2018 — Our grandson Wesley attending his first
Blue Jays game, at the Rogers Centre with his grandpa.

2018 — Receiving the Sports Media Canada Career Achievement
Award, with presenter Brian McFarlane and my son Joe.

areas, too, well before he gets to the ballpark. A true professional, on and off the field.

Blue Jay Al Leiter is another two-time World Series winner who went on to the TV broadcast booth. The lefty pitched in only one game in 1992 and got a ring but not a lot of the satisfaction that went with it. However, in 1993 he was a very valuable swing man, pitching in 34 games, 12 as a starter, and pitching to an ERA just over 4.00 at 4.11.

I admire two things about Al. First is his bigger-than-life personality. He just exudes a love for life and literally tackles friends when he sees them; you have to be on guard, or you'll get bowled over. He has great insight into people and his surroundings, which has allowed him to broadcast Yankees games for years with the YES Network and work for the MLB Network. Second is his patience and perseverance. He overcame blister problems on his pitching hand that restricted him to pitching in just nine games as a Blue Jay over four seasons from 1989 to 1992, but he finally won that battle, contributing significantly to the 1993 season. Al pitched 19 years in the major leagues.

Alfredo Griffin

One of the best trivia questions in baseball is: who was on deck when Bobby Thomson hit his famous walk-off home run, the "shot heard round the world," for the New York Giants against the Brooklyn Dodgers on October 3, 1951, to win the National League pennant? The answer: rookie Willie Mays.

If you know who was on deck in 1993 when Joe Carter hit his memorable walk-off home run to win the World Series, then you know your baseball. The answer: veteran Alfredo Griffin. Alfredo began his Blue Jays career winning the American League Rookie of the Year honours with Minnesota's John Castino in 1979.

I first met Alfredo in 1978 when I was broadcasting Triple-A games for the Salt Lake Gulls in the Pacific Coast League. Griffin was with Cleveland's top minor league club, playing in Portland, Oregon, at old Civic Stadium. He was very quiet and shy and spoke hardly any English at the time. I had no idea that we would later have many years together in Toronto. Or that he would be forever remembered by me for the love and care he gave to his stricken former teammate and fellow Dominican, Damaso Garcia. A year after Garcia retired in 1989, he started to have double vision. He was diagnosed with a malignant brain tumour and, in 1991, had the tumour removed and was told he had six months to live — it was at that time that Griffin went right to his bedside to be there for him. Garcia has defied those odds, but the effects of the tumour have left Garcia with limited speech and movement. Unfortunately, he is still unable to speak, and he rarely leaves his house in Santo Domingo. This friendship says far more about Alfredo Griffin than any career numbers, rings, or awards he ever won.

The Candy Man

One of the most significant contributors to the 1992 season was 15-year major league veteran outfielder Candy Maldonado from Puerto Rico. The "Candy Man" finished that regular season with a slash line of .272/.357/.462 while hitting 20 home runs and driving in 66. He played a very good left field. He showed his veteran expertise time and time again after starting the season on the bench in deference to rookie Derek Bell.

Candy was personable and friendly while being a fierce competitor who loved baseball. It was no surprise later to see him on the field as a radio and television broadcaster for ESPN Deportes, broadcasting games back to his native Puerto Rico. Maldonado had a way of climbing to the top of his profession without showing off his ego for everyone to see. This allowed Candy to mingle easily and freely with players, coaches, and managers, then take those conversations back to the booth, giving fans his field-level and clubhouse persepctive. In 2011, Maldonado was inducted into the Caribbean Baseball Hall of Fame.

Coaches Make a Difference

The 1992 Blue Jays under manager Cito Gaston were blessed with outstanding coaches. Right at the top of that list was pitching coach Galen Cisco. Galen was born in St. Marys. Not St. Marys, Ontario, the home of the Canadian Baseball Hall of Fame, but St. Marys, Ohio.

This close proximity to Columbus led Galen to attend Ohio State. In 1957, he was an All-American and All–Big Ten football star and captain of the National Champion Ohio State Buckeyes. He starred at fullback and linebacker as the Buckeyes went 9-1. Two years earlier, Galen had led the blocking for Howard "Hopalong" Cassidy in 1955, when Cassidy won the Heisman Trophy. Galen was also 12-2 on the mound his senior year, starring in two sports.

This confirms why as a basketball coach I always told parents to let their kids play all sports rather than just one in hopes of someday playing professionally. You can't hide talent. That sport will find you if you are good enough.

Cisco was the Blue Jays' pitching coach for six years, from 1990 to 1995, and he did it with a calming influence that everyone noticed and appreciated. There was another coach, also born in Ohio, who had that same quiet demeanour: hitting coach Larry Hisle.

Larry played 14 years with the Phillies, Twins, and Brewers. In our conversations at the batting cage, he gave me his undivided attention with thoughtful answers that I was able to use numerous times on the broadcasts. You could just feel the goodness in his heart. After his coaching career ended, he became a mentor to youngsters in the Milwaukee Public School system. "Clearly it was the most challenging part of my life. The kids were just so different than I imagined kids to be. Half of these young kids I worked with were considered 'at-risk' kids. If you took 70 percent of these kids in that environment and put them in a good one, they would be fine. They would have the life they deserved. And these kids deserve that."

Rich Hacker was the third-base coach in 1992. His energy and work ethic provided every player with extra opportunities to improve, and his desire and passion were second to none in his brief time as a Blue Jays coach from 1991 to July 1993. Sadly, his season ended during the 1993 All-Star break.

The 46-year-old was driving alone when he was struck head-on by a car that was drag racing in the wrong lane over the top of a bridge in St. Louis. Rich never knew what hit him. Conscious, he was admitted to the intensive care unit at St. Louis University Hospital at 1:35 a.m. with a head injury and a badly fractured right ankle. No longer able to throw batting practice due to permanent damage, Rich's coaching career came to an end.

When he was finally able to return for a visit to the clubhouse, I asked Rich about the experience. "I was lucky on a couple of counts. First, I had my seatbelt on, or I would have been killed instantly. Second, and perhaps more important, I have absolutely no recollection of what happened. The last thing I remember is starting my drive home from the airport, and that's it. My doctor told me that is a blessing. He said it happens all the time, where the mind just does not relive those awful moments, and for that I am grateful. And to be alive."

I have always been a "big picture" guy when it comes to my own life. This was another sobering reminder that while baseball is important, it is still just a game. A game that pales in comparison to life itself. While there would be no more coaching, Rich was alive. From 1996 to 2000, Hacker served as a scout for the San Diego Padres. In 2001, he was inducted into the Midwest Professional Baseball Scouts Association Hall of Fame.

The first-base coach was Bob Bailor, who was the second overall pick by the Blue Jays in the 1976 expansion draft after the Seattle Mariners selected Ruppert Jones first overall. Bailor played 11 seasons in the major leagues, including the years 1977 through 1980 with the Blue Jays. He later came back to Toronto as a coach from 1992 to 1995. Bobby played multiple positions in his career and could teach all aspects of the game. In his first season with the expansion Blue Jays, he hit .310, which was a record for an expansion team at that time. Bob was quiet, knowledgeable, and a good communicator, and his versatility helped him with all the players around him. As Pat Gillick remembers, "He always went about his job in a very professional manner."

Gene Tenace was an outstanding major league catcher who was part of Cito's coaching staff from 1990 to 1997. He later came back for a second tour of duty when Cito managed the club a second time in 2008 and 2009. "Gino" would tell countless stories that would have everybody laughing. His facial expressions were priceless. Bottom line, he knew baseball, and he could teach it and coach it. He could also manage, which he had to do during the 1991 season, when Cito had to undergo a back operation for a herniated disc. Tenace took over as the interim manager, posting a record of 19-14 in Cito's absence. The Blue Jays toed the line in those 33 games to maintain a position of strength and allow themselves a playoff berth that season.

Two stories come to mind with Tenace. He told us about the very well-known and much-talked-about 8th inning of Game 3 in the 1972 World Series, between the Cincinnati Reds and Tenace's Oakland A's. The Reds were ahead, 1–0, with runners on second and third and one out. Rollie Fingers ran the count full on Johnny Bench, prompting a visit to the mound from manager Dick Williams. "So I go to the mound to listen in, and our manager says he wants Rollie to pretend to walk Bench intentionally and for me to step out to catch the pretend pitch, and then jump back in behind the plate to catch the real pitch and a strike. But don't throw him a fastball because he's a fastball hitter. As I'm listening, I'm wondering what the hell is going on, and Rollie says, 'What? What are you talking about? Is this Little League or what?' I go back behind the plate and then stand up and hold my hand out for the intentional ball. I then jump back in behind the plate as Rollie snaps in a slider on the outside corner for strike three, and Bench is left standing there in disbelief. I'm saying to myself, *what just happened there?*" Inning over without allowing a run. The A's go on to win that World Series.

The second Tenace story has to do with Gene moving from behind the plate late in his career to play first base. That happens to a number of catchers nearing the end of their careers, to keep their bat in the lineup after a lot of wear and tear on their bodies. I asked Tenace how that went. "It went great. There was even one game where I made some major league history and I didn't even know it. The A's were in Detroit playing a doubleheader at Tiger Stadium. I played both games at first. After the doubleheader, the media came in and said, 'Hey, Gino, you made history today in game one.' 'What was that?' I said. They told me I had tied a major league record for a first baseman: I did not have one putout in the game. I began to think about that. I thought of all the strikeouts and fly balls hit to the outfield and infield. But there was not one ground ball hit where there was a throw to first base or a pop-up to me. Pretty amazing."

The other Blue Jays coach that 1992 season was John Sullivan — a.k.a. Archie Bunker. That was a nickname his fellow coaches had put on him for years, teasing him about his similar personality to the TV star. All business always, John was a baseball lifer, and it showed. He and his wife, Betsy, were such good people, but when it came to his profession, it was no nonsense. He was a crucial member down in the bullpen, where as an ex-catcher he enjoyed talking and working with pitchers to make them better.

As soon as the season was over, Sully would start growing a beard. In about three weeks it would be full and white, and he'd wear it all winter until spring training. The other fascinating thing about John was his love for deer hunting. Not with a rifle — with a bow and arrow. He would hunt deer in his wooded backyard, and there were even a few times he would fire his arrows from his kitchen door at deer running by.

John was in the bullpen in Game 6 of the 1993 World Series. He was the one who retrieved Joe Carter's memorable home-run ball. At the 1993 postgame celebration at the SkyDome, before more than 50,000 ecstatic fans, Sully announced that he was retiring from the game that began for him in 1959, playing with Erie in the New York Penn League. At the end of the festivities, John was asked to unfurl the 1993 World Series Championship banner. A great honour and momentous way to say goodbye.

The Blue Jays finished the regular season 96-66. It wasn't easy down the stretch. On August 25, the team had lost six of seven games and was only two games ahead of the Baltimore Orioles. That's when David Cone was acquired from the Mets. Cone would go 4-3 with an ERA of 2.55 to finish the season with his new team. Some people forget that heading into the last weekend of the season and a three-game series against the Detroit Tigers, the Blue Jays had only a two-game lead in the standings over the red-hot Milwaukee Brewers. Managed by Phil Garner, the Brew Crew had won 22 of 29 games going back to August 29. But on October 3 at home against Detroit, Blue Jay Juan Guzman pitched a one-hitter through eight innings. Duane Ward came on to pick up the save as the Blue Jays won the game, 3–1, clinching the American League East Division title.

The Playoffs: Alomar versus Eckersley

In the 1992 American League Championship Series against the Oakland A's, the Blue Jays lost Game 1 at the SkyDome, 4–3. They bounced back in Game 2 behind a well-pitched game by Guzman to even the series with a 3–1 win. Game 3 was in Oakland at the Coliseum. The Blue Jays flexed their muscles, pounding out seven runs to win, 7–5.

A defining moment came the next day in the 8th inning, when Eckersley struck out Ed Sprague to end the inning, leaving runners on base and preserving an A's lead. Dennis immediately looked over at the Blue Jays first-base dugout and threw a big sweeping celebratory fist pump. Not good.

But the key to the ALCS came in the 9th inning, when one future Hall of Famer homered off another. Eckersley had made the mistake of waking up the proverbial "sleeping dog." Roberto Alomar hit a game-tying two-run home run off A's closer Dennis Eckersley to dramatically tie the game, 3–3, and send it to extra innings. The Blue Jays won it, 7–6, in 11 innings to take a 3-1 series lead.

Top Five Blue Jays Home Runs

Many times in my broadcasting career, I have been asked, "Who hit the biggest home run in the history of the Blue Jays?" The expected answer, of course, is Joe Carter's walk-off home run in the 1993 World Series. When I tell people that I rank Joe's home run third in the history of the team, they gasp.

I have always felt the biggest and most impactful home run was Alomar's in Oakland against Eckersley. The Blue Jays had worn the "choker" label for a few years, whether deserved or not. The *Globe and Mail* had even run a headline the previous season that boldly proclaimed: "Blue Jays Choke." Until you win a championship, that label is going to stick. Roberto's dramatic 9th inning home run that led to the eventual extra-inning 7–6 win was the backdrop and first huge step to winning it all, once and for all shedding that choker label.

His home run in that most pressurized situation further established Alomar as one of the game's best-ever players and a deserved inductee into the Hall of Fame.

The second-biggest home run in team history, in my opinion, is rookie Ed Sprague's 9th-inning one-out pinch-hit two-run home run in Game 2 of the 1992 World Series in Atlanta, off veteran reliever Jeff Reardon. It turned a 4–3 deficit into a 5–4 lead. That was the final score as Tom Henke came on to close it in the bottom of the 9th. The Blue Jays evened the World Series at a game apiece. That one swing by Sprague was aided and abetted by Rance Mulliniks.

Rance studied pitchers his entire career. He had a well-deserved reputation for knowing what was coming from certain pitchers in key situations. The grateful Ed Sprague spoke about what led up to the biggest swing of his career. "Cito gave me plenty of time, which I think was probably the biggest key. He told me I would be hitting for Turner Ward in the 9th inning, which gave me an opportunity to talk to Rance about Reardon coming in."

Rance: "I had faced Reardon on a number of occasions. Ed came down and asked me, 'What do you look for?' What Reardon tries to do is get you out with the fastball. He was very adept at throwing that fastball letter-high. As a hitter, you see that very well and think you can be on top of it. You either swing through it, foul it off, or fly out. I told Ed if he flips you a little breaking ball early in the count, don't let that get in your head because that's not what he wants to get you out with. He's going to show that to you to put that pitch in your mind. What he wants to get you out with is his fastball up in the zone. Stay with the fastball no matter what and think belt or down." With Derek Bell aboard having drawn a walk, Sprague lined a first-pitch low fastball off Reardon into the left-centre field seats to win it. The professor was smiling, the student was smiling, their classmates were smiling, and so was the rest of Canada.

Then, of course, is Carter's walk-off home run to see the Blue Jays repeat as World Series Champions in 1993. But without Alomar and Sprague's home-run heroics a year before, there might never have been a 1993 World Series in Toronto. Prominent future Blue Jays like Dave Stewart and Paul Molitor might have looked elsewhere.

Jose Bautista's 2015 iconic three-run, no-doubt-about-it, bat-flip blast to beat Texas, 6–3, in the ALDS I rank fourth only because the others were so pivotal to winning two World Series. Edwin Encarnacion's dramatic 11th-inning shot to beat the Orioles in the 2016 Wild Card Game rounds out the top five biggest home runs in Blue Jays franchise history for me.

World Series Afterglow

When the Blue Jays returned home from Atlanta after winning the 1992 World Series, no one was prouder than manager Cito Gaston, who became the first African-American manager in the history of major league baseball to win a World Series. He did it again in 1993 to truly cement his place in the game. With Gaston, it was always about the players and coaches around him. He wanted the best for everyone, and it showed in how he managed. He let the players play and the pitchers pitch. Sounds simple enough. But not every manager does it.

Pitchers would often praise Cito when I asked them about him. It was not uncommon to hear about the confidence he inspired when they stood on the mound with runners on. They didn't continually feel the need to look over their shoulder to see who was up in the bullpen. No one was up. Knowing that Cito had their backs gave them so much more confidence to get hitters out in those situations. Hitters shared similar feelings: they didn't have to look back toward the dugout to see who might be coming out to the on-deck circle to pinch hit for them. They knew Cito felt that they could handle the at-bat, and they appreciated that.

Cito played in the major leagues from 1967 with Atlanta right on through to 1978, where he once again had returned to Atlanta, this time managed by young future Hall of Famer Bobby Cox. Bobby saw something in Cito he wanted to develop: after his playing days were over, Bobby extended Cito an invitation to become a minor league hitting coach in the Atlanta system. Cito quickly accepted. Just a few years later, when Pat Gillick hired Cox to manage the Blue Jays in 1982, Bobby brought Cito with him as his new hitting coach. That later led to Cito managing the club in May 1989 and to those two World Series Championships.

A First Nations Fan Letter

One of the best fan letters I ever received came shortly after the World Series ended. It was from a First Nations community in Northern Ontario. The fan politely asked me to please reconsider using terms like "Indians" and "Braves," out of respect for his people. "Jerry, I appreciate your work. But in the World Series, it was so offensive to hear and see the tomahawk chop and to have people talk about the powwows on the mound. And before that to see the Cleveland Indians' Chief Wahoo mascot with the red face and big white teeth. I would really appreciate it if you would just think about what you are saying when talking about teams like Cleveland and Atlanta and the Washington Redskins."

It is so easy at times to see things only one way without really thinking about it. When I read that letter from a fan who had lived dealing with demeaning comments and was so eloquent saying, "It's just so offensive and we don't like it," it touched my heart. I wrote him back and told him that for the rest of my career — no matter how long that would be — I was going to honour him and Indigenous peoples by no longer saying "Indians" and "Braves." From that point on, I never used those words again.

CHAPTER 18

HOW SWEET IT IS (AGAIN)

It is not easy to get to the World Series, let alone win it. The Seattle Mariners have never been to a World Series. If you are good enough to reach "the promised land" two years in a row, you also have to be lucky and catch your fair share of breaks. The talented Texas Rangers and the Los Angeles Dodgers were each heartbroken twice, losing back-to-back World Series in 2010 and 2011 and in 2017 and 2018, respectively. The Blue Jays had a most difficult challenge ahead of them entering the 1993 season.

The season also marked the first time that a manager from the Blue Jays would manage the American League team in the Major League Baseball All-Star Game. Played at Camden Yards in Baltimore, the American League defeated the National League by a score of 9–3. Cito Gaston and his coaches Galen Cisco, John Sullivan, and Gene Tenace were joined by starters John Olerud, Roberto Alomar, Joe Carter, and Paul Molitor. Pat Hentgen, Duane Ward, and Devon White were named as reserves to the team. When the team went out to centre field for a team picture, there were a total of eleven Blue Jays in uniform plus the trainers and equipment manager. Minnesota centre fielder Kirby Puckett had the line of the day. "Okay, everyone clear out! The Blue Jays are taking their team picture."

There was one All-Star Game episode that led to Cito Gaston being unfairly booed for years, whenever he came into Baltimore and Camden Yards. In the All-Star pregame meeting, Cito went over a number of things with his team, including the fact that with an abundance of pitchers, he would not be using Pat Hentgen or the Orioles' Mike Mussina. He wanted both of them to know that before the game so there would be no misunderstandings. As the game progressed and the American League was rolling along, all of a sudden Mussina got up and started to warm up in the American League bullpen, much to the delight of his Orioles fans. When Cito did not bring him into the game, the crowd booed unmercifully, feeling that Cito had snubbed one of their own by getting him up and then not using him. Mussina was the one to blame. Not Cito.

This wasn't the first time nor the last time that Mussina was involved in a story like this. There was the day my late radio partner, Tom Cheek, who was battling cancer at the time, saw his name go up on the Level of Excellence at the Rogers Centre. Tom was honoured before the game and gave a glowing speech before a very appreciative crowd. As a result, the game was delayed about 20 minutes. Mussina was the starting pitcher for the Yankees. He pitched very ineffectively and lost the game. Afterwards, he told the media that his poor performance was because he had to wait well beyond the start time due to the pregame festivities. That was Mike Mussina.

The Ignitor: Paul Molitor

On December 7, 1992, Paul Molitor inked a contract as a free agent, and the following day, so did pitchers Dave Stewart and Danny Cox. Stewart was a necessity with the loss of starter Jimmy Key. Molitor admirably filled the huge shoes of Dave Winfield as the DH. Tom Henke had departed as well, which meant that Duane Ward moved up as the closer. That left a void in the bullpen, and Danny filled it beautifully. It's not often that even a great team like the 1992 Blue Jays can take three big hits like that and repeat as World Series Champions. Once again, GM Pat Gillick filled those voids. He wasn't finished. In January, Pat signed free agent shortstop Dick Schofield. The Blue Jays were ready to report to spring training with hopes of repeating as World Series Champions.

When I think of Paul Molitor, one of the first things I recall was the team's daily stretch before batting practice, where they gathered in a big circle in the outfield to get loose: Molitor never missed a day. Sometimes, the big stars Alomar, Carter, White, and others would skip the stretch to do other things. Never Paul. When I then saw all the younger players, such as Olerud and Sprague, stretching every day, I knew who their role model was. If Molitor could stretch every day with his star-studded background, then so could they. With this kind of professional example, Paul was basically saying there are no short cuts in this game if you want to be great.

Paul and I have shared one Bible verse over our many years together that is easily the most meaningful for the two of us. It is short and sweet: "We all fall short of the glory of God." I had generally known about this verse for years and knew it was somewhere in the book of Romans. When we first started talking about the verse and how it influenced our lives, Paul quickly said: "Romans 3:23." We laughed because it was in both our hearts.

During the early years of his career, Molitor began using marijuana and cocaine. During the trial of a drug dealer in 1984, Molitor admitted that he had used drugs. "There are things you're not so proud of — failures, mistakes, dabbling in drugs, a young ballplayer in the party scene. Part of it was peer pressure. I was young and single, and hung around with the wrong people. You learn from it. You find a positive in it. It makes you appreciate the things that are good." Molitor, who was one of the very few Blue Jays to live year-round in Toronto, voluntarily visited schools during the offseason to talk about the dangers of drug use. Although he stopped using drugs in 1981, his addictions have been a part of his life and were not easy for him to overcome. He does not want young students to do what he had done but rather look at him as a real person with faults, not Paul Molitor the major league star. That took courage. Paul is one of the most courageous people I have ever met.

Molitor's nickname was "The Ignitor." It was easy to see why. He was one of the most effective leadoff hitters in the game. With his hands and body so still, he would suddenly be short and quick to the pitch-and-drill base hits all over the field. There was no wasted motion with his swing. He did in fact ignite many a rally with his Hall of Fame swing. Paul was named the 1993 World Series MVP, going 12-24 at the plate. Defensively, he played third base in the World Series games in Philadelphia where there was no designated hitter. Paul had come up as a second baseman and then played a lot at third base only to later become a full-time DH. He was very comfortable playing on the infield for the three World Series games in Philadelphia to keep his bat in the lineup.

Whenever the Blue Jays play Cleveland, and I visit with their fine TV analyst Rick Manning, a former Milwaukee Brewer, I immediately think of another Molitor moment. Paul had attracted national media attention in 1987 during his 39-game hitting streak. The streak ended at home in Milwaukee with Molitor in the on-deck circle. Manning won it with a walk-off game-winning hit to beat Cleveland. Fans booed Manning for driving in the winning run, thus depriving Molitor of one last chance to reach 40 games. The streak stands as the fifth-longest in modern-day baseball history and remains the longest since Pete Rose's 44-game hit streak in 1978. It might also be the only time in major league history that a hitter was booed off the field at home after his game-winning walk-off hit.

On June 11, 1999, the Brewers retired Molitor's No. 4. During the ceremony at Milwaukee County Stadium, Paul announced that if he went into the Hall of Fame, he would do so as a Brewer. On January 6, 2004, he was inducted into the Hall of Fame in Cooperstown in his first year of eligibility with 85 percent of the vote. True to his word, he joined Robin Yount as the only Hall of Famers to wear Milwaukee Brewers caps on their plaques.

Definition of True Greatness

It takes a lot to win a World Series, but the most important factor is talent. On the 1993 World Series Champion Blue Jays were four future Hall of Famers in Paul Molitor, Roberto Alomar, Jack Morris, and Rickey Henderson, who had come to the team in August. The talent did not end there. On most teams, there may be two or three players who stay in the game and contribute to baseball in some capacity after they retire. But for 11 players to use their unique ability to communicate the game they love to others? That's a feat.

Future major league coaches on that 1993 team included Darnell Coles, hitting coach with the Detroit Tigers; Turner Ward, hitting coach with the Los Angeles Dodgers; Randy Knorr, bench coach with the Washington Nationals; Pat Hentgen, bullpen pitching coach with the Blue Jays; Alfredo Griffin, first-base coach with the Angels; Molitor, a coach with both the Twins and the Mariners and later the Twins' manager. Dave Stewart became the Arizona Diamondbacks general manager. Darrin Jackson, Jack Morris, and Al Leiter all became longtime major league broadcasters. And Devon White is a Triple-A coach and getting close to becoming a major league coach. What an array of talent on one team.

Dave Stewart

Over a 16-year major league career, Dave Stewart put together four straight 20-win seasons from 1987 through 1990 with the Oakland A's. He was the 1989 World Series MVP, winning both of his starts against the Giants. Later he was named the 1993 American League Championship Series MVP after he defeated the Chicago White Sox in Game 2 and in Game 6 in Chicago to clinch.

After that clinching game that put the Blue Jays into their second straight World Series, I interviewed Stewart down on the field for our postgame show. It was so enlightening. Dave spent the entire interview talking about just one inning. He broke down nearly every pitch in the bottom of the 7th with the

Blue Jays clinging to a 3–2 lead. It is one of the most memorable interviews I have ever done. Dave gave us a glimpse of the thought process needed by a supremely talented pitcher who thought his way through every inning he pitched in his career. Mind over matter. That's what it takes to be great.

I have often told people that the great ones have both the talent and dedication to make their success happen. Years later, because of this interview with Dave and also reading about and listening to Greg Maddux and Roberto Alomar, I realized that there is a third dimension to greatness: the mental side. Being able to quickly think things through during the heat of the battle with a mental sharpness second to none is what it takes to reach Cooperstown. Dave Stewart that day in Chicago beat the White Sox with both his right arm and his mind.

And Along Came Rickey

At the July All-Star break, the Blue Jays were 49-40. GM Pat Gillick assessed his team and their chances for repeating as World Series Champions. Over the next two weeks, he tried to acquire tall lefty Randy Johnson, who is six-foot-ten, from the Seattle Mariners, putting a premium on the pitching that he had seen take the Blue Jays to their first World Series the year before. But the Mariners' asking price was too steep. So Pat went to Plan B and opted for more offence to go along with his potent lineup. He traded young pitcher Steve Karsay and minor league outfielder Jose Herrera to the Oakland A's for speedster Rickey Henderson.

As an aside here and a funny story, years ago, in the Mariners dugout before a game at the Kingdome, Randy and I were talking about photography, which was and still is his passion. Then the conversation switched to his height. "Jerry, one thing I always hear is 'Let's meet six-foot-ten Randy Johnson.' I have to tell people that my first name is not six-foot-ten. It's Randy." Ah, to be a star in this game.

If there was ever a case to be made for the decreasing significance of a batting average in modern-day baseball, I give you Rickey Henderson. It all started with Rickey's .215 average over his 44 games played with the Blue Jays that 1993 season. Remember, too, that he fractured a bone in his hand when hit by a pitch shortly after joining the team. I would hear many fans later say: "Well, he hit only .215." In those 44 games, Rickey collected 35 hits and walked 35 times, scoring 37 runs with an OBP of .356. He was on base 70 times, struck out only 19 times, and stole 22 bases. Case closed.

A perfect example of what we are talking about occurred in Game 5 of the 1993 ALCS at the SkyDome. The White Sox and Blue Jays were tied at two games apiece. In the 1st inning, Henderson opened with a double to left. That's when he started to taunt starter Jack McDowell, threatening to steal third. Already unnerved, McDowell walked Roberto Alomar to put two on. Rickey continued to draw numerous throws at second base. Finally, McDowell spun and threw the ball into centre field. Henderson raced around third and scored on McDowell's throwing error, and Alomar moved to second . . . 1–0 Blue Jays, just like that. All thanks to Rickey. The Blue Jays went on to win it, 5–3, clinching the division title two days later in Chicago. Rickey was a nuisance on the base paths, pure and simple. The Blue Jays were thrilled to take the .215 batting average.

Talking to Rickey at the batting cage one night at the SkyDome, I asked him about goals he had set for himself. I fully expected him to talk about being the all-time stolen base leader. Instead, he said his goal from the very beginning of his career was to pass Ty Cobb and become the all-time leader in runs scored. And, yes, he did want to lead the major leagues in stolen bases, too. He did both in his 25-year career, scoring 2,295 runs and stealing 1,406 bases.

No one had more fun talking with the fans during games at home and away in left field than Henderson. Between innings at the SkyDome, he would go over and rap with the fans with the biggest smile on his face, laughing and playing up to the crowd. If he was taunted on the road by fans in left field trying to get his goat, it didn't work. Quite the contrary. At the end of the game, those same fans were having a ball with Rickey, too.

The most electrifying moment for Rickey and his Blue Jays teammates is totally overlooked. It came in Game 6 of that 1993 World Series. The Blue Jays had a commanding 5–1 lead at the end of six innings only to see the Phillies score five runs in the 7th and take a 6–5 lead. The Phillies kept that narrow one-run lead going to the bottom of the 9th inning. That's when it happened: Rickey was sitting in the third-base dugout between innings when he looked up and saw the Phillies bullpen door swing open in right field. Out came lefty and closer Mitch Williams, a.k.a. "The Wild Thing," running to the mound. Rickey immediately went up and down the dugout, giving low fives to his teammates sitting on the bench. "I'm leading off, and he's going to walk me on four pitches! We're going to win this game!" Sure enough, that is exactly what happened. Williams walked Rickey on four pitches. Then, Mitch tried to counter Henderson's great speed while at the same time concentrate on throwing quality pitches. Not easy. The walk to Henderson was followed by a Devon White fly out and a single by Paul Molitor.

Up stepped Joe Carter. History was about to be made. Rickey had called it.

Rickey and I were both transplants to the Bay Area. Rickey was born in Chicago on Christmas Day in 1958. Then his family moved to Oakland, where he grew up. While I watched the Giants play in San Francisco and saw stars like Willie Mays and Juan Marichal, Rickey played in Oakland for the A's, where he was among the stars. I admire Rickey for what he did on the field over his long career, but that pales in comparison to my respect for Rickey and how he delivered his acceptance speech at Cooperstown the day he went into the Hall of Fame in 2009.

I will let Hal Bodley, senior correspondent for MLB.com, take it from here: "Rickey wanted to polish his admitted speaking deficiencies, so he went to school. That might be hard to believe, but that's what he did in the days leading up to the induction. For two weeks, he attended two summer classes at Laney Community College in Oakland. The courses? Public speaking and introduction to speech, both taught by Earl Robinson, a former major-leaguer with the Dodgers (1958) and Orioles (1961 to 1963). Robinson even went to Rickey's home some nights to help him polish the speech."

"It was great," Henderson told Bodley in a quiet corner two hours after the Sunday induction. "At Laney College, Earl kept telling me to slow down. You know, I tend to cut off my words in a sentence, and we worked on that. And he kept stressing, 'Slow down. Slow down.' You know I talk very fast, and Earl said I had a habit of talking about something, go off it, and not know how to come back. It was fun. The students in the classroom critiqued my speech, and then we would reverse our roles and I would critique them. The students were my 'live' audience."

That day at Cooperstown, Rickey Henderson was as brilliant at the microphone as he was on the diamond. He had to work extremely hard in both cases. Every season when the team was out in Oakland I was reminded about Rickey's talk at Cooperstown. The Blue Jays team bus goes right by Laney College each day on the way to the Oakland Coliseum. Huge green letters spell out the name on the grey building and I smile. *Way to go Rickey. Proud of you.*

It Takes a Village

In January 1993, the Blue Jays signed shortstop Dick Schofield as a free agent. His dad, Dick Sr., also known as Ducky, played shortstop for nine different teams in the major leagues from 1953 through 1971. I saw Dick's dad play against the Giants in San Francisco when his Pirates would play at Candlestick Park. I admired the little switch-hitter who could hit to all fields and was great with the glove. When his son signed on with the Blue Jays, it was fun not only to meet Dick, but to also talk about those days I enjoyed watching his dad play, too.

I was amazed at Dick's ability to recall all those players from a different era simply by hearing their numbers. We would be sitting across from each other on a bus going to a game, and I would throw out a number from his dad's playing days in the 1950s and 1960s, and Dick would rattle off the player and the team. Then he would give me a number from the same era, and I would do the same thing, naming the player and his team. We did this a lot and found it hard to stump one another.

In mid-May at the SkyDome, the Tigers' Milt Cuyler tried to steal second base. As Schofield came over to take the throw, the ball tailed into Cuyler, who went sliding in cleanly feet first. Schofield broke his arm in the collision and was lost for the season. It was such a bad break for both Dick and the Blue Jays, literally. Within a very short time, Pat Gillick realized he needed an everyday starting shortstop for the team to have any chance of repeating as World Series Champions. He went out and reacquired Tony Fernandez, who joined the team for a second time. Fernandez later would become a record four-time Blue Jay playing in 1998 and 2001. Tony was phenomenal as Schofield's replacement. He played a significant role in helping the Blue Jays reach the promised land for a second time. In this case one man's misfortune was truly another man's fortune.

The bullpen that season included a rookie of note named Woody Williams. Often kidded and called Woody Woodpecker by his teammates, there wasn't a finer person putting on the uniform. He was a devout Christian who lived his faith day by day and still does. A dedicated husband and father, he was the classic "late bloomer." In 1993, Woody pitched in 30 games. He also spent a great part of that season in Triple-A Syracuse, where he pitched for parts of seven years with various ailments, trying to find out if he was more than just a minor league pitcher. After spending 11 years with the Blue Jays organization, mostly in their minor league system and winning just 28 games at the major league level, he was traded to the San Diego Padres by Gord Ash for veteran pitcher Joey Hamilton. Woody went on to win 104 games with the Padres and St. Louis Cardinals. He pitched in five postseasons, including a trip to the 2004 World Series where the Cardinals lost to the Boston Red Sox. There is no substitute for character, and it is so important to hold on to a player who has it. The quiet and understated Woody Williams was one the Blue Jays let get away. It happens.

Huck and Darnell

A rookie left-hander, Huck Flener, pitched in all of six games in 1993, but that was enough to earn him a World Series ring. Flener pitched for the Blue Jays in 1993, 1996, and 1997. His major league debut was unique to say the least. It was a night game at Tiger Stadium: Huck was so excited about his call-up from the minor leagues that he left his equipment bag in his hotel room. Flener had to borrow Shawn Green's No. 15 jersey. It is noteworthy here that Shawn's jersey actually made an appearance in a major league game before Shawn did. Huck came on in the bottom of the 8th inning with two men on and two outs. On two pitches he induced Chad Krueter to fly out to centre field, ending the inning. Duane Ward finished up the 9–5 win in the 9th inning, rewarding the rookie with his first major league hold.

Huck: "When I went out for the game from our clubhouse, the guys were really laughing. Here I was with Pat Hentgen's shoes, Al Leiter's glove, and Shawn Green's jersey. I didn't care. I hadn't slept in a day and a half." Now that's how you make a major league debut.

On the Flener flip side, one of my saddest days happened when I read a story a number of years later about Huck, who had continued pitching in the minors and in winter ball. In January 2001, Huck lost his right eye after being struck by a batted ball while pitching in Venezuela that winter. I think of Huck Flener whenever a line drive is hit right back at a pitcher's face and how lucky, for the most part, all these other pitchers are to escape that kind of a serious injury.

Today, Flener is a proud and loving husband and father who lives his life to the fullest with great joy. He reminds me of basketball broadcasting legend Dick Vitale, whom I met years ago while I was emceeing a Special Olympics breakfast in Toronto. I had a long chat with Dick before I introduced him, then I listened to him speak so eloquently. It was only after Vitale had left Toronto that I learned that he, too, years earlier, had lost an eye. You could not tell the difference between his prosthetic eye and his good eye; they were matched so perfectly. Dick never brought it up. He did not want anyone to feel sorry for him. Huck Flener is cut from the same cloth.

Veteran Darnell Coles came to the Blue Jays in 1993, having spent the previous 10 years in the major leagues with five different teams. Veteran role players are essential for good teams to become even better — your chances of winning a World Series are that much better. Coles was very much like Pat Tabler, who'd starred in that role the year before.

Twice in Darnell's career as a Blue Jay, he hit three home runs in a game. In the afterglow of 1992, all of Canada wanted to see their reigning champions any way they could. So much so that during the 1993 season, the team travelled to Regina in early May to play an exhibition game at Taylor Field. Yes, the football field, home of the CFL's Saskatchewan Roughriders. The game was against young players from the National Baseball Institute. The NBI was founded by GM Pat Gillick. It was based in Surrey, B.C., to develop elite Canadian baseball players. That afternoon at Taylor Field, there wasn't a lot of distance from home plate down the left-field line, as you can imagine. On the other hand, you could see down the right-field line forever. It was in that game Darnell hit three fly balls to left field that all left the yard. In fact, the last home run that he hit was with an aluminum bat, much to the delight of over 26,000 excited fans, who loved hearing the "ping" off the bat. It capped the exhibition game and there was a great celebration and laughter afterwards in both clubhouses.

Two months later, on July 6, Coles did it again in Minnesota's Metrodome, but this time for keeps. The Blue Jays romped past the Twins, 14–3, as Coles hit a two-run homer in the 5th inning and solo shots in the 8th and 9th. All with a wooden bat. The team celebrated once again in the clubhouse. But this time there was no laughing or celebrating in the other one.

From a Baseball Family

After hitting his dramatic pinch-hit two-run home run off Atlanta reliever Jeff Reardon in Game 2 of the 1992 World Series in the 9th inning to win it, 5–4, Ed Sprague would become a fixture at third base for years to come. In 1993, Ed played 150 games, hitting 12 home runs and driving in 73 all while playing a very reliable third base and winning another World Series Championship. For Sprague, winning back-to-back championships was old hat. Ed was an NCAA college standout. He played third base, helping Stanford to win back-to-back College World Series Championships in 1987 and 1988. He collected a gold medal for Team USA in the 1988 Olympics in Seoul, South Korea. Sprague is the only baseball player ever to win championships in the College World Series, the Olympics, and the World Series. He was a very worthy first-round pick by the Blue Jays in the 1988 June Draft.

Sprague has a great family. I got to know them all very well during his playing days and have stayed in touch. The name Sprague is synonymous with both baseball and the Olympics. I watched his father, Ed Sr., pitch in the majors from 1968 through 1976. Ed Jr.'s wife, Kristen Babb-Sprague, won an Olympic gold medal in synchronized swimming in Barcelona in 1992. They have four children. Ed has given back to baseball in a huge way. From 2004 through the 2015 season, he was the head coach at the University of Pacific in Stockton, California, where he grew up. He is now back in the major leagues as the Oakland Athletics' coordinator of instruction.

So Proud to Be in Canada

Pat Borders was once again the principal catcher in 1993. He was backed up by Randy Knorr, who broke in with the Blue Jays in 1991 and played in 39 games in 1993. Knorr, like most catchers, had a lot to contribute to the game. He was a player, a minor league manager in Triple-A, and a major league bench coach with the Washington Nationals.

I recall an injury he sustained as a Blue Jay while playing Milwaukee at old County Stadium. With two outs in the inning, the Jays made a great throw and tag at home plate. Randy bounced up from the collision and ran to the third-base dugout as the inning ended. He did not come out for the next inning.

After the game, I saw him and asked what had happened. "I received the throw and made the tag on the sliding runner on a bang-bang play. Then I got up and went to the dugout as if nothing had happened. As I sat in the dugout, I was looking out on the field, trying to take my shin guards off like I have done a thousand times, but nothing was happening. That's when I looked down at my left thumb, and it was bent back to my wrist. I had no feeling in it at all. I was shocked to see how it had gone backwards. I had a torn ligament in my thumb, and I didn't even know it." Catchers are tough, but to see and hear about this kind of injury was a first.

Knorr caught 11 seasons in the majors. He finished his career with the Montreal Expos in 2004, becoming one of many who played for both the Expos and Blue Jays. In fact, Randy also played for the Edmonton Trappers, the Medicine Hat Blue Jays, and the Ottawa Lynx. On Canada Day 2004, in his final season of pro ball, the Trappers made him an honorary Canadian before a game against Salt Lake City. "They gave me a key to the city of Edmonton before all of the fans and gave me a certificate for a case of twelve beers. I'd been in Canada for close to twelve years, but I joked with them that it should have been a case of twenty-four because that's how it is in the U.S." What did Randy do to thank the Trappers and their fans? He hit a three-run homer as Edmonton pulled off a double-header sweep. It was the last year the Trappers played in the Triple-A Pacific Coast League. And it was the last year for the Expos in Montreal. Quite fitting that the Expos' Triple-A affiliate that season was in Edmonton. "I loved it in Edmonton," Knorr said. "I loved Canada, the whole country."

On June 23, 2015, Randy experienced the lowest point in his life with the sudden loss of his wife, Kimberly, at age 45. "Just when you think you're getting over it, something comes up some days to make you think of her. She had been battling rheumatoid arthritis. Her liver just gave out on her. She had a lot of migraines because of the arthritis. Her body couldn't take it anymore. Kimberly went to lie down and she never got up." Catchers are a special breed. They are strong beyond words, mentally and physically. Knorr is an example of that.

Turner Ward

When I watched the 2017 World Series between the Dodgers and the Astros, I had to smile when they would show the Dodgers' dugout. On TV, all the hitters were gathered around hitting coach Turner Ward. Turner played 12 years in the major leagues, three of those in Toronto.

As a Blue Jay from 1991 to 1993, Turner was continuously conversing with all of his teammates, especially with veterans like Dave Winfield. Turner was curious about the game and its nuances and was driven to be the best player he could be. He wanted to see his teammates get better, too. He was so easy to talk to and gave off positive vibes every single day. "Hey, Jerry! How you doing?" was always his greeting. Conversations with Turner helped to further my education in the game for our audience.

All of that due diligence paid off for him. After his playing days, Turner managed in the minor leagues, winning back-to-back Double-A Southern League Championships for the Arizona Diamondbacks in 2011 and 2012. He was named Manager of the Year. The D-backs brought Ward up to be their assistant hitting coach in 2013, then their full-time hitting coach in 2014 and 2015. That's when the Dodgers came a-calling, naming him their hitting coach in 2016, on his way to the 2017 and 2018 World Series. You could see this all happening from the very beginning. Someday, we could also easily be talking about manager Turner Ward.

And There Would Be More to Come

There were two kids who got their feet wet that season: a catcher and an outfielder. The catcher, who later turned first baseman, did all right for himself in his career. That was Carlos Delgado. The outfielder did all right, too. After going 0 for 6 in his three 1993 major league games and just 3 for 33 in 14 games the next season, he took off. His name was Shawn Green.

Yes, lest we forget, Delgado had come up through the Blue Jays system as a *catcher*. In 1993, he saw action in two games, catching three innings, and playing as the DH. The next year, Carlos started the season with the Blue Jays. He burst onto the scene, hitting eight home runs in April 1994. But by mid-May, his batting average was well below the .200 mark. He was sent back to Triple-A Syracuse. This proved just how hard it is to play this game at the highest level, even for the best young talent. In his 43 games in 1994, Delgado caught just one more game for two innings. Carlos played the rest of those games in left field. He did not move to first base until 1995, and that was for only four games.

Green was a right fielder from the beginning. After a rough start in the big leagues, he went on to star for 15 years. Shawn finished with a career .283 batting average, 328 home runs, and 1,070 RBIs. He won a Gold Glove with the Blue Jays in 1999, the same season he hit 42 home runs and drove in 123. He later had two 40-plus home-run seasons with the Dodgers that featured his four-home-run game in Milwaukee. That matched what Delgado did on September 25, 2003, at the Rogers Centre. Carlos is still the only Blue Jay to accomplish that feat. Both received World Series rings in 1993. A pretty good way to start two stellar careers.

The 1993 Blue Jays season was the 17th in their franchise history. It resulted in the Blue Jays finishing first in the American League East with a record of 95 wins and 67 losses. They were shut out only once in 162 games. Their repeat as World Series Champions made them the first back-to-back champions since the 1977–78 New York Yankees. The Blue Jays defeated their ALCS opponents, the Chicago White Sox, in six games and did the same against the Philadelphia Phillies in the World Series.

CHAPTER 19

FINISHING THE DECADE

1994: Becoming Canadians and the Season of the Strike

We started 1994 with a very significant and momentous event. On April 21, Mary, Ben, Joe, and I became Canadian citizens. The presiding citizenship judge was none other than Gina Godfrey, the wife of Paul Godfrey, former *Metro* chairman in Toronto and future president and CEO of the Blue Jays. That day, there were 52 of us, representing 13 different countries, who became new Canadians. What a proud moment. When I saw Gina begin to leave the room, I said for everyone to hear: "And *there she goes!*" That was quite a day for the Howarth family.

The year also saw the defending World Series Champions post an overall record of 55-60 when the season came crashing down around Major League Baseball on August 11. The Blue Jays were in New York and had just defeated the Yankees, 8–7. My postgame guest in the dugout that evening was Ed Sprague. At the end of the interview, I asked him what he thought might happen with the distinct threat of a players' strike looming over the game. He said he didn't know, but he was hopeful for a quick resolution between the players' union and the owners.

That did not happen. The strike lasted 232 days. It cancelled the rest of the season, including the World Series, for the first time since 1904. Although the strike was disappointing for the fans, it was devastating to the team with the best record in baseball at that time: the Montreal Expos. The Expos never recovered. Fans were incensed, and so were many of the players. That strike forever changed the course of history. Back in 2014, Dave Stewart, who in 1994 was in his second season pitching for the Blue Jays, told Bob Nightengale of *USA Today*: "I never felt the same way about baseball again after that. Even today, after all of my years in baseball, the passion I have for the game has never been the same. All because of that strike. It was one of the most embarrassing moments that's ever happened to Major League Baseball. I wish I had never come back."

You couldn't blame him. Not only was the 1994 season reduced to shambles, but the start of the 1995 season, too, with owners using replacement players for spring training games and any regular season games as the strike continued. The wealthy owners — who were hurting themselves — wouldn't concede to the players' demands. Finally, on April 2, 1995, the day before the season was scheduled to start with replacement players, the strike came to an official end. But the damage had been done to the players, the owners, and especially the embittered fans with teams playing an abbreviated 144-game season. Most apropos — and reflecting Dave Stewart's heartfelt thoughts — was a plane that flew over Riverfront Stadium, paid for by a Cincinnati Reds fan and carrying a banner that read: "Owners & Players: To hell with all of you!"

The Supporting Cast

The Blue Jays that season scored 566 runs but allowed 579. Without Duane Ward in the bullpen, many games were lost late in the game. The team signed veteran left-hander Dave Righetti on May 13 to help augment the bullpen. Darren Hall did a nice job, but the bullpen just wasn't as strong as it had been the two previous years. Joe Carter drove in 103 runs while hitting 27 home runs. He needed more of a supporting cast. In the midst of this crushing blow to the game itself, the Blue Jays were able to introduce to the fans three players who would become the future: Carlos Delgado, Alex Gonzalez, and Shawn Green.

Carlos Delgado

Delgado's name is on the Level of Excellence at the Rogers Centre, and for good reason. He hit 473 home runs in his career — a record 336 of those as a Blue Jay — while driving in 1,512 (a record 1,058). Carlos holds the all-time Major League Baseball home run and RBI records among Puerto Rican players. He is one of only six players in major league history to hit 30 home runs in 10 consecutive seasons. He is a testament to just how hard the game is to play at that level and what a player has to do to overcome the odds. He started out as a catcher and left fielder who was demoted to the minor leagues before becoming an All-Star first baseman.

On September 25, 2003, Delgado became the first-ever Blue Jay and 15th major league player to hit four home runs in a game.

He did it against the Tampa Bay Devil Rays in only four at-bats, making him the first player in history to do so. He would drive in only six runs that night. After his three-run home run in the first inning, he led off the 4th, 6th, and 8th innings. His first-inning three-run home run not only set the tone for the game, it also marked his 300th career home run. One other fascinating aspect about this game was the fact that Carlos did not feel that well beforehand — he took some antibiotics for a cold and then took a nap. Hard to believe, but only 13,408 were in attendance at the SkyDome that evening to see his historic accomplishment, in a season when the Blue Jays drew only 1,799,458 fans, averaging 22,216 a game.

Looking back at that memorable night, I realize there was a most unusual pattern to Delgado's milestone home runs. His first major league home-run hit on April 4, 1994, was the only home run hit in that game. His 100th career home run, in 1998 at Tiger Stadium, was the first of two that he hit in a game. His 200th home run in 2001 was one of three he hit that night in Kansas City. And the four home runs that he hit in 2003 included his 300th.

In retirement, in 2001, Delgado started his own charity called the Extra Bases Foundation. It aims to equip charitable organizations with the tools and resources necessary to offer healthcare, education, and physical activity in an attempt to better the lives of individuals in underprivileged communities or adverse situations. Carlos has always given back to the game he loves. In 2015, Delgado was elected to the Canadian Baseball Hall of Fame — an award richly deserved by someone who continually gives back to the city of Toronto since his retirement.

Young shortstop Alex Gonzalez's baptism by fire saw him play 15 games in 1994 to launch his career. He was born and raised in Miami, so I got to know him and his family very well, especially during spring training, when his mom and dad would come to see their son play. Alex told me stories about how his dad, Bill, a longtime university engineering professor in Miami, would make the time early in Alex's life to hit him one ground ball after another. It was Bill's sacrifice and love for his son that helped Gonzalez become one of the best fielding shortstops in the history of the franchise. It was often felt that his defence helped lower the staff ERA over the course of a full season by nearly half a run.

Shawn Green played 14 games in right field that 1994 season, on his way to a fabulous career. Two things stand out about Shawn. First, he was so respectful of everybody and especially of me as a broadcaster with a job to do. It was really easy for a player to say yes to a postgame interview request when the team won. But there were times after a tough loss that I felt the audience deserved to hear the Blue Jays perspective. I would ask a number of the players to help me out with this and be turned down by all — except for one. Whenever I asked Shawn to share his thoughts about these games, his answer was always, "Sure. Happy to do it." His thoughts and perspective were much appreciated.

The other aspect of Shawn's personality that I truly admired had nothing to do with baseball. After games, the families and friends of the players would always gather outside the clubhouse. This is how I met Shawn's parents, Ira and Judy. His mom was very outgoing and friendly and loved to talk about her son at these gatherings. I would look at Shawn and admire how he let her gush over him and tell stories about him before the group would leave the clubhouse area. He never rolled his eyes or got impatient or stopped his mother from joyously talking about him and the game. He let her be herself to the fullest.

1995: Ryan Freel and his CTE

The 1995 season was not pretty for either the 56-88 Blue Jays or Major League Baseball, using replacement players early on and playing just a 144-game schedule. Much to their credit, the Blue Jays refused to use replacement players. The season finally got started on April 26 and finished September 30.

One of the few bright spots that year occurred on June 1, when the Blue Jays selected pitcher Roy Halladay out of a high school in Denver, Colorado, in the first round, 17th overall. Three years later, "Doc," thanks to my partner Tom Cheek, who gave him that nickname, was in the major leagues winning the first game of an eventual 203; he dropped only 105 games over his 16-year career.

One other player drafted by the Blue Jays in 1995, in the 10th round, was Ryan Freel. Ryan did not go unnoticed by me — he was very likeable and positive. After playing just one season with the Blue Jays in 2001, Freel was traded to the Reds. There he played five different positions — all three outfield spots plus second and third — over four years. Then, I read in 2007, Ryan was injured in a game when chasing a deep drive to right-centre field. He and right fielder Norris Hopper collided, resulting in Freel's head and neck hitting Hopper as the two landed on the warning track. Ryan began getting random headaches and pains in his head, which delayed his return for another two weeks. That awful word concussion was beginning to rear in baseball. In 2009, with the Baltimore Orioles, Freel was hit in the head by a pickoff throw while on second base. He was put on the disabled list after the injury and officially retired a year later.

I would see Ryan on and off over the years and always enjoyed his enthusiasm and joy for life. I did not pick up any sign whatsoever of what he was going through mentally that would eventually lead him to take his own life. On December 22, 2012, Freel died at his Jacksonville Florida home as a result of a self-inflicted gunshot wound. He was just 36. After Ryan's death, his family donated his brain tissue to Boston University for research into chronic traumatic encephalopathy (CTE), a degenerative neurological condition associated with multiple concussions that has become rampant in football and can only be conclusively diagnosed postmortem. In December 2013, a postmortem examination showed that Freel was suffering from Stage II CTE, making him the first MLB player to have been diagnosed with the disease. Ryan was also diagnosed with various mental illnesses, including bipolar disorder, adult ADHD, depression, impulse control disorder, and anxiety. These mental illnesses are consistent with many athletes who also suffer from CTE once their playing careers are finished.

Ryan had gained some notoriety in August 2006, when the *Dayton Daily News* reported that he talked to an imaginary voice in his head named Farney. "He's a little guy who lives in my head who talks to me and I talk to him: 'That was a great catch, Ryan.' I said, 'Hey, Farney, I don't know if that was you who really caught that ball, but that was pretty good if it was.' Everybody thinks I talk to myself, so I tell 'em I'm talking to Farney." Freel later said that Farney's name arose from a conversation with Reds trainer Mark Mann. "He actually made a comment like, 'How are the voices in your head?' We'd play around and finally this one year, he said, 'What's the guy's name?' I said, 'Let's call him Farney.' So now everybody's telling me, 'Run, Farney, run,' or 'Let Farney hit today. You're not hitting very well.'"

It was a sad day when I read about Freel's death. He was a wonderful but troubled young man. Just like it was an awful day when I read that my friend and former Blue Jays pitcher Mike Flanagan had also committed suicide. And then there was Doug Ault, who took his life at 54. Three heroes in the game. Another reason to enjoy the moment — you are not promised tomorrow.

Crabtree, Perez, and Stewart

In 1995, one of baseball's greatest catchers arrived to play with the Blue Jays. It was in Toronto that Lance Parrish finished his brilliant 19-year career, playing in his final 70 games. Interestingly enough, that season also saw bright young rookie pitcher Tim Crabtree make his major league debut with the Blue Jays.

Tim was drafted by the Blue Jays in the second round of the 1992 June Draft out of Michigan State, and what a major league debut it was: June 23, 1995, at Yankee Stadium, in the bottom of the 8th inning. There were two on with two outs, and the Yankees were already ahead, 6–2, when Crabtree came on for lefty Ricardo Jordan. The first man he faced was former Blue Jay, now New York Yankee, Tony Fernandez. Tony singled on the ground between third and short. Left fielder Joe Carter threw out Danny Tartabull at the plate to end the inning as Lance made a great catch of the throw and applied the tag. I saw Tim after the game and congratulated him. "Jerry, I grew up in Jackson, Michigan, and followed the Tigers from the very beginning on radio and TV. My all-time favourite Tiger was catcher Lance Parrish. As a kid, I first thought about catching myself but liked pitching better. I had a huge poster of Lance over my bed for years. And who is behind the plate tonight when I make my major league debut but Lance Parrish. I couldn't believe it. It was a dream come true."

Another rookie on the 1995 team who would go on to play in the major leagues for 12 years was Tomas Perez, who was born and raised in Barquisimeto, Venezuela. Tomas was just 14 years old when he dropped out of school — he had no choice. He had to go out and find any work he could along with his brothers and sisters to literally put food on the table. He wasn't the first player I had met who fit that scenario.

One of my most memorable postgame interviews was with Perez in his first season. Tomas spoke very little English at that time and he had trouble understanding it, too. After a game he'd helped win, I asked him to join me on the post-game show. By now I thought we knew how to communicate well enough to try to pull this off. Well, think again Jerry. After running down the totals, Tom threw it down to me from the booth, and away we went. With every short and slowly spoken sentence, I tried to elicit a simple answer from Perez for our audience. It actually turned out to be one of my funniest interviews. I would ask him a question that he would not fully understand, then he would mumble something back that I didn't quite understand. This went on for about three minutes. Tomas and I began laughing as the interview ended and I said, "Tom, I am going to send this back to you. This is the first interview I have ever done where our audience won't understand anything that was said — and we were both speaking English."

Lastly, in 1995, a rookie debuted at the tender age of 21. He went on to play 10 seasons with the Blue Jays and 14 overall. That was outfielder Shannon Stewart. Shannon was a Blue Jays first-round pick in 1992 out of a high school in Miami, Florida. His quick hands, excellent knowledge of the strike zone, and speed led to a lifetime slash line of .297/.360/.430. Along with that went 196 stolen bases, caught just 71 times, for a good 73 percent stolen base percentage.

In high school Shannon was a good student and a letterman in football, baseball, and track. In football as a junior and baseball as a senior, he was an All–Dade County selection. Stewart reflected what I always tried to preach to parents when I coached high school basketball: let your kids play all the sports while emphasizing academics. You can't hide talent. If you are that good in one of those sports, the colleges and universities will find you. Playing the additional sports will also force you to concentrate more on your studies in the fewer hours allotted to you. Plus, you will play for different coaches, learning something different from each one of them. This will help you to open up all the doors. Shannon epitomized that.

He had *Moneyball* numbers before there ever was *Moneyball*. In his 10 seasons with the Blue Jays, Shannon hit .298, with an on-base percentage of .365 and a slugging percentage of .440, for a solid OPS of .805. It was the .365 OBP that really stood out as Stewart quietly went about his business, allowing him to steal his 166 bases, caught only 55 times, for a 75 percent success rate.

1996: "Q," Otis, and Charlie's Hockey Mask

The Blue Jays finished the 1996 season fourth in the American League East with a record of 74 wins and 88 losses, marking a third-straight losing season. In December, before the season began, the Blue Jays traded infielder Howard Battle and pitcher Ricardo Jordan to the Philadelphia Phillies for right-handed pitcher Paul Quantrill. That same month came two more free agents in outfielder Otis Nixon and veteran catcher Charlie O'Brien. The last roster move occurred on February 10, just before the opening of spring training with free-agent pitcher Dane Johnson coming aboard.

Paul Quantrill pitched 14 years in the major leagues, pitching at "home" with the Blue Jays for six years. Born in London, Ontario, Quantrill lived in nearby Port Hope. Yes, it was a long commute, but he happily made it over all those years. A few things stand out with "Q," as he was known. I had many happy times with both Paul and Dan Plesac, who came to the Blue Jays from Pittsburgh the following season. They could be found side by side in the Blue Jays clubhouse and bolstered the bullpen year after year with their pitching skills. I loved teasing them, and they loved teasing me back — that's the way I like it. There is an old saying: "You only tease people you like." Well, I like a lot of people, so I do a lot of teasing. During the years Quantrill pitched with the Blue Jays, he would always have his son, Cal, with him at the ballpark. The little man was five or six years old, running all around the outfield. The two had one loving father-son moment after another. Cal, who had to be all of three feet tall at the time, rose to a height of six-foot-two. He went out west and pitched very effectively at Stanford University until he had to undergo Tommy John surgery on his right elbow. Despite that, seeing his future potential, the San Diego Padres drafted Cal eighth overall in the 2016 Draft. He is hopeful of a major league career like his dad.

Another Quantrill memory takes me to a weekend retreat in Port Hope one November, with members of our church group. I had heard about Quantrill Motors in Port Hope for years. During one of our breaks, I drove over on a Saturday afternoon, hoping to find Paul. He wasn't there, but one of his family members gave me a quick tour of their dealership. Right there in the garage, I saw a smooth plywood mound that was perfectly sculpted to duplicate a pitcher's mound at a height of 10 inches and sloped beautifully downward. For years at his family's dealership, this is where Paul would come indoors in the offseason and work out, pitching baseballs 60 feet away to a catcher he would bring in with him. It was so amazing to see this mound that he had specifically built so he could stay sharp all year round. Paul pitched in 80 or more games out of the bullpen during five of those 14 years in Major League Baseball. He was known for his durability and great control. He did not walk more than 25 batters in a season from 1996 through the end of his career in 2001. I finished the dealership tour asking the obvious question: "Did Paul ever miss the catcher's target and break a window?" The answer came with a smile: "Not too often."

Another newcomer that 1996 season was Otis Nixon. It was the veteran Nixon who made the last out of the 1992 World Series, when he tried to bunt his way on only to be thrown out at first base by Mike Timlin. One day in the Blue Jays clubhouse, I sought out Otis to ask him a question about the game the night before, where he had played so well. I noticed that he was quietly sitting in front of his cubicle, writing in a small book. I asked him what he was doing. He was so honest with me that day, talking about something I knew nothing about. "For years, I have had to battle being an addict — cocaine and other drugs I have used. It has been awful, and I have always had trouble trying to stop and live my life daily without these issues. I have had a lot of counselling and therapy, and it was suggested that I keep a daily journal to just write down my thoughts and go over them each day to try and get better. This is helping me to just take some quiet time and slow everything down to try and cope with my addiction one day at a time. And it is helping me."

I had so much admiration for Otis from that day forward, and I still do. Living the life of an addict or alcoholic is clearly difficult. It requires not only a strong diligence to work on recovery but persistence as well — there are no days off. That is so difficult to maintain consistently. It is so easy to slip back just one day and have to start all over again.

In another of our conversations, Otis told me all about how he would get a lead at first base, having already read a pitcher's moves in order to best steal a base off that pitcher. I asked him what he looked for. "With left-handers especially, there are six different moves I am looking for as I scout a pitcher before I ever reach base. I look at his overall throws over from the rubber: the soft toss for show, the quick throw over to get an out, the kick and pretended delivery where at the last moment he throws to first, the step off and throw to first, the long pause and stare to try and disrupt my timing, and the quick pitch. I study his footwork and mechanics to try to get a read on all of these moves to help me out. Once I have solved that, I feel confident that I can steal a base off him."

Sure enough, when the Blue Jays went to Detroit to play the Tigers, they faced tough left-handed starter C.J. Nitkowski.

When Nixon reached first base, I was astonished to see C.J. use all six moves to try to stop Otis from stealing second base. All to no avail. With patience and diligence, Otis finally got the jump he was looking for and stole second. It was so enlightening to see the teacher down on the field show the pupil up in the booth what made him so successful. In his major league career, Nixon stole 620 bases, including an Atlanta-record 72 in 1991. In one minor league season, he led the league, stealing 94.

Veteran catcher Charlie O'Brien came to the Blue Jays in 1996 for the first of two seasons in Toronto. It was all part of his 15-year major league career that saw him finish in 2000, playing with the Expos. He was destined to be a Blue Jay and catch in Canada. Why do I say that? As a first-year Blue Jay in 1996, Charlie was hit in his conventional mask by two consecutive foul tips in a game. That was the proverbial last straw for O'Brien. While in Toronto, Charlie was watching hockey games when the light went on. He came up with an idea for a new catcher's mask which would help deflect all those nasty foul balls. He worked with Van Velden Mask Inc., in Hamilton, Ontario, to develop his idea. The new design, called the All-Star MVP, was approved in 1996 by Major League Baseball. Thus was born baseball's catcher's hockey mask, used by so many today. It is also noteworthy that the second major league catcher to use the new hockey mask was also a Blue Jay: Gregg Zaun.

To wrap up the season, the fourth-place Blue Jays saw Mike Timlin save 31 games. Otis Nixon reached enough times to steal 54 bases. Ed Sprague was a great run producer in the lineup as he hit 36 home runs and drove in 101. Pat Hentgen won the Cy Young Award when, in his last start of the year, he won his 20th game to edge out the Yankees' 21-game winner Andy Pettitte.

An amusing postscript: at the All-Star Game in Philadelphia that season, there were boos for All-Star outfielder Joe Carter when he came to the plate. Phillies fanatics still remembered the sting of that 1993 World Series walk-off home run Joe hit in Game 6 off Mitch Williams.

1997: Interleague Play Begins

The 1997 season started and finished at opposite ends of the spectrum. Pitcher Roger Clemens was signed as a free agent to start it, and to end it, with a week to go, manager Cito Gaston was fired. Pitching coach Mel Queen took the reins in the final week, and Joe Carter was released, ending his outstanding run as a Blue Jay.

Another veteran who joined the team, signing a free agent contract in December, was catcher Benito Santiago. It's funny how hearing a certain name can cause one thing to immediately pop into your mind. When I hear Benito's name, I think of the number he wore. When the season started, I looked down from the radio booth and saw something I had never seen before or since. Benito was wearing No. 09. I always thought that Al Oliver's 0 and Cliff Johnson's 00 were the two lowest numbers worn in Blue Jays history. Wrong. Santiago's 09 was easily the lowest number — a negative number.

I asked him one day in the clubhouse, "Why do you wear zero-nine? I have never seen that before in all my years broadcasting."

"I like to have everybody see my number nine. But when I am catching and put on my chest protector, the strap goes right over my number and people can't see it. So I went to zero-nine. Now the strap goes right down the middle between the two numbers and everyone sees the nine." That was a first for me.

On June 30, 1997, the first-ever interleague game between the Blue Jays and the Montreal Expos took place at the SkyDome. The Expos won, 2–1, as both starters went the distance. Montreal's Pedro Martinez spun a three-hitter, allowing only the one run, while tough-luck loser Pat Hentgen went that route, too, allowing only two runs on six hits. Just 37,430 took in the two-hour-and-three-minute game that saw Carlos Delgado and Vladimir Guerrero hit home runs. The next day, which was Canada Day, the Blue Jays broke out their brand new red uniforms for the first time. They have been wearing them at home on Canada Day ever since.

Delgado emerged as an everyday player at first base that year, playing in 153 games, hitting 30 home runs, and driving in 91 on his way to greatness. Right fielder Shawn Green played in 135 games, hitting .287 while cracking 16 home runs and knocking in 53. The future was now.

1998: Manager Tim Johnson

In 1998, the Blue Jays hired a new manager: Tim Johnson. The club finished with their best record since 1993, winning 88 games and losing 74. There were two oddities. One was Tim himself. The other was that even with their 88 wins, the Blue Jays finished a distant 26 games behind the first-place New York Yankees. The Bronx Bombers won a whopping 114 games that year.

Before the season started, the Blue Jays went on their annual two-week winter caravan. I was asked to be the emcee for the first week to help introduce Johnson to various provinces across Canada. I had never met Tim, who had played for the Blue Jays at the end of his seven-year major league career in 1978 and 1979, and thought getting to know him would be very beneficial to me as a broadcaster.

That week on the caravan is one of the most enjoyable weeks I can remember, all because of the very outgoing and likeable Johnson. We spent a lot of time together and found out we had a lot in common. We had both been in the military. We both loved basketball. I was in awe of Tim's military background and the graphic and detailed stories he told about his tour of duty in Vietnam. In most all of them, he had come to the rescue and saved someone's life — it was amazing. It was also completely untrue. When our conversations turned to basketball, I talked about coaching high school basketball, and Tim told me about how he had been a star high school basketball player in Los Angeles, averaging 26 points per game and winning city championships. Then he really got my attention. He told me that legendary UCLA head coach Johnny Wooden had actually visited Tim at his house. Wooden tried to convince Tim and his parents to accept a full scholarship to play basketball for the Bruins as a starting guard. Tim told me he turned Wooden down, telling him that baseball was his first love, and instead he was going to sign a baseball contract out of high school and turn pro.

All these stories on the caravan carried into the 1998 season. However, their authenticity was being questioned more and more with each day. Roger Clemens and others did some research after hearing yet another Vietnam story. They discovered that Johnson had not served in Vietnam. As for John Wooden coming to his house, a phone call to Tim's high school made it clear he had never played basketball. It was all made up.

The capper occurred in a night game in Texas during the season, when reliever Dan Plesac was in trouble, surrounded by Rangers in a tight ball game. Tim came to the mound and had a long visit with Plesac. He then turned and went back to the dugout. On the next pitch, the Rangers had a surprise bunt play that was read beautifully by Plesac. Dan knocked the hitter down with runners going and turned it into an inning-ending double play that eventually led to victory. The next day in the Texas newspapers, I read all about it when Tim took complete credit. He had thought it all out and told Plesac about a counter-move to a possible play by the Rangers, and Dan had executed it brilliantly.

That night in the clubhouse, I congratulated Plesac on what he had done to contribute to the win the night before and what a great call it was by his manager to set it all up. "Jerry, when Tim came to the mound, he had no idea what the Rangers might do. So he asked me what I thought. I carefully explained everything we might do in the event they tried a bunt play. He said, 'Great, let's do it.' And he left the hill. After the game, he took all the credit for it as if it were his idea. That's why no one in here has any respect for him." When I asked Dan at season's end about the final record of 88 and 74, he was very quick to answer. "We would have won ninety-three or more games if we had had another manager."

In late November, Johnson finally confessed. He told several Toronto newspapers that all of his stories were completely made up. In truth, Johnson had been in the Marine Corps reserves throughout the war and trained at Camp Pendleton while playing in the Dodgers' farm system. And the UCLA basketball story and being an All-American high school basketball player weren't true either. During the 1998 December baseball winter meetings, Johnson said that admitting the truth was like having "a 50,000 pound weight" taken off his shoulders. He said he'd lied because he felt guilty about going to spring training with the Dodgers while many of his friends fought in the war. He entered therapy and called several of his players to apologize for lying.

The Blue Jays were initially willing to stand by Johnson and let him return for 1999. During spring training, he apologized to the entire team. It was too late. On March 17, less than a month before Opening Day, Blue Jays general manager Gord Ash fired Johnson and replaced him with Jim Fregosi. Ash said, and rightfully so, that Johnson's presence had become too much of a distraction.

Free agents Randy Myers and Jose Canseco joined the 1998 team, as did catcher Darrin Fletcher. For a third time, shortstop Tony Fernandez came back into the fold as well. The 1998 team had three players drive in 100 runs or more, in what turned out to be a very potent offence. Carlos Delgado drove in 115, Canseco knocked in 107, and young, emerging Shawn Green had an even 100 RBIs.

Roger Clemens

Roger Clemens won a second straight Cy Young Award, simply dominating the league for a second consecutive year. He once again won the pitcher's Triple Crown, posting the lowest ERA with the most wins and strikeouts. It was men against boys. I had never seen anything like it, and I doubt if I ever will again.

These were the same two years that Clemens was working with Blue Jays trainer Brian McNamee. Clemens was alleged by the *Mitchell Report* to have used anabolic steroids, mainly based on testimony given by McNamee. Clemens firmly denied these allegations under oath before the United States Congress, leading congressional leaders to refer his case to the Justice department on suspicion of perjury. On August 19, 2010, a federal grand jury at the U.S. District Court in Washington, D.C., indicted Clemens on six felony counts involving perjury, false statements, and contempt of Congress. Clemens pleaded not guilty. The proceedings were complicated by prosecutorial misconduct, leading to a mistrial. The verdict from his second trial came in June 2012. Clemens was found not guilty on all six counts of lying to Congress in 2008.

After Clemens's 1996 season ended with the Red Sox, GM Dan Duquette was asked if he would try to re-sign him. "I feel that Roger is in the twilight of his career. We will not be bringing him back to Boston." That season, Clemens had gone 10-13 with an ERA of 3.63. He was 34 years old. He had won 192 games in his career up to that point, mostly in his prime. That included winning three Cy Young Awards. The next season he came to Toronto as a free agent. Roger promptly went 21-7 with an ERA of 2.05, followed by a 20-6 season and an ERA of 2.65. From the time he joined the Blue Jays in the "twilight of his career," as noted by Duquette, Clemens won another 162 games from ages 35 to 45 and four more Cy Young Awards. He retired in 2007 with 354 wins.

"The Sarge" and Darrin Fletcher

This was the year the Blue Jays added new hitting coach Gary Matthews, also known as "The Sarge." I had never met

Gary, but I had followed his career when he was with the San Francisco Giants from 1972 to 1976. After coaching two years, Gary then worked in our radio booth for two more years in 2000 and 2001. He was the analyst alongside Tom Cheek and myself. We had a ball. Matthews related all kinds of stories and insights from his playing days, laughing all the while. He later had a long TV career as the analyst for the Philadelphia Phillies. Gary got his legendary nickname with the Chicago Cubs in 1984, when he became a Wrigley Field fan favour- ite right through to his last season with the Cubs in 1987. In 1984, he had led the league in walks, on-base percentage, and sacrifice flies. He was fifth in runs scored and ranked fifth in the National League MVP voting. "The Sarge" came from his habit, developed early in that 1984 season, of saluting the legions of left-field bleacher fans at Wrigley, who would cheer his every appearance in the outfield. In August, he arranged for caps with "Sergeant stripes" and his name on them to be distributed to all the bleacher fans.

One sunny and hot afternoon at U.S. Cellular Field in a game against the Chicago White Sox, I was calling the play- by-play in the top of the 4th inning. Gary, in his second year on radio, was sitting right between Tom and me as we called the game. "What a play made just now by catcher Darrin Fletcher to block that pitch and save a run. Gary, it doesn't get any better than that." There was total silence. "Here's the next pitch, and it's outside. An unbelievable play by Darrin, Sarge," as I opened up the floor once again for him to comment. Still nothing. I looked to my right. There was Gary with his sunglasses on, chair pushed back about a foot from our counter, head tilted back and resting on the wall of the little area we sat in. He was sound asleep!

As I called the next pitch, I used hand gestures to get Tom's attention, who was just to the right of Gary. Tom noted what was happening, and he started laughing as I continued, "Here's a strike, and it's two and one. Ladies and gentlemen, you are probably wondering why Tom just laughed out loud. Well, it's because our analyst has fallen asleep." Now we were both laughing. All of a sudden, Gary's head came off the wall as he moved forward to see what was happening. I couldn't resist. "Welcome back, Gary. We missed you. You just took a nap here in the fourth inning." All three of us burst out laughing, none harder than Gary.

Another free agent on the 1998 team was catcher Darrin Fletcher. In Montreal, Fletcher became a fixture in the lineup, regularly playing in over 100 games a year from 1992 through 1997. Then, with the Blue Jays, he had some of his finest seasons, including a game on August 27, 2000, when he hit three home runs against the Texas Rangers. Those home runs were three of the 20 Darrin hit that year. Seven Blue Jays hit 20 or more in 2000 as Toronto tied a major league record set by the 1996 Baltimore Orioles. When his playing days came to an end, Fletcher worked as a Blue Jays TV colour commentator on Rogers Sportsnet. He had an easy way about him on the air, providing interesting insights into the game. Catchers usually do. They often end up as either managers or broadcasters. Darrin Fletcher was one of 56 men to play for both the Expos and the Blue Jays.

On Sunday July 5, 1998, just before the All-Star break, my sister, Anita, called me from California. She was crying so hard over the phone, I couldn't understand her at first. Her daughter, Traci, her only child, went to lie down with a little bit of a headache, and half an hour later, she was gone, having passed away from an aneurysm. Traci was only 24. I had just seen her on a Blue Jays road trip to the Bay Area. She was blossoming into such a beautiful young lady with so much to look forward to in life. I couldn't believe it. The next day I flew to California to spend that entire week with my sister. It was one of the saddest weeks in my life.

1999: Two Newbies, Vernon Wells's Dad, and the One that Got Away

Jim Fregosi took over running the club in the spring of 1999. The team went on to post an overall record of 84-78 that season. The offence was outstanding. The Blue Jays set franchise records for most runs scored in a season, with 883, and most hits collected, at 1,580, topping the two previous marks set in 1993. Unfortunately, the club could not match what had happened in those two World Series years. The pitching staff allowed the most runs in Blue Jays history.

One newcomer to the clubhouse was quiet shortstop Tony Batista, who would take over for Alex Gonzalez. A couple of things stood out with Tony. First was his swing. I had never seen anything like it before, but it sure worked for him. He had such an extremely open batting stance that he would literally stand almost directly facing the pitcher during his delivery with both heels on the back chalk line before stepping into his swing. That season he hit 26 home runs and drove in 79. The next year, Tony hit 41 home runs while driving in 114. Amazing how he could do that. His unique swing and corresponding numbers proved once again that it is unwise to try to copy someone. What is comfortable for one person is not the same for the next. Young hitters are taught to do what makes them most comfortable swinging the bat, then work on that swing to keep improving it. Batista hit 221 home runs in his career and drove in 718, with a batting average of .251. Had he been able to walk more and improve his career .298 OBP, his numbers would have been even greater.

Batista was a devout Christian. He lived his life quietly, going about his business, excelling on the diamond and off. Tony made time for people, from teammates to perfect strangers. One day in Baltimore before batting practice, I saw Batista reading his Bible at his cubicle, as he often did when he had quiet moments in the clubhouse. I had wanted to ask him a question about his faith and the Bible, and this was my opportunity. "Tony, if you don't mind my asking, I see you reading the Bible all the time. With all that is in there, from the Old Testament to the New Testament, how do you read it? What do you read?"

"Each morning I open up the Bible and read a few pages from anywhere in the book. Then from those pages, I pick out one sentence and try to live it that day, doing what it says. This way I am always doing something that God asks me to do."

Another Blue Jay to make his debut in 1999 was infielder Chris Woodward from Covina, in Southern California. Chris turned out to be the best 54th-round pick the Blue Jays ever made, or will ever make for that matter. In 2017, the June Draft was down to 40 rounds. Chris and I hit it off right from the beginning. He had a smile on his face and a way of making you feel very comfortable around him. It was admirable to see him turn his baseball skills on the diamond into a 12-year major league career, the first seven with the Blue Jays. Four other teams followed, including the Seattle Mariners, who must have been impressed after what they saw and then heard on August 7, 2002, the day Chris hit three home runs against them at the SkyDome in a game the Blue Jays lost in part due to his fielding error. "It would have been a lot better had we won. My error in the third inning helped me in a positive way. I was mad. It got me more focused, and it made me step it up a notch." Sage words of advice on how to turn a negative into a positive.

Woodward retired in November 2012, but not before meeting his wife, Erin, who grew up in Aurora, Ontario. They have three beautiful children. I was at their wedding reception and later get-togethers with Erin and their young kids throughout his career. One of the happiest moments in my career came in 2014, when I walked onto the field at Safeco Field in Seattle, and there was Chris in his first season as a major league coach. "Look at you!" I said. He was beaming from ear to ear. In 2015, the Dodgers hired Woodward as their third-base coach. Two years later, Chris helped coach the Dodgers to the seventh and deciding game of the 2017 World Series, won by the Houston Astros in one of the most exciting World Series ever played. And in 2019, he became the new manager for the Texas Rangers. All part of being a 54th-round pick.

I distinctly remember standing at the batting cage one afternoon at the SkyDome in the summer of 1997, when I was introduced to a young man who had just been drafted in the first round and fifth overall by the Blue Jays. Out of high school in Arlington, Texas, he was quiet and shy and didn't say much. But in the cage, you could see an outstanding swing. Two years later, in 1999, Vernon Wells made his major league debut, skyrocketing from Class-A Dunedin to Double-A Knoxville to Triple-A Syracuse to Toronto. You rarely see that kind of one-year ascension through a team's minor league system.

Vernon married his high school sweetheart, Charlene, out of Bowie High School in Arlington, and together they have two boys: Jace and Christian. The name Christian is very appropriate; Vernon has lived his Christian faith his entire life. An outstanding quarterback in high school, Vernon shared with me a story that every kid growing up in football-dominated Texas dreams about. "My greatest thrill playing football came when our team reached the Final Four for the Texas State Championship. We were able to run out onto the field from the tunnel at Irving Stadium, the home of the Dallas Cowboys, before a sold-out crowd." I got goosebumps just hearing Vernon tell that story. As good as Wells was in football, baseball was his first love. He turned down many college football scholarships to sign with the Blue Jays.

Vernon's dad, Vernon Sr., is an accomplished artist. "My dad is the artist," Vernon laughed. "All I can draw are stick men, and they aren't very good." For years, I would see many of his dad's oil paintings; Vernon Sr. would bring them into the clubhouse not only to show players, but to encourage them to have their paintings done, too, for their family and friends. When Vernon finished with the New York Yankees and retired after the 2013 season, his dad would still come to spring training in Dunedin.

That is where, several years later, I caught a break when I saw Vernon Sr. and learned about some major league history that I was totally unaware of and have shared with our audience ever since. He handed me his latest brochure of paintings of players he had done that winter. As I thumbed through it, I saw one great painting after another. I stopped when I saw the one featuring Rajai Davis. The former Blue Jay was swinging the bat four times on one canvas. "Why do you have Rajai painted here four times?" I innocently asked. "Last year, Jerry, he had a walk-off triple in Detroit. Rajai is the only player in major league history to have a walk-off cycle."

At Comerica Field in Detroit on September 22, 2015, the Tigers and the White Sox were locked up in a great pitcher's duel in the bottom of the 10th inning when, with two outs, the speedy Anthony Gose drew a walk. Rajai was the next hitter. He promptly tripled into the right-field corner, sending Gose sprinting to the plate. Anthony beat the throw to win it. As he was sliding across the plate, there was Rajai going into third, standing up with the walk-off triple. It was Rajai's seventh career walk-off hit and first triple, making him the only player in the history of the game to have a walk-off single, double, triple, and home run. What a cycle — what an artist.

One other Blue Jay of note in 1999 was catcher Mike Matheny. Mike had great character and maturity beyond his years. You could easily see that he might someday transition into a manager's role. He was too quiet, in my opinion, for a broadcasting career, but he had a certain presence about him that exuded excellent leadership skills with all the intangibles. Mike was one the Blue Jays let get away — not once, but twice. In 1988, he was drafted in the 31st round by the Blue Jays out of a high school in Ohio. GM Pat Gillick saw something special in him and tried to sign him as if he were a second-round pick, but it didn't work out. Three years later, Milwaukee drafted him in the 8th round out of the University of Michigan and signed him.

In 1999, he came to the Blue Jays as a free agent. Mike played in 57 games as the backup catcher to Darrin Fletcher. He hit just .215, with low numbers across the board. Defensively he was outstanding, not only catching but guiding and help-ing every pitcher on the staff. It was then that the Blue Jays let him get away a second time, releasing him after the 1999 season. Matheny went on to catch five years with the St. Louis Cardinals and two more with the San Francisco Giants. Mike began his managerial career with the Cardinals in 2012 and became the first manager in MLB history to guide his club to the postseason in each of his first four full seasons, which included a trip to the 2013 World Series against Boston.

Though not a great hitter, in Matheny's 13-year career, he was one of the most accomplished defensive catchers of his era, winning four Gold Gloves. He retired from playing due to persistent concussion symptoms and has since become an advocate for its prevention and for improved catcher safety. Mike wore the hockey mask for years, including during his one season with the Blue Jays. Even though the hockey mask was designed to help create more glancing foul balls than the conventional mask, in 2006, Mike still had to retire prematurely.

After he retired, Matheny coached his son's Little League team, and he later wrote a book about his experiences. It was written for parents, so that they could see their kids in a different light and understand the difference between playing the game for fun and just trying to win. The book is entitled *The Matheny Manifesto: A Young Manager's Old-School Views on Success in Sports*. It is an excellent and informative read.

CHAPTER 20

TRYING TO KICK-START THE ENGINE

Prior to the 2000 season, which saw the Blue Jays finish third in the A.L. East with a record of 83-79, the club traded Shawn Green to the Dodgers for outfielder Raul Mondesi and left-handed pitcher Pedro Borbon. The next time the Blue Jays went out to Los Angeles to play the Dodgers, Shawn hit a home run against his old team. Okay, that happens. But then I saw something I had never seen before.

As Shawn was trotting back to his own third-base dugout, he peeled off both his batting gloves and gave them to a young fan near the dugout, where the kids were all cued up, hopeful they would get a surprise keepsake from their idol. The following day down on the field during batting practice, I asked him about what had happened. "My first year with my new team, I hit a home run here at Dodger Stadium. But I was so disappointed because I had torn one of my batting gloves on the swing. So as I hit home plate and headed for our dugout, I ripped off both gloves and flipped them into the crowd. I didn't think anything about it. But the next inning, when I came off the field, the young boy who caught the gloves yelled, 'Thank you, Shawn!' I was so touched, I decided right then and there I would happily take off my batting gloves after every home run I hit here at home and hand them to a fan." And he did that often, much to the delight of many a young Dodgers fan.

The 2000 season marked the second and last year that Jim Fregosi would manage the Blue Jays, despite the fact that the team finished in third place and above .500 in each of his two years in Toronto. Fregosi completed his two-year final managerial position in Major League Baseball with a record of 167 wins and 157 losses. He had previously managed the Angels and the White Sox and was in the Phillies dugout during the 1993 World Series.

Fregosi was feisty and sarcastic, congenial, very opinionated, and at times condescending. Jim had a love for both baseball and life that was second to none. He was very well read in many areas outside of baseball. But when it came to baseball, you wouldn't want to cross him. I remember one time in his office, he was addressing all the members of the media and fielding questions about a loss the night before. Finally, yet another reporter began a question with, "If you had done *this* instead of *that*," to which Jim tersely answered, "And if my aunt had balls, she'd be my uncle." The room erupted with laughter.

Doing the manager's show each day for years allowed me to really get to know a person as more than just a manager. Fregosi was an eye-opener. We would sit and talk well before and well after the five-minute show. There were many times I would just listen in awe at various aspects of the game that I had no idea about. It was such a good education. In February 2014, Fregosi was a part of an MLB alumni cruise when he suffered multiple strokes. The cruise docked in the Cayman Islands, where he was rushed to a local hospital. His condition was stabilized by doctors, and he was then moved to Miami. However, Fregosi's condition took a turn for the worse, and he died on February 14.

The coaching staff in 2000 included two pitching coaches: Dave Stewart and Rick Langford. Stewart, of course, needed no introduction to the city of Toronto, having been a prominent member of the 1993 World Series Championship team. On the other hand, I did not know Langford, although I found him fascinating. In 1980, when Rick was pitching for Billy Martin's Oakland A's, he had done the seemingly impossible. He not only completed 28 games of his 33 starts that season, but he also reeled off 22 consecutive complete games. That unbeliev-able streak ended September 17 in Texas, in a game in which he pitched eight and two-thirds innings.

Here is what the ever-gracious Langford had to say about the end of his remarkable streak when Billy Martin came to take him out that night. "I remember him standing there, like it was yesterday. He didn't ask me, 'How are you?' or 'You can do it,' or whatever. His comment was, and God bless him, 'I think it's time now.' Those were his words. I said, 'Yes, it is.' I handed him the ball and walked off." Lefty Bob Lacey came on to get the last out, saving Langford's 17th win. That season, Rick went 19-12 with an ERA of 3.26, working 290 innings.

Injuries can also go hand in hand with pitching that many innings. The *Sports Illustrated*'s cover of April 27, 1981, was headlined: "The Amazing A's and Their Five Aces" featuring Langford, Mike Norris, Steve McCatty, Matt Keough, and Brian Kingman. Years later, in 2015, a book was written by Bill Pennington, entitled *Billy Martin: Baseball's Flawed Genius*. In it, Pennington saw another side to the five starters' terrific 1981 season. "Of the five, only Steve McCatty had a winning record in 1982, and he was 6-3. Baseball historians have looked back and unequivocally come to an assessment: Billy Martin and his pitching coach, Art Fowler, burned out an entire staff." That was roughly when a starter's pitch count had begun to be taken very seriously.

2001: Manager Buck Martinez

The 2001 season started with a new manager as Buck Martinez replaced Jim Fregosi. The club finished 80-82, in third place. Buck and I have known each other for years. Two Northern California boys who found careers in Canada, one as a broadcaster and the other as a player, manager, and broadcaster. We both know how fortunate we are to have lived the dream. Buck was hired as manager by GM Gord Ash after Fregosi's contract was not renewed.

The Blue Jays got off to a solid 16-9 April but then slid to 10-18 in May, putting the team just under .500 after two months. The team finished strong, going 16-12 in August and 15-12 in September/October. Sadly, this was also the year that six games were rescheduled in September after the 9/11 attack on the World Trade Center in New York.

In his new job as manager, Buck surrounded himself with good coaches. That included pitching coach Mark Connor, first-base coach and former teammate Garth Iorg, and Buck's longtime mentor Cookie Rojas as bench coach. Cito Gaston remained as the hitting coach while Terry Bevington, a veteran baseball man, coached third. Gil Patterson was the other pitching coach out in the bullpen.

When Pat Hentgen was named the new Blue Jays bullpen coach in 2011, I asked him if he had an early role model to follow now that he was a coach.

"Years ago, Roy Halladay told me that one of the best pitching coaches he ever had was Mark Connor, back in 2001, when he came to the Blue Jays. Roy said that Mark never said anything negative to him or any of the other pitchers. He would teach you something and then ask you to do it. As you did it and made mistakes, he would encourage you, saying *try this* or *try that*. And then when you finally got it, he would say, 'That's it. Perfect. Way to go!' Roy said you never heard, 'Don't do that or don't do this.' Everything Mark said was positive or he didn't say it. That is what I want to do now in my career as a coach."

Hentgen did an outstanding job the two years he was bullpen coach in 2011 and 2013. He stepped down twice for family reasons and the passing away of his dad. Someday you might be reading about manager Pat Hentgen, who will still be using those Mark Connor principles.

Buck and Cookie played together with the Kansas City Royals from 1970 through the 1977 season. Buck caught and Cookie played second. Cookie was great for Buck. Every manager needs a strong bench coach and friend who can help smooth out the long haul of a season. I remember Tony La Russa once telling me: "Managing is so difficult, Jerry. You have to make all kinds of sacrifices, and that includes your family. There are so many ups and downs in a season, plus the scrutiny that goes with all the losses. Even when you win it all, it can be a thankless job."

At the end of the 2001 season, after eight years as GM and no playoff appearances, Gord Ash was let go. You could see the handwriting on the wall for Buck, as J.P. Ricciardi became the Blue Jays' fourth general manager in their history. Fifty-three games into the 2002 season, with a 20-33 record and coming off a three-game sweep against the Detroit Tigers, Ricciardi replaced Buck with Carlos Tosca, whom Ricciardi had originally brought in as a third-base coach.

After his firing, Buck went to Baltimore, where he worked for years as an analyst on the Orioles TV broadcasts. When Ricciardi was fired after eight years as the club's GM, it paved the way for Buck to return to Toronto as their new voice on TV. I have always admired Buck, who went from a player to an analyst on radio to the lead play-by-play broadcaster on TV. It takes a lot of hard work and discipline to become a play-by-play broadcaster. Buck is one of the few ex-athletes in our business to pull it off.

In his first season back as broadcaster, we were on the field one day during batting practice at the Rogers Centre, and Buck said something to me that I have appreciated and used from that day on.

"I am so happy I had the chance to manage for many reasons, and one of them is that now, as a broadcaster, I am so much more aware of how complex situations are. Having sat in on so many meetings where we were discussing all the possibilities for our decisions has made me a better broadcaster. It looks so easy from the outside. As a broadcaster the first time, I got caught up in all that as well, saying, 'Do this and do that, and everything will be fine.' Well, it doesn't work that way. Now I check myself on the air. I am a lot more aware of what is really going on as opposed to what I think is going on."

Those honest words from Buck helped to clarify things in my outlook, too. This is a tough game to play on the field and even tougher to orchestrate from the front office — when you come to that realization, it makes life a lot easier.

2002: J.P. Ricciardi

Although never able to lay claim to a playoff game during his eight years as general manager, Ricciardi had great bookend trades. His first ever deal in December 2001 saw him move closer Billy Koch to the Oakland A's, where J.P. had worked for years under GM Billy Beane, for third baseman Eric Hinske and pitcher Justin Miller. Hinske went on to become the American League Rookie of the Year while Miller, known as "Tattoo Man," would sadly take his own life at the age of 35 in 2013. In 2008, Ricciardi pulled off the biggest trade in his eight years when he sent minor league catcher Robinzon Diaz to the Pirates for an unknown named Jose Bautista.

The 2002 season saw the Blue Jays go 74-84 under two managers: Buck Martinez for the first 53 games (20-33), and Carlos Tosca (58-51). Roy Halladay went 19-7 with an ERA of 2.93. Homer Bush played second base. Years later, Homer became a fixture with the Honda Super Camps across Canada as he gave back to kids across the land. There were two catchers in young Kevin Cash, who would eventually go on to manage the Tampa Bay Rays, and Tom Wilson. Wilson was originally a second baseman but had been groomed in the New York Yankees system. "The Yankees were so deep at that position, they took two of us off that bag and converted us to catchers. I was fine with that, and so was the other infielder, Jorge Posada." Yes, the same Jorge Posada who helped the Yankees get to six World Series appearances and four wins. Tom, meanwhile, has been a longtime scout for the team that initially signed him, always looking for that next great infielder turned catcher for the Yankees.

Rookie second baseman Orlando Hudson made it "to the show," as they say, where he was greeted by his best friend, who was also from South Carolina, outfielder DeWayne Wise, who was already in his second year as a Blue Jay. Their dads were so funny when talking about their sons and what they could do on a baseball diamond. Orlando's father would gently take off his cap and say in that South Carolina drawl of his, "Jerrrrrrry . . . how did my son everrrrr catch that ball?" Those two dads had me in stitches every time I was around them.

Gibby, the NBA, and East Lyme

The new first-base coach that season was John Gibbons. Gibby had initially come to the Blue Jays in spring training as the team's bullpen catcher. He and Ricciardi had been teammates and roommates back in their first years together, after they had signed with the New York Mets, and had become close friends. In his first year as the GM, J.P. had put in place two people he could see as future managers: Tosca and Gibbons. Sure enough, both eventually did manage the team. Gibbons replaced Tosca in 2004.

I really didn't get to know John during spring training; he was busy with all the pitchers. Spring training sees an inordinate number of pitchers in camp with a ton of catchers to help them out. Then, as the season started, John was once again out in the bullpen. One day, when I was standing at the batting cage having just talked with Tosca, there was Gibby at my elbow. He said, "Jerry, I know some baseball, too," and we both started laughing. I had been busy and he had been busy, and we hadn't formed much of friendship.

He went on to tell me in that folksy Texas way of his: "Ask me anything you want about the game. There is no right or wrong in baseball — everything can be talked about and debated and broken down from so many different points of view. I'm good with anything you bring up." John has been true to those words since the day we met.

He and his wife, Julie, have three terrific kids: Jordan, Troy, and Kyle. After Jordan graduated from college, she formed her own band in San Antonio, Texas, called Southtown. She is the lead singer, writes her own lyrics, and plays guitar. In May 2017, her band was featured during the pregame show on Country Day, performing on the West Jet Flight Deck. The crowd loved it, and so did a proud dad watching from the third-base dugout. I love people who follow their hearts and turn hobbies into careers. Jordan Gibbons is doing that, and in December 2017, she started a new band called The Barrens.

John has forever been family first, which is the best way to handle long seasons as a manager: it puts the game into its true and proper perspective. Not only do you have to manage 25 players and delegate responsibilities to all of your coaches, but you have to deal with the media and fans and front office daily. Not easy. In the grand scheme of things, when considering family first, you're ready for whatever comes along. John has done that admirably, not once but twice, managing the Blue Jays.

The 2002 season also brought with it someone unique. That was six-foot-nine, 240-pound left-hander Mark Hendrickson. Hendrickson pitched 10 years in the major leagues, the first two of those years as a Blue Jay. Mark was also a power forward in the National Basketball Association. He is one of just 12 athletes to play in both the major leagues and the NBA. Mark passed up baseball after high school when he was selected by Atlanta in the 13th round of the 1992 Draft. Instead, he chose to attend Washington State University, and upon college graduation, he was selected by the NBA's Philadelphia 76ers (second pick, second round, 31st overall) in the 1996 Draft, and by the Blue Jays (20th round) in the 1997 Draft. He elected to play basketball. Unsigned by the NBA prior to the 1998 season and frustrated by his inability to get more consistent work, he decided to give up basketball and concentrate on baseball.

Mark was easy to talk to. Although, I did most of my visiting with him in the clubhouse when we were both sitting, so we could talk eye to eye. My most vivid memory of Mark occurred in his second season in 2003. The Blue Jays were playing at Olympic Stadium in Montreal just before the All-Star break. With one swing, Hendrickson became the first pitcher in Blue Jays history to hit a home run — a drive to deep right-centre field. I'm guessing that probably felt better than any slam dunk he ever had in the NBA.

One other pitcher slipped under the radar in 2002. He was a 10-game winner that season, but there would be a lot more to come for Pete Walker. He enjoyed the best season of his eight-year career, going 10-5. Years later, Walker would be named the Blue Jays' bullpen coach and eventually pitching coach. As a testament to the person and coach Pete is, when lefty J.A. Happ became a free agent after the 2015 season and entertained numerous offers, he settled on Toronto. Why? "Because of pitching coach Pete Walker and manager John Gibbons." Happ went 20-4 and reached the American League Championship Series in his 2016 return to Toronto, under the guidance of one and the leadership of the other.

One interesting note centred on Walker and another Blue Jay, John McDonald. They both went to East Lyme High School in East Lyme, Connecticut, located between Boston and New York. They were five years apart, Pete being older.

I asked Pete one day, "Where did you go to see your first major league game?"

"We always went to Boston to see the Red Sox at Fenway Park. I was born in Beverly, Massachusetts, so my family liked the Red Sox."

I asked Johnny Mac the same question. "We always went to New York to see the Yankees play. My dad liked the Yankees, so I became a Yankees fan, too." A few years later, I asked Rajai Davis, who was born in Connecticut and raised near East Lyme, the same question. He replied, "Both!"

2003: Wells, Bordy, the Cat, and Reed

In 2003, Carlos Tosca's one-and-only full season as the Blue Jays manager, the team finished third with a record of 86-76 and 15 games behind the pace-setting New York Yankees. Roy Halladay went 22-7 with an ERA of 3.25, winning the A.L. Cy Young Award. Carlos Delgado, who finished second in the A.L. MVP voting to the Yankees' Jason Giambi, hit 42 home runs and drove in 145.

Vernon Wells hit 33 home runs and drove in 117 while collecting a franchise record 215 hits, easing by Tony Fernandez's previous record of 213 hits, set in 1986. Wells still holds that franchise mark. Only three other Blue Jays have collected 200 or more hits: Paul Molitor, 211 in 1993; Shannon Stewart, 202 in 2001; and John Olerud, 200 hits in 1993, when he won the batting title, hitting .363.

Sadly, the rookie of the year from the 2002 season, Eric Hinske, broke his hamate bone and finished the year batting just .243 with 12 home runs and 63 RBIs. On the flip side, the

Blue Jays signed two free agents, Mike Bordick and Frank Catalanotto, who both did yeoman work that year and helped to solidify the team on the field and in the clubhouse. After attending the University of Maine, where he played college baseball for the Black Bears, Bordick was signed as an amateur free agent with the Oakland Athletics in 1986 by none other than scout J.P. Ricciardi. Mike made his major league debut in 1990 with the Athletics, and later succeeded Hall of Fame and Gold Glove shortstop Cal Ripken in Baltimore as Cal moved to third base.

The humble and self-effacing Bordick set American League records with the Orioles for most consecutive errorless games played (110) and total chances (543) by a shortstop in a season. He did it with an unusual technique: after catching a ground ball, he never tapped the ball back into his glove before making the throw, as you see so many infielders do. The game is extremely fast at the major league level, and this technique helped Bordick to unload his throws quicker to get his extra share of outs on close plays at first. "I have done that from the very beginning. The other way of tapping is okay, too. But this worked best for me. Do what's comfortable for you." Following the end of his playing career, Bordick worked as a roving minor league instructor for the Blue Jays. Since 2012, he has served as colour analyst for Orioles telecasts on their MASN TV network, alternating games with Jim Palmer.

Frank Catalanotto had a wonderful 14-year career, playing both on the infield and in the outfield. He spent four of those seasons, from 2003 through 2006, with the Blue Jays. A few great memories come to mind when I think of "The Cat," as he was known. One has to do specifically with his name. It happened on the Blue Jays' first-ever Dog Day promotion at the ballpark. Before the game, hundreds of fans paraded along the warning track with their dogs. That day, Catalanotto went 5 for 5 against the Detroit Tigers to help the Blue Jays win it. The headlines the next day screamed: "The Cat goes 5 for 5, on Dog Day!" The very next season, in May, Frank would top his 5 for 5 game setting a Blue Jays record going 6 for 6 in the second game of a doubleheader in Chicago against the White Sox. Over his 14 years, Catalanotto hit .291 with an OBP of .357 and a SLG of .445.

Frank was born and raised on Long Island, and whenever the Blue Jays played the Yankees in New York, Frank's dad would come to see his son play, and I'd get to talk to his dad during batting practice. One day this led me to ask Frank if he'd been a Yankees fan or a Mets fan growing up — and what about his brother, Mike?

"When Mike and I were growing up, we would always be arguing at the dinner table about what team was the best: Yankees or Mets. I was a big Yankees fan, and I couldn't stand the Mets. Mike loved the Mets and didn't care at all about the Yankees. This went on and on for years, until one day Mike said, 'But Frank, what if the Mets wanted you to play for them? What would you do then?' I answered: 'Mike, I would never play for the Mets, and that ended the conversation. At the end of my career, I played 25 games for the Mets!"

Every spring training, as it gets closer and closer to Opening Day, teams will dip into their minor league system and call up players who were not invited to camp to give the other players a breather. I was at the microphone in Dunedin for one of those games in 2003, when in the middle innings, a kid just called up went in to play centre field. That day, he put himself on the map not once but twice, making two spectacular running catches in centre field up against the wall. His name was Reed Johnson.

After that game, it was discovered that Reed had somehow slipped through the cracks after spending four years in the Blue Jays system. He had an injury in 2002, when he slid into second base head first, and played only 44 games, going basically unnoticed. No one took him in the Rule 5 Draft that December, which clearly benefited the Blue Jays.

Reed played 13 years in the major leagues, his first five years with the Blue Jays. He was a terrific outfielder with an outstanding arm and great makeup to play the game at the highest level. In his first season in 2003, he did something that only six other players in major league history have ever done. On June 15, against the Cubs at the Rogers Centre, Reed hit a leadoff home run to begin the game and a 10th-inning walk-off home run to end the game. Talk about bookend home runs.

Historic Inside-the-Park Home Runs

The team used three catchers that season: Ken Huckaby, Greg Myers, and Kevin Cash. What are the odds that a catcher would hit an inside-the-park home run? Pretty low, considering that catchers are notoriously slow. What are the odds that catchers would hit inside-the-park home runs in back-to-back years? Virtually impossible. But it happened.

The year before, on July 17, 2002, Huckaby hit a fly ball down the right-field line in a game at home against the Orioles. Gary Matthews Jr. raced over from right to get it and slid trying to make the catch. As the ball bounced away from him, he thought the ball hit foul. Matthews stayed on the ground, messing with the crowd. Meanwhile, Huckaby raced around the bases as the crowd was laughing at Matthews in the corner.

By the time Matthews realized the ball was fair, his throw to the plate was too late. Ken Huckaby had hustled around the bases for an inside-the-park home run. Ken had earned the distinction of being the only catcher in Blue Jays history to do so. He also saw the humour in the moment. "I don't think there are too many guys slower than me."

Well, guess what? There was one: Greg Myers. The very next year, Ken's teammate became the second catcher in Blue Jays history to hit an inside-the-park home run. It took place on September 13, once again at the Rogers Centre and again with the Orioles in town. Talk about "déjà vu all over again," as Yogi Berra would say. In the 4th inning, Myers hit a looper to centre field that looked as if it would be a single. Orioles centre fielder Tim Raines Jr. charged the ball and got too close to it. The ball bounced high off the spongy artificial turf and over his head, rolling all the way to the wall as Myers rounded the bases and scored standing up. Huckaby and Myers. Who would have guessed? Inside-the-park home runs in back-to-back seasons. Both catchers. First time in Blue Jays history for a catcher — not once, but twice. Baseball's version of Ripley's Believe It or Not.

2004: Remembering Tom Cheek

One of the most difficult and saddest years in my career as the Blue Jays radio announcer was 2004. The Blue Jays finished last in the A.L. East with a record of 67-94, marking their worst record since 1980, but the difficulty had nothing to do with the team on the field. That happens. I have never ridden the waves of winning or losing — that is out of my control. All of that paled in comparison to what happened to my longtime radio partner Tom Cheek and my close friend and Blue Jays TV broadcaster John Cerutti.

The Blue Jays had just finished a series in Seattle to start the month of June and had flown down to Oakland. On the morning of June 4, I was in my hotel room when the phone rang. There was no mistaking that deep, loud, and distinctive voice. But this time it was without the usual energy that went with it. "Jerry, I won't be broadcasting the game with you tonight. I just got a call from my dad's wife. My eighty-six-year-old father died of a heart attack while taking a shower this morning. I am going to drive over to nearby Monterey about an hour away to see her and then spend the day and night with her to help her out."

That day, Tom not only suddenly lost his father, who had been in very good health at the time, but he also saw his amazing streak of calling 4,306 consecutive games on radio come to an end. Tom had called every Blue Jays game from the team's inception on April 7, 1977 to June 3, 2004, and the number is memorialized right beside Tom's name on the Level of Excellence at the Rogers Centre. A remarkable feat spanning 27 and a half seasons.

Tom returned to the broadcast booth in Oakland the day after missing the one game. However, I noticed something wasn't quite right. His calls were a little bit off. That happens to all of us, and we move on. But this continued, with more mistakes here and there. I attributed it to the stress and strain of losing his dad so unexpectedly. The eventual bigger picture was the last thing on my mind. The road trip ended, and the team flew back to Toronto to open a series against the Dodgers the following night. During the home stand, Tom continued to make mistakes on the air. We all make mistakes as broadcasters, but I could see these were becoming more and more magnified: he had Eric Hinske leading off first base when he wasn't in the game, followed by a score that included Seattle, and we weren't playing Seattle — I knew something was seriously wrong.

I came to the booth the next day and sat beside him in my customary seat to his right. Tom was about to write out his opening for the sign-on that night, but he looked confused. He took out a blank piece of paper and began writing. After a word or two, he tore it up and started over again. He did this about four or five times as the wads of paper mounted. He couldn't get past "Live! From the Rogers Centre . . ." Five words. Our engineer Bruce Brenner saw all this, too. With Tom's last wadded up piece of paper tossed in the garbage can, Bruce called down to our clubhouse to ask Ron Taylor, the Blue Jays' team doctor, to come up and see Tom. He was taken over to Mount Sinai Hospital, where they found a malignant brain tumour. A few days later on June 13, his birthday, no less, Tom had surgery. He was told he had six to 16 months to live. It was crushing. Sixteen months later, Tom passed away on October 9, 2005, at the age of 66. My wife and I still keep in touch with his wife, Shirley, celebrating all Tom did in his wonderful career for everyone in Toronto and across Canada.

I asked my friend Nelson Millman, who headed up our radio broadcasts, what he wanted me to do in the second half of the season without Tom. He graciously left it in my hands. I chose to have nine different minor league broadcasters I had mentored join me when the Blue Jays played their parent clubs. This allowed them to call their first major league games. They appreciated the opportunity, and I enjoyed seeing their faces glow as they did something that would continue to motivate them to realize their dreams. One of those young pups, who was calling games on the radio for Cleveland's top farm club, was Jim Rosenhaus, who is now their radio play-by-play broadcaster. Jim sits right beside veteran Tom Hamilton. Steve Klauke in Salt Lake City joined me when the Blue Jays played out in Anaheim. Steve has gone on to call a number of games for the parent Angels, as did Triple-A broadcaster Johnny Doskow for the Oakland A's.

I took the liberty to reach out to the other teams' general managers and have them join me for games as well. They did a great job highlighting their teams for our audience. Cleveland's young GM Mark Shapiro was one of the most gracious guests and impressed me greatly both on and off the microphone. Another GM who was exactly the same way was Brian Cashman of the Yankees. Brian always makes it a point every season to find me and say hello to see how I am doing.

People have asked me over the years, *when was Tom's last broadcast?* I can tell you specifically when it was because of how special it was for Tom and me. The Blue Jays opened up the 2005 season in St. Petersburg, Florida, against the Rays. Tom and Shirley lived in nearby Oldsmar, and Shirley brought Tom to the game. My new radio partner, in his first year, was the analyst Warren Sawkiw. I did all the play-by-play. After three innings, the Rays led, 1–0, as the Blue Jays had been set down in order all three innings. Much to my surprise, Tom came into the booth at the end of the 3rd inning to say hello. He asked me if he could do an inning of play-by-play. I said sure.

As we went to the top of the 4th inning, Tom sat right in the middle of the two of us, with me to his right and Warren to his left. "Ladies and gentleman, with the Rays leading 1–0, it gives me great pleasure to welcome to our radio booth my partner, Tom Cheek, who is going to call this inning for you."

With that, Tom took over. The first batter up was leadoff hitter Frank Catalanotto. Tom called his double, which was shot up the gap into right-centre field. The very next batter, Orlando Hudson, cracked a two-run home run as the Blue Jays took the lead, 2–1. The next hitter, Vernon Wells, belted a home run off the catwalk in deep left-centre field to make it 3–1. We were all laughing. "Tom, look at you. I'm at the microphone for the first three innings, and it's nine up and nine down. You sit down, and the first three hitters give the Blue Jays the lead. Wow." Tom was so happy. Warren was sitting there in awe. He hadn't said a word so far and this, too, did not go unnoticed by Tom.

Tom called the rest of the top of that inning. Over the course of the next three hitters, who were all retired, Tom looked to his left at Warren. "Do you ever say anything up here?" Again more laughter. Warren finally said on the air, "Tom, I grew up listening to you and Jerry. And now I am just watching and listening to the two of you and taking it all in. It is so awesome." Warren's facial expression said it all. No doubt he was transplanted back into his childhood for a moment and was thinking, *Is this all happening?*

During the commercial break, Tom said that was enough. He was tired and appreciated being able to sit down with us and call that half inning. It was meant to be. The Blue Jays went on to win that season opener over the Rays, 5–2. It was the last inning Tom Cheek ever broadcast in his long and distinguished career.

Let me put an exclamation point on all of this. The following year in 2006, the Blue Jays opened the season at home against the Minnesota Twins. Tom had passed away the previous October. He was honoured before the game with Shirley and their three now-adult children, Tom Jr., Lisa, and Jeff. At the bottom of the 4th inning, Jeff came into the booth to join me on the radio to talk about his dad. Divine intervention happened again. The Twins were ahead, 1–0. The Blue Jays put runners at first and third with no one out as Jeff and I continued to reminisce about Tom. A sacrifice fly tied the game at 1–1 when, with one on and one out, catcher Bengie Molina came to the plate. This time I had the pleasure of being at the microphone. "Here's the pitch to Molina. Hit high and deep down the left-field line. A towering shot. It is up, and *there she goes*! A ball that almost hit Tom Cheek's name on the Level of Excellence on the fourth level here at the Rogers Centre! Blue Jays 3, Twins 1." As Molina hit third base, I looked at Jeff, who was smiling. "Jerry, somewhere up there my dad had a hand in that one." He sure did. Just like he'd had a hand in so many other memorable Blue Jays moments. *You touched us all, Tom. They'll never be another one like you.*

A Class Act Truly Missed

The other very sad moment in the 2004 season came out of nowhere, on the very last day of the season, at home against the Yankees. When I arrived at the Rogers Centre, it didn't take long for me to hear the shocking news that Blue Jays TV broadcaster John Cerutti had passed away in his Rogers Centre hotel room.

I could not believe it and neither could anyone else. This was on the heels of what Tom had gone through just months before. Cerutti was supposed to broadcast this last game but missed an 11 a.m. TV meeting, which was very unlike him. The production staff began to worry and started calling him. After numerous attempts, the police were brought in to break open the door of his stadium hotel room. He was found without any vital signs, his hands tucked together under his chin, holding a cross he wore around his neck. His death at the age of only 44 was officially declared to be of natural causes: a ventricular arrhythmia.

Born in Albany, New York, John was selected out of Amherst College in the first round of the 1981 amateur draft, by the Blue Jays with the 21st overall pick, and pitched seven seasons in the major leagues, with the Blue Jays (1985 to 1990) and the Detroit Tigers (1991).

He was a great storyteller and a great golfer — everybody liked John and his wife, Claudia, and their three children. People forget that on June 7, 1989, Cerutti recorded the first-ever Blue Jays win in their new home, at the then SkyDome. After his playing career, he went into broadcasting. John started calling Blue Jays games alongside Brian Williams on CBC. It was after the 2001 season that Scott Moore, the program director at Rogers Sportsnet, made a great call for both John and me. I had worked all 30 televised Blue Jays games in 2001 as the analyst alongside Rob Faulds, who did the play-by-play and did it well, and I had broadcast the rest of the games on the radio. The next season, Scott sat down with me and explained that the network was expanding to 120 games, and they were going in a different direction with a former player as the analyst. That was going to be Cerutti.

I was 100 percent in agreement — the analyst definitely has to be a former player — and went back to radio full time. I had met so many great people in my one year on TV, and it paved the way for enduring friendships. In hindsight, I was so happy I wasn't chosen to continue in my TV role as the analyst, and I was just as happy I was not asked to be the TV play-by-play broadcaster. I am happiest and most comfortable in radio and always have been. John Cerutti did a great job on TV for Sportsnet. Sadly, just not long enough.

Frasor and Towers and Zaunie

The 2004 campaign saw the Blue Jays add a smallish five-foot-nine, 180-pound rookie right-hander to their bullpen. Years later, on July 17, 2011, Jason Frasor made his 453rd appearance for the Blue Jays, passing Duane Ward to become the team's all-time appearance leader. A starter in the low minors from 1999 to 2002, Jason was converted to a reliever in 2003. The Blue Jays acquired him from the Los Angeles Dodgers prior to the 2004 season in exchange for Jayson Werth. While Werth went on to have a very good career, Frasor was worth a lot, too. Not only did he set the Blue Jays record for most appearances, pitching in a total of 505 games, he later pitched for the Kansas City Royals. Frasor helped the Royals reach two straight World Series in 2014 and 2015, winning the ultimate prize and ring in 2015.

Frasor was a tremendous competitor who had a great disposition. We joked around a lot in the clubhouse over the years. He came from Southern Illinois University, the same school that produced Dave Stieb, and grew up a White Sox fan, pitching for the Sox in 2011 after the Blue Jays traded him to Chicago. Frasor might have been the slowest pitcher to work in Blue Jays history, but it worked for him. I asked him about trying to quicken his pace, and he said that he had been advised to do that many times and had even tried to be quicker between pitches, but it wasn't comfortable for him. In his nine-year career in Toronto, he pitched to an ERA of 3.73. Over 504 innings, he allowed just 445 hits, with 479 strikeouts and only 216 walks. Some pretty amazing numbers bolstering the premise: do what is comfortable for you and don't try to copy anyone. Pretty good for the 1999 Detroit Tigers 33rd-round pick.

Another pitcher worth noting was right-hander Josh Towers. Towers signed with the Blue Jays as a minor league free agent midway through the 2003 season and went on to have a very successful run, appearing in 14 games (eight starts), finishing the year 8-1 with a 4.48 ERA.

But there was more to that story. While with the Blue Jays, Towers was assigned uniform number 7. That made him the only pitcher in the major leagues at that time with a single-digit uniform number. Years later, Kyle Drabek would wear the lowest number ever as a Blue Jays pitcher: 4. Most recently, the outstanding five-foot-eight hurler Marcus Stroman, who is a tower of strength in his own way, has been wearing No. 6 since the 2015 season. More on that later.

Catcher Gregg Zaun also joined the team in 2004. The 16-year major league veteran went on to follow in his uncle Rick Dempsey's footsteps. Dempsey caught 24 seasons, 12 of them with the Orioles. Upon retirement, Rick moved right into the Orioles' TV booth, and Gregg followed suit — in 2006, Zaun became an on-air personality with Sportsnet TV, joining host Jamie Campbell. In 2008, during his last season as a Blue Jay, Zaun hit a game-winning grand slam in the bottom of the 13th inning off Rays closer Troy Percival. That came with two outs in the inning, wiping out the Rays 7–4 lead. It was only the second game-winning grand slam at that time in Blue Jays history, but the first in extra innings. George Bell had hit the first walk-off grand slam in September 1988 in the bottom of the 9th inning against the Texas Rangers at old Exhibition Stadium. Blue Jay Steve Pearce in 2017 topped all of that as he became one of just three players in major league history to hit two walk-off grand slams in the same season, joining Cy Williams who did it in 1926 and Jim Presley, Steve's former hitting coach, who did it 60 years later. But Pearce is the only player to do it in one *homestand*. Pretty good work for Boston's 2018 World Series MVP.

I bring up Gregg and the slams because of something he said to me early in his career as a Blue Jay. I noticed he had big base hits with the bases loaded. "I wasn't always that good at the plate with the bases loaded. In fact, I was pretty bad. Then one day, my manager Frank Robinson pulled me aside as I was about to go to the plate with the bases loaded. He told me very firmly, 'Remember all the pressure is on the pitcher out there. Not you at the plate. So relax.' I got a base hit and never forgot what he told me. It did help me to relax. I was a much better hitter with the bases loaded after that, thanks to Frank."

When he was behind the plate, Gregg also shared the fact that whenever there was a pitch in the dirt with nobody on base, he would aggressively block it as if there were runners on base. I saw him do this repeatedly. This way he developed the muscle memory needed to always do that. Zaun saved many a runner from either scoring or advancing because of his constant working on fundamentals. A great lesson for all catchers.

On August 8, 2004, after a game at Yankee Stadium, GM J.P. Ricciardi told first-base coach John Gibbons not to go anywhere. Ricciardi then went into the manager's office and relieved Carlos Tosca of his duties. Gibbons was named the club's new manager that afternoon. It was quite a year.

CHAPTER 21

MOVING IN THE RIGHT DIRECTION

2005: A New Broadcast Partner

Before the 2005 season began, on February 2, Rogers Communications renamed the SkyDome the Rogers Centre. At the same time, Rogers Sportsnet hired Warren Sawkiw to be my full-time partner on the radio broadcasts. Born in Toronto, Warren was a 20th-round pick in the June Draft in 1990 out of Wake Forest University. He later signed with the Blue Jays organization, getting as high as Triple-A Syracuse. He played 11 games at that level in his nine-year minor league career. Warren did a good job as analyst during his two seasons while I did the play-by-play. He was very personable with everyone and did his homework. It was a great experience for him and for me.

After Warren's two seasons at the microphone, Alan Ashby became available. He replaced Warren for the 2007 season. Ashby caught for 17 years, including time with the Blue Jays in 1977 and 1978. He later broke into broadcasting on radio with the Astros and veteran play-by-play broadcaster Milo Hamilton. Alan lent a lot of insight and baseball experience to the broadcasts. He did a very good job for six seasons and was continually praised by Blue Jays fans. He departed at the end of the 2013 season for Houston, where he'd been offered a job as their new TV analyst.

Aaron Hill

The Blue Jays finished third that season at 80-82 under John Gibbons in his first full season as manager. The team featured one player who I liked from the very first day I met him, rookie second baseman Aaron Hill. Aaron was born in Visalia, California, the central part of the state. The Blue Jays made him a first-round pick (13th overall) in the June 2003 Draft out of Louisiana State University: a great baseball school. The next year at spring training, I went up to him at the batting cage to introduce myself. "Aaron, Jerry Howarth, one of the Blue Jays radio announcers and a fellow Californian. It's nice to have you here. Enjoy your time as a Blue Jay." Aaron then said something to me that no else ever had. "Thank you, Jerry. It's nice to meet you. I am so happy to be here. It is an honour to put on this uniform." For years afterwards, I would remind Aaron that he "honoured" that commitment in a career that spanned 13 years. He would always say, "It's been my pleasure."

During our years together, he openly talked about what happened to his mother when he was 15 years old. He and his friends were participating in a soccer tournament in Park City, Utah. While on their way to a round of golf, a college student narrowly missed Hill's car but slammed into his mother's car, following behind him. His mother, Vicki, died in that crash. Aaron later introduced me to his dad, who was such a great father and inspiration to his son, especially after losing his wife.

Hill told me about his neighbour just down the street in Visalia, who became a second dad to him after he lost his mom. That was Brad Mills. Yes, the same Brad Mills who played for the Montreal Expos from 1980 to 1983. Brad was the bench coach in Boston, winning two World Series Championships in 2004 and 2007 for manager Terry Francona's Red Sox. Mills went on to manage an outmanned and fledgling Houston Astros team that was in the throes of losing 100 games annually, prepping for what turned out to be a World Series Championship in 2017. Brad saved his best calls for a young man who needed him the most.

Looking back, I see so clearly why concussions are so damning — and this does not even take into account what lies in store for athletes after their careers are over. On May 29, 2008, Hill suffered a grade two concussion in a collision with teammate David Eckstein during a game against the Athletics in Oakland. I called the play and their collision and didn't think too much about it. That is, until Aaron missed the remainder of the season; that was a sobering reminder of the dangers of a brain injury. When Hill came to spring training the next season, he told me that he'd still felt the effects through the middle of the offseason before he finally began to feel normal again. It was an eye opener to realize how a concussion could have such long and lingering effects.

Fortunately, Aaron was able to put all that behind him. On July 5, 2009, he was selected by managers and players to play in the MLB All-Star Game in St. Louis. When you talk about survivors in baseball and in life, you begin with Aaron Hill.

In 2005, the Blue Jays introduced pitchers Gustavo Chacin, Brandon League and Dustin McGowan. They were all unique in their own way. Gustavo's last name reminded people of a cologne. Sure enough that led the Blue Jays to have a "Chacin Cologne" Night on June 27, 2006. Brandon was born in Sacramento, California, but raised in Honolulu. Growing up there, League would surf to strengthen his body. Dustin, unfortunately, has had to battle diabetes with inhalers and pumps, but they helped him pitch 10-plus years in the major leagues.

There was one very unusual trade that took place on July 22. The Blue Jays dealt infielder John McDonald to the Detroit Tigers for cash and a player to be named later. The player to be named later turned out to be . . . John McDonald. What goes around comes around.

2006 and 2007: Slowly Getting Better

The 2006 season saw the team improve to 87-75 under John Gibbons. First baseman Lyle Overbay was acquired from Milwaukee. A power-hitting third baseman, Troy Glaus, and shortstop Sergio Santos came in a deal with the Arizona Diamondbacks. Added to the pitching staff was lefty Scott Downs and right-hander Casey Janssen. Kevin Barker was a September call-up. Mickey Brantley became the new hitting coach.

Downs and Janssen

Scott Downs pitched 13 years in the major leagues, including three with the Expos. His best years were the six he enjoyed in Toronto. Scott and I got along great: lots of teasing, lots of laughs, lots of mutual respect.

Scott shared with me that he'd had to undergo Tommy John surgery early in his career. Then in 2004, with the Expos Triple-A club in Edmonton, everything clicked for him, both on the mound and off. Scott not only threw a seven-inning no-hitter for the Trappers, but he did it before his pitching coach Tommy John. "Tommy encouraged me so much that season. He told me I was ready to pitch effectively again in the major leagues. To be confident and know I could pitch for a long time — that changed everything for me. That and my wife, Katie, supporting me. I'm a positive person and so is she. We did it together." Scott and Katie have two kids, a daughter, Katherine Grayson, and a son, Harrison. When Downs would come in from the bullpen to pitch, he would first write their initials on the back of the mound.

Casey Janssen was from Orange, California, just a short distance from Anaheim Stadium. As someone from San Francisco, I would seek out these Californians first and tease them about coming from "that other part of the state." Casey was a pretty good hitter, both in high school and at UCLA. In his first spring training in Dunedin, Casey told me about his freshman year at UCLA, where he pitched as a fourth starter and long reliever. He excelled in his relief appearances, which was a barometer of things to come. Then he smiled when he told me about one particular at-bat.

"I came up my freshman year and hit a home run to right field as a pinch hitter. It was the only home run I hit in college. UCLA has won all kinds of NCAA Championships, but they have never won one in baseball. There was a good reason for that. Our baseball program always stressed the fundamentals and doing things the right way. It wasn't about winning or losing and running up pitch counts for that extra win. We repeatedly worked on fundamentals. It was the best preparation I could ever ask for now that I am a professional." For the record, UCLA finally won its first NCAA Baseball Championship in 2013. Janssen made his major league debut against the Baltimore Orioles on April 27, 2006. The best was soon to come. On May 7 in Toronto, Casey won his first major league game, against the team he'd grown up rooting for. Ten days later, he did it again, this time in front of family and friends in Anaheim.

Three Former Diamondbacks

Lyle Overbay became a Blue Jay in 2006, after spending his first five years with Arizona and Milwaukee. He would go on to play five of his 14 years at first base for the blue and white. When he played for the Blue Jays, he and his wife, Sarah, had three very young boys who were each about two years apart, but they looked almost identical — I could not believe it! When I interviewed Lyle after he retired, he told me they now had five kids. He was going to show me a picture, but I said, "No need! I know exactly what the last two look like." Whenever I saw Lyle taking ground balls while I was on the field, I'd yell, "Overbay! You bum!" That's how our days together on the diamond started — with smiles on both our faces. In his quiet way, Lyle was a key contributor each season to what the Blue Jays were trying to do: win 90 games and hopefully qualify for the playoffs. Unfortunately, they just kept falling short of the mark.

At the end of 2005, the Blue Jays engineered a trade with the Arizona Diamondbacks. On December 27, third baseman

Troy Glaus was sent to the Blue Jays along with shortstop Sergio Santos in exchange for Miguel Batista and Orlando Hudson. Troy had the build and power of the prototypical third baseman. He was six-foot-five, 220 pounds. He hit 320 home runs in his 13-year career and drove in 950. He was with the Blue Jays for just two years. In 2006, he hit 38 home runs with 104 RBIs. The next season, he hit 20 more home runs with 62 RBIs. Two things stood out with Troy: First, he was a UCLA Bruin like his new teammate Casey Janssen. That told me he was very skilled in his fundamentals. Second, for all of his size, power, and dynamic force in the game, he was as quiet and shy as a church mouse.

That was backed up by his mother. I mentioned to her how well Troy was doing in his new surroundings and that I was a Californian, too. "There aren't too many Californians who are as quiet and shy as your son is, let alone being an outstanding major league player."

She laughed and said, "Jerry, he has always been that way. I remember when he was very young, he would be on the phone with a friend or family member. He was always nodding. After he hung up, I said, 'Honey, they can't see you nod. You have to tell them how you feel and speak up some more.' That's my son." When I told Troy that story, he nodded. Some things never change.

The other player the Blue Jays acquired from Arizona had a most interesting story to tell that ended far too quickly. Sergio Santos, of Mexican-American descent and raised in Southern California, was drafted in the first round of the 2002 June Draft as a shortstop. Santos played three seasons in the Blue Jays system. The best he hit was .244 and the lowest .214. In 2007, he was claimed off waivers by the Minnesota Twins and eventually wound up with the Chicago White Sox. With the Sox, major-league star Buddy Bell, who was director of minor-league instruction and player development, encouraged him to pitch. What a transformation that was. In 2011 with the White Sox, Santos saved 30 of 36 games and dominated the opposition.

At the end of that season, the former Blue Jays farmhand came back to the Blue Jays in a trade. Sadly for both Santos and the Blue Jays, he pitched in only six games with two saves, plagued by right shoulder problems that required surgery. Over the rest of his career as a Blue Jay, he pitched in only six more games, and in another 14 games after that with the Dodgers and the Mets.

I appreciate all that Sergio had to do in his career to reach the pinnacle on the mound. As a kid, he never dreamt he would be a pitcher, let alone an outstanding closer, if ever so briefly. He was the same gentle, kind, and hard-working person he was from the first day I met him, without any rancour or "woe is me" attitude for what happened to him. I have the utmost respect for Sergio Santos.

Chase Said What?

September 2006 ended with a call-up, Kevin Barker, whose first hit as a Blue Jay was a home run off Red Sox starting pitcher Josh Beckett at Fenway Park. After retiring from baseball, Kevin married sportscaster Hazel Mae. Both do an outstanding job covering the Blue Jays for Sportsnet. Kevin co-hosts *Blue Jays Central* on TV with Joe Siddall and host Jamie Campbell while doing the same on radio with *Baseball Central* host Jeff Blair. Hazel has anchored the morning edition of *Sportsnet News*, hosted *JZone* — a weekly magazine show dedicated to all things Blue Jays — and works Blue Jays games as a sideline reporter, interviewing the players. After recording one of her interviews, Hazel was at home that night watching TV with her then four-year-old son, Chase. When Hazel's interview came on, Chase looked at the TV and then looked at his mommy and said, "Are there two of you?"

The Big Hurt, Tomo, and Joe

In 2007, the Blue Jays finished just above .500 at 83-79, good for third in the A.L. East. Twelve Blue Jays ended up on the disabled lists, requiring 12 surgeries. It was one of those years. One highlight occurred on June 28, when Frank Thomas, known as "The Big Hurt," put a big hurt on a baseball and hit his 500th career home run. Frank became only the 21st player in major league history to accomplish that feat.

Tomo Ohka pitched for the Blue Jays just this one season. Seven years earlier, he had pitched a nine-inning perfect game for the Triple-A Pawtucket Red Sox. Ohka retired all 27 batters he faced in a 2-0 win over the Charlotte Knights. He threw only 77 pitches to toss the first nine-inning perfect game in the International League since 1952. His catcher was Joe Siddall, my radio partner. Joe had come to the park that day to announce his retirement. Asked to catch Tomo, he put off announcing his intentions until after the game. Not wanting to take anything away from the moment, Siddall celebrated Tomo's wonderful accomplishment that night and retired the next day, ending a 13-year career that included 73 major league games with the Expos, Marlins, and Tigers. A perfect way to go out.

2008: Ricciardi's Best Trade

The 2008 season saw John Gibbons replaced by the returning Cito Gaston. The Blue Jays were 35-39 in their first 74 games under Gibby and finished 51-37 under Cito's leadership. It turned out to be a history-making year. A young Jose Bautista was supposed to be the Pirates' starting third baseman and backup outfielder in 2008. That didn't happen. On August 21, the Pirates traded him to the Blue Jays for a player to be named later. That player was young minor league catcher Robinzon Diaz.

With the help of new hitting coach Dwayne Murphy and Cito himself, Bautista immediately made adjustments to his swing. Murphy taught him how to leverage his pull power by starting his swing with what would become a very familiar high leg kick. In September, he finally broke through, hitting 10 home runs with 21 RBIs and a .606 slugging percentage. It provided a glimpse of what was to come. In 2010, he led the major leagues with 54 home runs. Jose led the majors again in 2011, this time in five categories, among them home runs (43), walks (132), and OPS (1.056).

Canada's Own and Scott Rolen

Matt Stairs was in his second season as a Blue Jay. Born in St. John, New Brunswick, Matt played for Team Canada in the 1988 Summer Olympics in Seoul, South Korea. Later he launched his 19-year major league career with the Montreal Expos, where he played for two years in 1992 and 1993. Matt holds the record for the most pinch-hit home runs in major league history with 23. His pinch-hit home run with the Philadelphia Phillies in the 8th inning of Game 4 of the 2008 National League Championship Series off Dodgers reliever Jonathan Broxton was called "One of the most memorable home runs in Phillies history." It helped Philadelphia get to the World Series and beat the Tampa Bay Rays.

What it also did was put Stairs on the map in the City of Brotherly Love. Philadelphia fell in love with Matt, who became a longtime Phillies TV broadcaster and later their hitting coach. In his career, Stairs played for more teams — 13 with 12 different franchises, which included both the Montreal Expos and the Washington Nationals — than any position player in MLB history. Octavio Dotel holds the record for pitchers and all players at 13 franchises. I would ask all the players every spring training what they did in the offseason. Stairs was the only one I talked to who spent the entire offseason coaching high school hockey and winning championships in Fredericton. He was equally good in skates and spikes — tremendously gifted on the ice and on the diamond.

Veteran Scott Rolen also arrived on the scene in 2008 from the Cincinnati Reds. The Reds had traded Rolen to the Blue Jays for Troy Glaus in January of that year. We talk often on radio about having a presence in the lineup or in the clubhouse. Scott had that presence. He was a seven-time All-Star who won eight Gold Gloves. We got along great, teasing one another all the time. In his first spring training in Dunedin, he was taking ground balls in batting practice off the bat of coach Brian Butterfield. All of a sudden, everybody stopped doing what they were doing. Rolen had suffered a non-displaced fracture of his right middle finger reaching into his glove, as he had done thousands of times before. But this time, the ball got him. Rolen missed the beginning of the regular season, recovering from the surgery that inserted a screw in his broken finger. In

April, Scott was activated from the 15-day disabled list. Two days later, against the Kansas City Royals, he hit his first home run as a Blue Jay.

Near the end of the season, he had a big game at the Rogers Centre, helping the Blue Jays to a victory. After the game, as I was walking to my car in the stadium's underground parking lot, I saw Scott sitting in his car. He had the window down. His five-year-old daughter, Raine, was sitting in the back seat. "Great game, Scott. Is that your little girl in the backseat?"

He looked back at his daughter. "Raine, this is the man on the radio who says bad things about your daddy every night." That was Scott and Jerry every day.

2009: A Confusing Alphabet

In 2009, under Cito, the team slipped to a record of 75-87. Midway through the year, the Blue Jays traded Rolen back to the Cincinnati Reds for Edwin Encarnacion and left-handed pitcher Marc Rzepczynski. Six years later, Edwin would help the Blue Jays to the American League Championship Series in both 2015 and 2016. The rookie Rzepczynski pitched with the Blue Jays into the 2011 season before being traded that year to the St. Louis Cardinals, where he helped the Cards reach the World Series.

A funny thing happened in Rzepcyznski's first week as a Blue Jay. Late in one game, he was pitching very effectively. I was calling the inning, and I needed to find something specific about Marc's past, so I went to the media guide as I often do during the play-by-play. I became frustrated sorting through the entire guide trying to find his name, and it wasn't there. His nickname was "Zep," which seemed to fit perfectly with his last name. Wrong! The next day I went to the Blue Jay's vice president of communications, Jay Stenhouse. "Jay, I couldn't find anything on Marc last night. I even went to the minor league sections as well. Is he in the guide?"

"Did you look under R?"

I said: "Why would I do that?"

"Because his last name begins with R." Sure enough, everything I was looking for was right there under Rzepczynski. Jay had the final word. "You're not the first, Jerry."

Funny how you can see a name all around the stadium and up on the Jays Vision Scoreboard and even look at the name on the back of the uniform but not really take the time to read it, because in your mind all you hear is Zep-chinski. RRRRR!

The Arrival of Alex Anthopoulos

J.P. Ricciardi was fired as the general manager the next-to-last day of the 2009 season. Young assistant GM Alex Anthopoulos took over the reins. What an ascent he had made. In 2000, Anthopoulos was hired by the Montreal Expos as an unpaid intern. His first job was sorting out fan mail for the players. After working in the mail room, Alex would then sit with the scouts during games and take notes. Thus began his journey toward becoming one of the best general managers in baseball. Alex would leave the Expos at the end of the 2003 season while working as the assistant scouting director to join the Blue Jays later that year as their scouting coordinator. "Jon Lalonde hired me from the Expos. He had just been promoted to the director of scouting and needed someone to take over for him as a scouting coordinator. We had met at the MLB Scout School in 2000, in Arizona, and then kept in touch when I was with the Expos, at industry scouting meetings and games."

Anthopoulos had put in the time. Now he was ready to run his own team.

CHAPTER 22

MEMORABLE MOMENTS

The 2010 team, starring Jose Bautista, who led the major leagues in home runs with 54, posted a record of 85-77. They finished a disappointing fourth place. Bautista was moved to right field, permanently, where he excelled defensively with both his arm and his range.

Being Constructively Critical

Left-handed starter Brett Cecil had a very good 2010 campaign. He started 28 games, going 15-7 with an ERA of 4.22. In 2011, he slipped to a 4-11 season with an ERA of 4.73. He was overweight. In February 2012, he reported to spring training in Dunedin having dropped 33 pounds. Longtime coach Brian Butterfield was stunned when he saw him. "In all seriousness, Brett, I didn't recognize you." Cecil said he knew what people had said in 2011 when he struggled after showing such promise in 2010.

"When I had a bad game," Cecil said, "they said I was too heavy. If that was right or wrong doesn't matter. I had to make changes. What I am doing right now makes for a much healthier lifestyle. I weighed two hundred fifty-two pounds by the end of 2011. I'm two hundred nineteen today. My foot quickness is so much better, everything is so much better."

Did he feel like a new man? "Yes," Cecil said. "Yes, I do."

I share this story for a reason. And it ties in to what I have done on the radio and what I encourage other young broadcasters to do as well. Our profession, whether you are a player or a broadcaster, demands a certain routine and discipline to do the job right every day. For a player, it extends even further to the offseason, when after taking a month off you must get back to your routine and not let yourself go as Brett did. One day in spring training 2012, Brett came up to me and asked if he could talk to me. We leaned against the chain-link fence. In a very calm way, he proceeded to tell me, "My wife was listening to you, and she told me that you were critical of my training and weight gain and pitching ability in 2011 because I wasn't applying myself. Did you say those things?" I answered: "Yes, I did. And now I am happy to see you are ready to hopefully have a much better year." We talked amiably for a few more minutes and then he said, "Thanks for telling me that," and walked away. I was totally fine with that, even though it did cool our relationship from that point on.

I tell young broadcasters that there is a way to be constructively critical of a player when you are up in the booth. This is what works for me: when you feel you must be critical, pretend that player is sitting right beside you as you say it. That way you can walk into the clubhouse the next day or mingle at the batting cage and not be afraid of what a player might say to you. Why? Because you are just repeating what you have already said to that player. You aren't ducking the issue or regretting what you said. You're not making it personal. You are simply being fair, using all the facts you have at your disposal. What Brett's wife heard was exactly right. I did not have to backtrack or cover my words or retract anything when Brett and I talked. It's called professionalism and standing by what you said the first time.

John McDonald — and His Father

John McDonald — "Johnny Mac" as he was affectionately known — had just returned from his father's bedside, remembering his last words, "Hit a home run for me, John," as he quietly slipped away. John was not a home-run hitter. He was revered across Canada for being such a classy professional and modest person. He gave it his all on and off the field. On this Father's Day, he definitely gave it his all. With the San Francisco Giants leading, 9–3, the game moved to the bottom of the 9th inning. Having entered the game earlier at second base for Aaron Hill, McDonald came to the plate for his first at-bat since being with his dad. He lined a pitch down the left-field line toward the corner. When the ball cleared the wall for a home run, I looked at John as I was making the call. He rounded first base with a huge fist pump. He headed toward second on his way to what would be the most loving trip he would ever make around the bases. We knew his dad had passed away. None of us, however, knew what his father had said to him days before. Johnny Mac stepped on home plate a little teary-eyed and pointed to the sky for his father. I had tears in my eyes, too.

J.P. Arencibia — and His Mother

Catcher J.P. Arencibia was promoted to the Blue Jays on August 4, 2010, to replace the injured John Buck, who had been placed on the 15-day disabled list for a right thumb laceration. Three days later, J.P. started in his first major league game against the Tampa Bay Rays. What a start it was in front of his mother, Irene, who had raised J.P. and his sister as a single mom.

In his first major league at-bat, Arencibia hit a two-run home run on the first pitch he saw from Rays right-hander James Shields. J.P. became just the 28th player in major league history to hit a home run on the first pitch he ever saw. He wasn't finished. Not by a long shot — which went deep to right field to cap his day. In his follow-up plate appearances, he hit a double, a single, and then another home run, going 4-5 with three RBIs in a memorable 17–11 win. J.P. was just the fifth player ever to hit two home runs in his first major league game. The stunned rookie sat at the podium postgame and struggled to keep his emotions in check. With his mom watching from the back of the interview room, the young catcher tried to comprehend everything that had just taken place. "I could never have imagined this," Arencibia said. "I could never have imagined this — ever."

I got to know the Arencibia family very well. Irene became an ardent listener. Even when her son was not doing well, she would always praise the honesty she heard. I really respected that. I saw how loving she was to J.P. and his sister, also named Irene, and her family with their six children. Irene was a woman to admire for her positive outlook on life and her strength of character. In November 2016, when I had my prostate cancer surgery, the first three people to call me to see how I was were Paul Beeston, Alex

Anthopoulos, and J.P. Arencibia. Like mother, like son. Two years later on Opening Day, April 5, 2012, Arencibia hit a game-winning three-run home run in the top of the 16th inning against Cleveland to win that game, 7–4. It was the longest Opening Day game in major league history in terms of innings.

2011: New Manager John Farrell

The 2011 season marked the hiring of John Farrell to manage the Blue Jays when Cito Gaston retired after holding the position for a second time. Farrell had served as the Red Sox pitching coach from 2007 to 2010, and under Farrell, the Jays went 81-81. We did the manager's show together for two years. I liked John, but we also had our moments. Farrell was all business; he was very intense and could be sharp with his responses. I was okay with all of that, until I found out, after the first year of his three-year contract, he'd expressed an interest in managing the Red Sox. This put GM Alex Anthopoulos in an uncomfortable situation and led to a strained relationship. After John's second year, he wanted out of his three-year agreement, to go to Boston for his "dream job." This led to an unusual and costly exit for the Blue Jays.

On October 21, three weeks after the 2012 season ended, compensation negotiations saw Red Sox shortstop Mike Aviles traded to the Blue Jays for veteran reliever David Carpenter and Farrell. Two weeks after that on November 3, the Blue Jays traded Aviles and catcher Yan Gomes to Cleveland for pitcher Esmil Rogers. Ouch. The club had lost a manager and, more importantly, an outstanding young catcher. Rogers was a major disappointment, going 5-9 with an ERA of 4.77 before being designated for assignment the next season, while Gomes helped Cleveland reach the playoffs three times, including the 2016 World Series, where they lost in Game 7 to the Cubs. It is why Farrell was booed so loudly by the fans when he came back into Toronto with the Red Sox.

I later softened my stance about John when he was diagnosed with stage-one lymphoma in August 2015. In announcing his diagnosis, Farrell indicated that he would begin chemotherapy later that month. Bench coach Torey Lovullo would manage the Red Sox for the rest of the 2015 season. The cancer was discovered when Farrell underwent surgery for a hernia. John described his cancer as being localized because it was discovered early and indicated that his treatment would take approximately nine weeks. The Red Sox announced on October 22, 2015, that Farrell's cancer was in remission. He resumed his managerial duties for the 2016 season.

Langley, B.C.

On August 4, 2011, Brett Lawrie was called up to the Blue Jays. He made his debut on August 5 against the Orioles. In his first career at-bat, he recorded his first hit and RBI. He finished 2 for 4. Two games later, he hit his first home run. In his second game at home, he belted his first grand slam. The early accomplishments continued: a first triple and stolen base days later, and then, on September 5, Brett hit his first walk-off home run, finishing the season batting .293, with nine home runs, 26 runs scored, seven stolen bases, and 25 RBIs in 161 plate appearances in only 43 games.

I had never seen a Blue Jay break into the major leagues

like Brett Lawrie. And I haven't since — not yet. He was Mike Trout before there was Mike Trout. In fact, Trout broke in with the Angels in 2011, playing in 40 games, hitting .220 with five home runs and 16 RBIs and four stolen bases. Sadly, Brett never came close to his glowing 2011 numbers again, which included an OBP of .373 and SLG mark of a whopping .580.

Injuries plagued Lawrie throughout his career. He was too tense physically and very tense mentally. That is never good in anything, let alone when you're playing major league baseball. While playing high school baseball for the Langley Blaze in Langley, British Columbia, Lawrie was selected 16th overall in the 2008 June Draft by the Milwaukee Brewers. That selection made him the fourth-highest Canadian ever drafted, behind pitchers Jeff Francis, Adam Loewen, and Phillippe Aumont, and the first position player. Brett was like a comet, which was so beautiful to watch in 2011, but quickly disappeared after that.

Best Rookie Interview

One of my all-time favourite interviews took place in the first-base dugout in Detroit at Comerica Park in May, when the Blue Jays called up young rookie Eric Thames. Eric was born in Santa Clara, California, where I had gone to school at the University of Santa Clara. We had that in common from the start. In our interview, he spoke quickly but without rushing his words or thoughts. Honestly, I was mesmerized and surprised by this rookie's boundless enthusiasm in our five-minute interview.

Thames had a good first year in 2011, hitting .262 with 12 home runs and 37 RBIs in 95 games. Then to his detriment, he took all his enthusiasm home in the offseason, where, and even by his own admission, he overdid his workouts. He became too tight the following season and lost his flexibility. Eric hit just three home runs, driving in only 11 with an OBP of .288 and SLG .365 in 46 games in 2012, before he was traded mid-season to the Seattle Mariners for pitcher Steve Delabar.

There are no guarantees of continued success for teams or players going from one season to the next. So much is dependent upon what a player does in his offseason. For Thames, it was doing too much, which many young players do; for Brett Cecil, it was not doing enough in the offseason; in the middle of this spectrum was Adam Lind. Adam talked with me about his very good start in 2006, which was followed by just an average year in 2007. "I worked out the same way in the second offseason doing the same things I had done the previous offseason. But it was without the intensity and drive and concentration that I had done before. It wasn't the same." I appreciated his honesty. It doesn't take much for the pendulum to swing for any athlete between seasons. It takes a lot of hard work. And intensity.

One very happy footnote to Thames's career ties into his joy for playing the game and his renewed and more disciplined offseason approach, making the necessary adjustments to get better. After his 2013 season in the minor leagues, Eric played in the Venezuelan Winter League, where he was scouted by the NC Dinos of the KBO League in South Korea. He signed a one-year contract in 2013 for $800,000 that he parlayed into three outstanding seasons, capping it off in 2015, when he became the first player in KBO history to hit for the cycle twice in one season. He was named the league's Most Valuable Player, winning a Gold Glove as well.

He told me after his three years in South Korea that he had planned on playing in Japan, an upgrade from the professional baseball played in South Korea. That is, until the Milwaukee Brewers said they would like to sign him to a three-year contract for $16 million. "How could I turn that down? I said goodbye to Japan and went to the Brewers." In his first year in Milwaukee in 2017, Eric Thames hit 31 home runs, drove in 63, had an OBP of .359, and a SLG of .518. That's what you call putting it all together and reaping the benefits of all your hard work and discipline with a lot of joy and enthusiasm.

2012: Omar Vizquel

The Blue Jays' 2012 campaign ended with only 73 wins against 89 losses to finish fourth in John Farrell's second and last season as manager. The Blue Jays featured two players who stood out: the oldest player in the major leagues, and the first-ever Brazilian.

Omar Vizquel was 45 when he put on a Blue Jays uniform to play in his 24th and last major league season. Although there has always been the feeling that the city of San Pedro de Macoris in the Dominican Republic is the baseball capital of the world for shortstops, I believe the same can be said for the country of Venezuela. The succession of shortstops from that country has been phenomenal, starting in 1950 with Chico Carrasquel. Chico was followed by Luis Aparicio, Davey Concepcion, Ozzie Guillen, Omar Vizquel, Marco Scutaro, and Elvis Andrus, among many.

In his final game of the season, Brett Lawrie gave his No. 13 to Omar to wear as Brett took No. 17. This allowed Vizquel to wear the same number he'd worn through most of his career. A great gesture by Lawrie. Omar retired after the season. At the time of his retirement, he was the oldest player in the major leagues and the only active player with service time in the 1980s. He is one of only 29 players in baseball history to play in major league games in four decades and the only one who played shortstop. Earlier in the season, Omar became the oldest player to play at shortstop in major league history. I enjoyed being around all of that history.

First-Ever Brazilian

On May 17, the Blue Jays optioned a struggling Adam Lind to Triple-A Las Vegas and called up catcher Yan Gomes. In his debut that day, Gomes became the first Brazilian-born player in major league history. He singled off Yankees starter Phil Hughes for his first hit. The next night the New York Mets came to the Rogers Centre, and Yan drilled his first home run. It came on the first pitch he saw off starter Jon Niese in a 14–5 win. The following day, the modest Gomes told me how proud he was to be the first Brazilian in the game. We started talking about his family. He was born in São Paulo and, like so many of his friends, he played soccer and baseball. At the age of 12, his family moved to Miami. After high school, he went to the University of Tennessee to catch behind J.P. Arencibia, who was the starter in his third year with the Volunteers. Now they were teammates once again.

Yan told me about the young lady he was dating and later married. Her name was Jenna Hammaker, daughter of former pitcher and All-Star Atlee Hammaker. Atlee was an outstanding left-handed starter with the San Francisco Giants and became a good motivator and source of information for Yan. At the end of the 2012 season, the Blue Jays traded Gomes to Cleveland for pitcher Esmil Rogers in a deal that clearly favoured Cleveland. Yan helped the Brazilian National Team qualify for its first-ever berth in the World Baseball Classic, by leading them out of the 2013 WBC qualifying round. Gomes was the only major leaguer on Brazil's team.

2013: Surprises Abound

In 2013, the Blue Jays finished last with a record of 74-88. The season started with a complete surprise. John Farrell was out as manager, and John Gibbons was back in. In the offseason, GM Alex Anthopoulos had John fly into Toronto from his home in San Antonio, Texas, to talk some baseball. Gibby speculated that he might be offered the job as bench coach for the new manager, never dreaming the new manager would be him.

Mark Buehrle

At about the same time in November, pitcher Mark Buehrle was traded to the Blue Jays along with Josh Johnson, Jose Reyes, John Buck and Emilio Bonifacio, in exchange for Jeff Mathis, Adeiny Hechavarria, Henderson Alvarez, Yunel Escobar, Jake Marisnick, Anthony DeSclafani and Justin Nicolino. A blockbuster 12-player deal. If that wasn't enough, in December, the Mets agreed to trade the reigning N.L. Cy Young Award winner and first knuckleball pitcher ever to win that award, R.A. Dickey, to the Blue Jays. R.A. came along with two personal catchers in Josh Thole and Mike Nickeas. Going to the Mets were Travis d'Arnaud, John Buck, Noah Syndergaard and Wuilmer Becerra.

Everyone in Toronto was so excited. The Las Vegas oddsmakers picked the team to win the 2013 World Series.

Buehrle turned out to be the best of those acquired. He was the quickest worker among all major league pitchers. Mark let the catcher call the entire game without ever shaking off a pitch. I asked him about that when he joined the club. "Ten years ago when I was with the White Sox, my catcher was A.J. Pierzynski. I shook him off. On that pitch I gave up the game-winning hit to beat me. I told A.J. that would never happen again. Whatever he called after that, I threw. I have been doing that for ten years. Catchers work so hard to prepare for a game, studying the other team's hitters, I want to completely respect their work and let them call the game."

Mark pitched 200 innings in 14 consecutive seasons (2001 to 2014), tying Hall of Famers Greg Maddux, Phil Niekro, and Christy Mathewson. In his last season and with a chance to pass those three, he pitched in 198 and two-thirds innings, just missing the mark. He recorded at least 10 wins in 15 straight seasons. Buehrle was one of my all-time favourites to put on a Blue Jays uniform. He was the epitome of having fun in a very tough business. He embodied Brooklyn Dodgers catcher Roy Campanella's famous line: "You have to have a lot of little boy in you to play this game." Buehrle was thoroughly professional in everything he did, and he let the game come to him, setting the bar high for other pitchers to work with their catchers. Mark was not condescending or patronizing, realizing what worked for him might not work for the next pitcher, and that was okay. He was one of the best role models the Blue Jays ever had. If you happened to see him on the day he pitched, he would engage you in conversation without any reservations. He was that comfortable and confident in his abilities: a manager's dream.

Ryan Goins

Rookie Ryan Goins was called up by the Blue Jays on August 22, 2013. He made his MLB debut the next day, batting ninth and playing second base against the Houston Astros. Goins tied a Blue Jays franchise record, beginning his career with hits in eight consecutive games and tying the great Jesse Barfield, who had done that in 1981. In my opinion, Ryan is the second-best fielding second baseman in Blue Jays history, behind Hall of Famer Roberto Alomar. He plays an outstanding shortstop, too. His parents, Robert and Melissa, have always supported him, taking many trips around the two leagues to see him play. Goins can play relaxed in front of his parents; not many players can. Ryan has been able to get the very most out of his abilities and has had fun doing it. He is a valuable role player.

If Goins were a career .250 hitter, as he showed over a handful of games his rookie year, I believe he would have been an outstanding everyday second baseman. His lifetime .228 average, even with glowing numbers when hitting with runners in scoring position, presents one of the widest discrepancies between a player's offence and his defence that I have seen in my career. With all of his ups and downs, he has always remained positive.

Munenori Kawasaki

The Blue Jays had another versatile infielder on the 2013 team, who became as popular with the fans across Canada as anyone — right up there, in fact, with John McDonald. That was Munenori Kawasaki, or "Moonie" as he was affectionately known. Kawasaki was born in Japan and went relatively unknown as a high school baseball player. He signed professionally after that and played 11 seasons in the Japanese Professional League. One of his best friends was the great Ichiro Suzuki, who played professionally in Japan for nine seasons before he left for the Seattle Mariners in 2001, the same year that Kawasaki started his professional career in Japan. The longer Munenori played, the more he wanted to finish his career as a teammate of Suzuki's in Seattle. In 2012, at the age of 30, Kawasaki left Japan to play in Seattle with his friend. He played one year with the Mariners, hitting just .192 in 61 games. The best was yet to come.

Moonie played with the Blue Jays for three seasons at second, short, and third. The crowds loved him. His bows and enthusiasm were infectious. And could he ever charm the media. Just ask Sportsnet's Arash Madani, who interviewed Kawasaki immediately after his game-winning hit at the Rogers Centre and got this initial response: "Thank you. Thank you very much, Arash. My name is Munenori Kawasaki. I come from Japan. I am Japaneeeeese. My teammates gave me an opportunity, so I wanted to do something about it." Everybody was in stitches, including Arash.

Then there was a memorable moment on the team's charter flight. We were on the plane, parked at the terminal waiting for the luggage and equipment to be loaded onto the plane. I was sitting at the front of the plane, when all of a sudden I heard all this commotion and laughing and clapping. As I looked back, there was Munenori dancing up and down the aisle and almost doing cartwheels. Everybody was loving every minute. That was the first and only time I have ever seen that on a plane.

After Kawasaki's three years as a Blue Jay, he played his fifth and final season in the Chicago Cubs organization. Munenori was called up during that historic 2016 season to play in 14 games, going 7 for 21, drawing 4 walks, and stealing two bases in two tries. Cubs manager Joe Maddon took note of his presence. Maddon had Moonie in uniform during the Cubs' magical playoff run, lending his support and happiness on the bench to his teammates who were on the playoff roster. Kawasaki finished his major league career slipping on a Chicago Cubs World Series ring that was 108 years in the making. How about that to cap your five-year overseas major league career? He went back to Japan and played another season in 2017 before retiring and becoming a broadcaster. He was a delight for all of us.

One postscript to Kawasaki's remarkable career: When the Blue Jays played the New York Yankees in August of that 2013 season, Ichiro Suzuki, then a Yankee outfielder, singled through the infield in the first inning for his 4,000th hit in his professional career playing in Japan and the major leagues. The Yankees spilled out of their first-base dugout to celebrate. Curtis Granderson was the first to reach Ichiro, enveloping him in a big hug.

Ichiro bowed to the crowd to acknowledge his standing ovation. Then he looked at second base, where John Gibbons had started Munenori Kawasaki. The two longtime and fast friends looked at one another as Kawasaki put his hands together and bowed to the iconic Suzuki. Gibby had done it again — he wanted to make sure these two were on the field when history was made that day at Yankee Stadium. Following the Chicago Cubs' 2016 World Series championship, Kawasaki joined Daisuke Matsuzaka and Koji Uehara as the only Japanese players to win championships in the World Baseball Classic, Japan Series, and World Series.

2014: And We Bring You . . . Joe Siddall

Just before leaving for spring training in 2014, I read a story by Bob Elliott in the *Toronto Sun* on February 11 that noted the passing away of 14-year-old Kevin Siddall. Kevin died one week shy of his 15th birthday on February 4, in Windsor, Ontario, after a brief but courageous battle with non-Hodgkins lymphoma. Over the years when the Blue Jays played the Tigers in Detroit, I had on occasion briefly said hello to Kevin's father, Joe, who would be working with various Tiger players during batting practice. I just wanted to introduce myself to a fellow Canadian who had played professionally for 13 years, mostly in the minor leagues.

After reading about his son, I emailed Elliott and asked him if he had an email address for Joe. He did and sent it to me. That prompted this email exchange with Joe:

Hi Joe . . . This is Jerry Howarth here in Toronto. Today, I read about your son, Kevin, in Bob Elliott's column and asked Bob for your email address. Knowing you and what a good man you are and such a good father as well, my prayers and thoughts are with you and your family right now. We all have the greatest respect for you, Joe. God Bless you, Tamara, and Brett, Brooklyn, and MacKenzie. I will look forward to seeing you throw batting practice at Comerica when we arrive there in the first week of June. You take special care. Jerry

Joe immediately responded:

Hi Jerry, Thanks so much for reaching out to me. It is very much appreciated. Our lives have changed forever. As you can imagine, I was so looking forward to coaching Kevin in high school. My wife and our three other children will miss him dearly. We will find a way to move forward. Baseball will be a very important avenue for me to deal with life after this loss. I look forward to seeing you in Detroit as well. And who knows? Maybe a broadcasting career is in my future. I always thought I would enjoy that. Joe

My quick reply:

How about now? My partner, Jack Morris, has left after a year, to spend more time with his family. I am happy to say that I encouraged Jack to do that and especially with his eight-year-old son, Miles, back in St. Paul, Minnesota. So if you are interested at this very moment for this season, let me know and I will give you the name of the person to email in all of this. My pleasure, Joe. Thinking of Kevin. Jerry

Two weeks later, Don Kollins at Sportsnet 590 The Fan hired Joe to replace Jack and become my on-air partner. Joe's first major league broadcast with me was a webcast that took place in Clearwater, Florida, on February 26, as the Phillies hosted the Blue Jays. In the 6th inning, the Phillies brought in a young pitcher named Kevin Munson from their bullpen who had just been selected by the Phillies in the Rule 5 Draft that December from Arizona. The Phillies quickly took the lead, making Kevin the pitcher of record to win it. An inning later, it began to rain, and the umpires temporarily halted play as the grounds crew covered the infield with a tarp.

As the delay continued and we were quietly up in the booth, I began to think about one scenario that could occur. "Do you realize, Joe, if this game is called right now, who the winning pitcher is? *Kevin* Munson." Twenty minutes later, the game was called. Through some amazing divine intervention, a young pitcher named Kevin was the winning pitcher in Joe Siddall's first-ever major league broadcast.

Over the years, Joe has grown into an outstanding major league broadcaster, which includes his play-by-play and TV work. He has a certain gift for sharing his knowledge with the fans in a very articulate manner without his ego getting in the way. He was meant to do this, and that was clear in his very first game — a most special game for the Siddall family.

The 2014 season marked the Blue Jays' 38th. The 25th at the Rogers Centre. The team finished 83-79, in third place.

Roy Halladay came back to Toronto to sign a one-day contract to finish his illustrious career as a Blue Jay before retiring. Edwin Encarnacion hit 16 home runs in the month of May to tie an American League record set by Mickey Mantle in 1956 for most home runs hit in May. A couple of young pitchers arrived on the scene in Aaron Sanchez and Marcus Stroman. They would both help the Blue Jays reach the playoffs for the first time in 22 years.

New Coaches

The Blue Jays added first-base coach Tim Leiper, a former outfielder who spent 12 years playing in the minor leagues. That included playing in London, Ontario, with the Tigers Double-A team. Tim collected over 1,000 hits in 1,166 games. He never did get a major league call-up. Despite that, he persevered and started coaching in the minors. His Canadian connection continued as Tim worked in the Expos organization, eventually managing their Triple-A Ottawa Lynx team in 2002.

After so many stops along the way, the Blue Jays named Leiper their first-base coach in 2014. Opening Day, Tim made his major league debut after spending 29 years in the minor leagues as a player, coach, manager, and instructor. It is amazing what he has done in the game for Canada: a coach on the 2004 Canadian Olympic team, on Canada's 2006, 2009, and 2013 World Baseball Classic squads, on the Baseball Canada staff that won bronze medals at both the 2008 and 2011 Baseball World Cups, and on the gold medal–winning team in the 2011 Pan-American Games.

Third-base coach Luis Rivera is another treasured friend. Born and raised in Puerto Rico, he signed with the Montreal Expos as an international free agent. After spending four years in the minors, Rivera made his MLB debut as an Expo on August 3, 1986. Luis played parts of three seasons with the Expos before he was traded to the Boston Red Sox, where he had his most productive seasons in his 11-year career. Luis has been with the team since 2010, and he and his wife, Carmen, and their three children have deep roots in Canada.

And so the 2014 season ended. Twenty-one years and counting without a playoff appearance after the magical two World Series years in 1992 and 1993. In the offseason, GM Alex Anthopoulos acquired Marco Estrada, Devon Travis, Josh Donaldson, and Michael Saunders via trades. In the free-agent market, the Blue Jays signed Russell Martin to a five-year contract. Justin Smoak was claimed off waivers from the Mariners. The Blue Jays were set to finally end 22 years of playoff frustrations.

CHAPTER 23

BREAKING THE POSTSEASON BARRIER

Spring training 2015 began with a splash thanks to Josh Donaldson. After introducing myself to Josh at the batting cage, it took only a minute or two to realize that we were going to get along just fine. He was bigger than life. Donaldson loved to tease, going back and forth with me at whatever level I set the conversation. In fact, I once had to tell him to back off — before I knew it, I was pinned up against the batting cage like a rag doll with everyone from Gibby to his teammates howling.

After my prostate cancer surgery in November 2016, I arrived in spring training that next February. The first player to come over with arms wide open to give me a big hug and ask, "How are you?" was Josh. He has a heart of gold, with feelings and a sensitivity that go well beyond the fierce competitor you see every day on the field. It makes Donaldson a complete person and wonderful teammate and leader. He is the one who famously coined: "This is the 'Get it done' league." No excuses. Play hard. It's all about winning. Josh is the one who started the ball rolling toward two straight playoff appearances.

Anthopoulos had stolen him away from the Oakland A's, and with four years left on his contract.

I have a lot of respect for players raised by a single mom. In my 25 years coaching basketball, the first five at Islington Middle School and the remaining 20 at Etobicoke Collegiate Institute, I coached many players who were raised solely by their mothers. Every Sunday night for years, I would call each player at home to remind them about Monday practices, which were often first thing in the morning. The purpose of these calls was twofold. One, no excuses if you missed practice. Two, I got to talk to all the parents, including those single moms. It gave me a greater appreciation of what the players as well as their moms were going through.

Donaldson was raised by his mom, Lisa. There was no father in his life. In fact, Donaldson's father was serving time in prison. It was ugly. Yet Josh continued to persevere with his mother's love, a very strong work ethic, and a burning desire to be the best he could be, despite what was happening in his young life. That is the person I know and have grown to respect, who goes far beyond his outstanding baseball accomplishments. Marco Estrada's mother, Sylvia, gave her son what he needed, too, and all on her own. Josh and Marco are a tribute to single mothers everywhere.

The Jose Reyes Story

The advice I give to young broadcasters about constructive criticism bears repeating here: There is a good way to be constructively critical of a player when you are up in the booth. Pretend that player is sitting right beside you as you say it. That way, you can walk into the clubhouse the next day or mingle at the batting cage and not be afraid at all of what a player might say to you. You've already said it to him. In my encounter in 2015 with shortstop Jose Reyes, many of you might be thinking, *Did Jerry do the same thing with Reyes?* The answer is: yes, I did. The only qualifier I would add is that a few days later, on a morning show with Dean Blundell on our flagship station Sportsnet 590 The Fan, I wish that my tone of voice had not been so harsh and angry. However, when I spoke to Dean about the situation, all the facts were still on the table.

I liked Reyes as a person. He was friendly and happy and smiling all the time. But as the 2015 season wore on, his play at shortstop began to slip badly. A couple of times, routine ground balls went right through his legs, costing his team wins and pitchers losses. I didn't say anything at that time. But as I went through the clubhouse on a daily basis, I began to sense how it was affecting his teammates, who were losing games as a result. The Blue Jays went to Minnesota for a weekend series at the end of May. It happened again. With classy Mark Buehrle on the mound Friday night, Twin Danny Salazar led off and hit a ground ball to short. As Reyes bent down to field it, the ball went right through his legs. On the air I said, "That is the third time this season a ball has gone right through Jose Reyes' legs." I left it at that. But I was feeling for Mark and his teammates. Buehrle escaped that inning, and the Blue Jays went on to win it, 6–4.

Two days later, the Blue Jays led, 5–4, going to the bottom of the 7th inning. Twins outfielder Aaron Hicks led off and hit a ground ball to short. Reyes fielded it and threw it wildly to first base, allowing Hicks to reach on the throwing error. As the inning unfolded, Minnesota scored twice to take a 6–5 lead, aided and abetted by Jose's error. Near the end of the inning, TV shots showed Reyes smiling. After the commercial break, I came back on the air. "Jose Reyes is hurting this team with his play at shortstop. He is hurting his teammates and the pitchers on the mound. They are not seeing even routine plays made behind them. Something has to change at shortstop, or the Blue Jays will not have a chance to make the playoffs this season." I was firm and direct and didn't mention a thing about the smiling. And, yes, I also pretended that Reyes was sitting right next to me, in case he had an issue with what I was saying. Nothing was said as we boarded the plane and headed home. And nothing was said to me over the next two games at home. What I had said was fair and honest and spoke volumes.

On Wednesday, I was asked to go on the morning show. I agreed. I also knew what Blundell was going to ask me, and that was about Reyes and my comments on Sunday. I could have easily said, "I said what I said and have no regrets. Let's move on." But I did not. Instead, for the next six or seven minutes I told Dean what Jose was doing to his team and teammates. The longer I went, the harsher my voice got, to the point of anger. For the first time, I also brought up the fact that I thought his laughing was totally uncalled for and unacceptable. When I was finished with the show, I had mixed feelings about how my attitude may have come across but not about the content.

That night at the game, Paul Beeston, the president of the Blue Jays and a loyal friend of mine from day one, going back to 1982, called me into his office. "Jerry, I am not here to fire you, even though I am disappointed in you and what you had to say this morning. It was your tone of voice that bothered me the most. You have been around a long time, and I respect what you have done here, but that was not good."

We had a good talk. "Paul, I am disappointed in myself, too. And you are right about the tone of voice. I was angry and upset. I should have just let it go and let my words on the broadcast stand alone for what I saw happening."

That night, I looked for Reyes to apologize to him for what I had said that morning and how I had said it. I did not see him in the clubhouse before the game, so I pulled my good friend and third-base coach Luis Rivera aside and asked him if he would please ask Jose if he would see me after batting practice. He came up to me later and said that Reyes did not want to see me. That did not surprise me. A few days later, when the team was in Boston, I waited in the tunnel that leads from the clubhouse to the playing field — there was no other way for Reyes to get to the field. After some time, he came into the tunnel and started to the dugout. Halfway to the field, I stood right in front of him. "Jose, I'm sorry for what I said, and I am especially sorry for how I said it. You are a great young man and you love playing the game. Again, I am sorry." He looked at me and said, "Okay." I moved aside as he continued to the dugout. That was the last time we spoke.

Sometimes even when we pretend that a player is right there next to us, there can be extenuating circumstances that can factor in. I have no regrets about what I said. I do, however, wish I had softened what I said a few days later and not let my emotions and feelings get the best of me. In the big picture, I also learned a valuable lesson about honesty. That came from Alex Anthopoulos. "You sure made that trade of Reyes to the Rockies a lot more difficult for me because the Rockies kept asking what was going on with Reyes. That deal took a few more weeks than I expected, but we pulled it off." I had never thought about that. My words could have negatively affected a transaction that was paramount to the Blue Jays' future success in 2015, bringing Troy Tulowitzki and LaTroy Hawkins to the Blue Jays.

"Tulo Tulo" and the Price Was Right

The 2015 season really started on the night of Wednesday, July 29, at the Rogers Centre. Up to that point, the Blue Jays were just 50-51 and going nowhere fast for a 22nd straight season. Then it happened. That night in his first game as a Blue Jay, shortstop Troy Tulowitzki led off. Troy went 3 for 5 with a home run and two doubles. That sparked an 8–2 win over the Phillies before just 27,000 fans. Four days later 45,736 fans — only the fourth sold-out game of the season at that time — saw the Blue Jays begin an 11-game winning streak, defeating the 2014 World Series Champion Kansas City Royals, 5–2. It was only fitting after 22 years of futility that 22 more sellouts would follow. The Blue Jays were back, and so were the fans.

The very next day, August 2, 2015, I saw and heard something from the fan base that I had not experienced in my entire career as a Blue Jays broadcaster. *Passion. Enthusiasm. Anticipation. Youth. Energy.* Left-handed veteran David Price was making his Blue Jays debut before nearly 46,000 fans. It was the 4th inning. Game tied with the Twins, 1–1. Minnesota's Trevor Plouffe opened the inning with a double. Price then walked Miguel Sano and Torii Hunter back to back to load the bases with nobody out. What happened next was the story of the season — and the next season, too, for that matter.

The young crowd rose to its feet and began a thunderous roar never before heard that early at a home game. Price responded by inducing Eddie Rosario to pop-up on the infield. One down. He struck out Aaron Hicks looking. Two down. He struck out Kurt Suzuki swinging. The inning was over. Price had left the bases loaded on his way to a convincing 5–1 win. David enthusiastically left the mound and applauded all the way to the third-base dugout, pounding his left fist into his glove time and time again as the crowd roared. That inning was the benchmark of what was to come. The crowds never stopped their boisterous standing ovations. This beautiful frenzy continued right through to the end of the 2016 season.

The 1992 and 1993 crowds were more corporate. The Blue Jays drew 50,000 a game in those years: attendance averaged better than four million fans a season for three straight years. All well and good. The fans cheered when they should have cheered. They stood and raised their voices to the max only when there were two outs in the top of the 9th inning, and many of those times when there were two strikes on the hitter. There was no sense of anticipation, no feeling that the game was on the line even as early as the 1st inning, or that the fans could make a difference. That all ended August 3 with Price's 4th inning. That inning was well received by the players in the clubhouse. A new era of fandom had begun in Toronto. Starting pitchers were now getting loud standing ovations running out to the bullpen to warm up 25 minutes before game time, "Tulo! Tulo!" was echoing through the Rogers Centre, Price was on his way to going 9-1 with an ERA of 2.30, the club finished August 21-6, then went 19-12 the rest of the way. The Blue Jays went 43-18 after their 50-51, start to finish 93-69 and win their first American League Eastern Division Championship since 1993. Along the way, they won the hearts of their adoring fans. The loudest and most energetic crowds I had ever heard in my years in Toronto.

In early August, I spoke with GM Alex Anthopoulos. This was just after the July 31 trade deadline, when over the course of a few days Troy Tulowitzki and LaTroy Hawkins had been acquired from Colorado, David Price from Detroit, pitcher Mark Lowe from Seattle, and outfielder Ben Revere from the Phillies. Alex was very open and honest. "I wanted more character players. I had always looked at numbers. They were good to know, but I wasn't getting a full return. So this season I started to change my thinking and look at players differently. That started with the offseason acquisitions like Josh Donaldson. I am doing the same thing right now, adding character players. I had to be better."

Great players need to make adjustments to get better. So do great general managers.

Russell Martin

What are the odds that Donaldson, a catcher — who made his major league debut with the Chicago Cubs — turned third baseman would be paired with a third baseman turned catcher in Russell Martin? Together as teammates for the first time, they helped to end a 22-year playoff drought. Martin was born in Toronto and raised in Montreal. He was selected in the 35th round of the 2000 June Draft by the Expos but did not sign. Instead, he attended Chipola Junior College for two years, where he played alongside future teammate Jose Bautista. In 2002, Martin was drafted by the Los Angeles Dodgers as a third baseman and later converted to a catcher. When Russ was a Dodger, they came in for a three-game series at the Rogers Centre. I sought him out to introduce myself. I asked him if he liked to be called Russell or Russ. "Either is fine with me. I'm good with Russ." I like to ask the player directly about his name and especially last name. I had to learn that the hard way.

In my first month broadcasting games in 1974 for the Triple-A Tacoma Twins, Spokane came to town. I asked their manager, Del Wilber, about a few names on his roster. "Who is your first-base coach?" He replied: "Jose Mart-i-NEZZ." I said thanks and went up to the radio booth. I learned real fast to go straight to the person. I set the stage early and noted that skipper Del Wilber was coaching at third, and Jose Mart-i-NEZZ was coaching at first. After the game I went back to the station. The engineer came running up to me. "Jerry, the phone lines lit up all night. Callers were saying 'Doesn't he know the name is pronounced Mar-TEE-nez?'" That was the last time I ever asked a manager for help with names.

Martin was one of the keys to the Blue Jays' success, both as an outstanding receiver and swinging the bat. Russ is unassuming and loves to compete, a personality I found typical of catchers who have ended up as managers or broadcasters. My own radio partner Joe Siddall fits that mould perfectly as an excellent communicator on both radio and TV. Russ is an excellent communicator with his pitchers.

It didn't take Martin long to receive his first standing ovation from the fans. It came at Olympic Stadium in Montreal on April 3, 2015, in the first of two final spring training games. You could see tears in Russell's eyes as he stood at home plate with all his catching gear on, watching his dad out at the mound play the two national anthems on his saxophone. His father, who used to play the saxophone in Montreal metro stations to help pay for his son's baseball training, had done this at a game in Los Angeles when Russ broke in with the Dodgers. Two weeks later, Russ caught lefty Jeff Francis from Vancouver, B.C., in Jeff's debut as a Blue Jay. It was the first all-Canadian battery in franchise history. The year was off to a rousing good start.

One of the Good Guys

Speaking of Canadians, prior to the 2015 season, the Blue Jays acquired Michael Saunders in a trade. Sadly, the pride of Victoria, B.C., tore the meniscus in his left knee on one of the back fields at the Bobby Mattick Centre just as spring training was beginning in late February. He played in only nine games.

The next season, Saunders bounced back with such a strong first half and was named to the All-Star team. In June against the Orioles, he hit three home runs for the first time in his career. He joined Joey Votto, Justin Morneau, and Larry Walker as the only Canadians to hit three home runs in a game and the first to do it for a Canadian team. For whatever reason, after the All-Star break, Saunders struggled, hitting only .178 with eight home runs and 15 RBIs. Despite the poor second half, he appeared in eight postseason games for the Blue Jays, batting .381.

Throughout the good times and the bad, Saunders remained the same very decent human being I had met years earlier. Saunders has the right disposition to play this game, taking the highs and lows in stride. He does not get too cocky or full of himself when he excels, nor does he get too low or depressed when things are not going well; he is what I like to call a battler. It has held him in good stead as an athlete.

Significant Contributors

The other catcher in 2015 was in his second season as a Blue Jay: Dioner Navarro. When news broke that the Blue Jays had signed Martin as a free agent to a five-year, $80-million contract, Navarro immediately made it known that he wanted to be traded. He wanted to be a starting catcher and not just a backup to Martin. Nothing happened on the trade front. Navarro began spring training without making anymore negative statements. In fact, to the contrary: "I am happy to be a Blue Jay and will help the team win any way I can to get to the playoffs." He meant it.

When I arrived in spring training, Dioner was one of the first players I talked to. He told me not being traded meant nothing in the big picture of his life. Born in Caracas, Venezuela, Dioner married his wife, Sherley, at age 18. On September 27, 2003, their first wedding anniversary, she suffered a cerebral aneurysm in Tampa. Doctors gave her less than a 5 percent chance of surviving surgery. They said it was likely she would die three days later on September 30. Sherley survived and made a full recovery. Dioner has worn the number 30 in her honour ever since.

Not only was Navarro happy backing up Martin all the way to the playoffs, he did something else with Russ, too. They would have a blast before games, kicking a soccer ball all over the field. Dioner wore his Venezuelan soccer jersey and Russ his Canadian one. Other teammates would join in. It became a pregame ritual to see that soccer ball flying all around the many ball parks. It was the Blue Jays' version of the Premier League.

Two pitchers in camp were from Southern California. Marco Estrada was born in Mexico and raised by his mother in California. Sylvia wanted her son to have opportunities to grow and mature, both as a person and as a student athlete.

Marco did just that, starring at Long Beach State with his teammates Evan Longoria and Troy Tulowitzki. Young Aaron Sanchez was expected to pitch out of the bullpen and compete for the closer's role. But after Marcus Stroman suffered a torn left ACL on March 10 in a spring training pitcher's fielding drill, Sanchez pitched in the rotation the rest of spring training, earning the fifth starter spot. Aaron recorded his first win as a starter on April 22, defeating the Baltimore Orioles, 4–2. There would be many more wins to come and an American League ERA title.

Both Estrada and Sanchez are cut from the same cloth: soft spoken, kind, respectful, and competitive. Aaron is also a reflection of great parenting. He, like Estrada and Donaldson, was always among the first ones to come over and see me on the field or in the clubhouse each spring, and in particular after my surgery, to see how I was doing. Sanchez was able to take in stride his fabulous 2016 season leading the American League in ERA with the same grace and dignity he did the following season when plagued by blister problems and making only eight starts. It's easy when you are on top. In back-to-back seasons, Aaron showed he could handle the good and the bad with great professionalism, grace, and patience.

Acquiring a Glass Overflowing

In addition to trading for Donaldson, Estrada, and Saunders, Anthopoulos pulled off one more deal, bringing second baseman Devon Travis to the Blue Jays from Detroit for young outfielder Anthony Gose. This was clearly a trade that saw Alex's new philosophy put into practice. So many times in my talks with Anthony, I heard nothing but his negative thoughts. "I can't do this. I can't do that. Nothing works." I even used the glass-half-empty analogy to try to tell him how much he was hurting himself. He wasn't coming close to maximizing his God-given abilities. I liked Anthony, but he was easily the most negative player I had ever met in my career. His constant glass-half-empty attitude and lack of self-confidence directly led to his demise. What a shame.

At the other end of the spectrum, coming to Toronto was glass-overflowing Devon Travis, who is one of the most positive people I have ever met. When working as a speaker, I sometimes tell a story to get an audience laughing: "It is so nice to hear such a positive audience. Reminds me of the time my son, Ben, came home one day from the third grade and said, 'Dad, I'm afraid I flunked my mathematics test.' I said, 'Ben, that's negative. Around our house we want you to be positive.' He said, 'Dad, I'm positive I flunked my mathematics test.'"

And I'm positive that if Travis could stay healthy, he would be an All-Star.

There's an old saying in baseball: "He's injury-prone." For all his admirable positive traits and skills, Devon has unfortunately fallen into this category. He is such a force on the field when healthy. In May 2017, he hit .364 with a .373 OBP and .646 SLG, scored 17 runs, drove in 19, and hit .409 with runners in scoring position. The Blue Jays finished that month 18-10. It was their only winning month all season long. Travis did not play after that, logging only 50 total games due to a nagging knee injury. Had he played all season in 2017, the odds of the Blue Jays going back to the playoffs for a third straight year would have been greatly enhanced. Devon remains glass-overflowing to this day despite his setbacks.

Discovering a New Closer

Finally, in spring training that year, there were two kids not expected to make the 25-man roster; instead, they were expected to get acclimated to major league baseball for their future, then return to the minors: Roberto Osuna and Miguel Castro. For one — Osuna — the future was now. The other — Castro — had to bide his time and eventually move on to another organization.

Osuna was signed by the Blue Jays out of Mexico as a 16-year-old. In March 2013, at the tender age of 18, Roberto injured his right elbow; he would require surgery later that season. "I got injured at the best time of my career. It was hard for me. The doctors told me that I needed the Tommy John surgery immediately. I cried, I wasn't focused, I didn't understand anything. I wanted to seek a second opinion and avoid the operating room. I took therapy, tried everything." On April 8, 2015, the 20-year-old Osuna became the youngest pitcher ever to appear in a game for the Blue Jays. He was the first player born in 1995 to play in the major leagues.

It's not often that at the age of 12, you have to quit school to help support your family, but that was Roberto. He helped pick vegetables with his father, who pitched in the Mexican League for 22 seasons. Roberto's dad taught his son how to pitch at the end of those long days. Osuna's uncle, Antonio, pitched in the majors for 11 seasons, mostly with the Dodgers.

The youngest reliever in major league history to reach 75 career saves, at age 22 and 134 days in 2017, Osuna became the youngest Blue Jays player in franchise history to play in an All-Star Game. His 2017 season thrilled fans with 21 consecutive saves, the fourth-longest save streak in franchise history.

In September of that same year, I had a joyous moment in the Blue Jays clubhouse. Osuna — just back from Mexico — called me over and pulled out his phone. "Jerry, you are one of the first to see a picture of my daughter, Kaylie, who was born just a couple of days ago." A gentle reminder that these players have personal lives, too, with all-consuming responsibilities that go far beyond playing baseball.

A not-so-joyous moment occurred in May 2018, while the finished manuscript for this book was with my publishing house ECW Press. Osuna was arrested and charged with a domestic violence incident in Toronto. He was issued a 75-game suspension without pay that ran through August 4, for violating the Joint Domestic Violence, Sexual Assault and Child Abuse Policy of Major League Baseball and the Major League Baseball Players Association. The 23-year-old was traded to the Houston Astros on July 30 of that season.

I was shocked to hear this about someone I called a friend and still do. My hopes and prayers are that Roberto will learn from this and go forward as a positive role model against domestic violence. Romans 3:23.

The Iconic Bat Flip

October 14, 2015, will always be remembered for the bat flip, and it was a cherished moment in my Blue Jays career at the microphone. Yes, that was the day that Jose Bautista, in the 7th inning of the final and deciding game of the ALDS against Texas, finished off one of the most famous and bizarre playoff innings in major league history. An inning that took a phenomenal 53 minutes to play.

Texas had taken the lead in the top of the 7th on a throw back to the mound by catcher Russ Martin that hit the bat of Shin-Soo Choo in the batter's box. Rougned Odor was allowed to score from third base after the ball was initially ruled a dead ball. Texas took a 3–2 lead. The crowd went berserk. In the bottom of the inning, three softly hit ground balls amazingly led to three straight Texas errors loading the bases. It reminded me of the old adage in baseball: "There's no such thing as a routine ground ball."

With the infield drawn in, a little pop-up out behind second base resulted in a force out at second as a run was scored to tie the game, 3–3, leaving runners at the corners. Up stepped Jose Bautista against right-handed reliever Sam Dyson. On the 1-1 pitch, Bautista hit the biggest home run of his career. As the ball sailed toward deep left-centre field, I simply said: "Yes, Sir! THERE! SHE! GOES!" The thunderous applause filled our crowd mic for close to a minute. Bautista paused for a moment as he watched the ball fly over the wall. As the crowd erupted, Bautista then tossed his bat high over his shoulder toward the Rangers first-base dugout. His famous — or infamous depending on which side you came down on — bat flip was the exclamation point.

People have asked me many times how I feel about Jose's bat flip. I tell them I feel exactly the same way former Blue Jays pitcher and later Arizona Diamondbacks general manager Dave Stewart felt about it: "In today's game — what Jose Bautista did — that's acceptable. I've got to tell you, there's no better professional than he is. There's no better guy and no better teammate than he is. So I don't think it was to show up the other side. I don't believe that. I just think that's how they play today, and displays of emotion when you do something great — especially on that platform in that moment — that's just today's game."

The season ended on Friday, October 23, at Kauffman Stadium in Kansas City with a heartbreaking 4–3 loss in Game 6 of the American League Championship Series. In that game Bautista hit two home runs and drove in all three Blue Jays runs. His two-run home run in the top of the 8th inning dramatically tied the game, 3–3, only to see the Royals score a run in the bottom of the 8th and then hold on to win it in the 9th as Toronto left runners at second and third.

Joey Bats

Over his 10 seasons in Toronto, I really enjoyed Jose and what he meant to the Blue Jays and to the fans who adored him on and off the field. That was all very evident when I had the pleasure of taking Bautista off the field in the top of the 9th inning at the Rogers Centre in what many felt would be his last home game as a Blue Jay on September 24, 2017. The hugs started in centre field with Kevin Pillar and went on from there as the ovation grew louder and louder. Manager John Gibbons said it best in his postgame scrum with the media. "The focus was on Jose today, what he's done for this town, this country. He helped rebuild the team, was the face of the franchise for a number of years, and he did it the right way."

A six-time All-Star and two-time Hank Aaron Award recipient, Jose helped his team break through the 22-year postseason barrier by hitting 40 home runs and batting in 114 runs while crossing the plate 108 times and leading the league with 110 walks. I respected how Bautista grew up with an emphasis on education that later enabled him to apply mind over matter to persevere when he needed it the most, not only staying in the game he loved, but starring in it.

Jose attended the private De La Salle high school in Santo Domingo, in the Dominican Republic. Although he invested a lot of time pursuing professional baseball, he continued to study business at Mother and Teacher Pontifical Catholic University in case a career in baseball did not materialize. While in school, Bautista even created a highlight tape of himself and sent it to various colleges in the United States.

There was no response until he received a call from Oscar Perez, whom he had known from the Quique Cruz Baseball League in the Dominican Republic. Perez informed him of the Latin Athletes Education Fund, founded by Don Odermann, designed for players from Spanish-speaking countries aspiring to play college baseball in the United States. Perez connected Bautista with Odermann, a businessman in the San Francisco Bay Area. Don knew that Chipola Junior College in Marianna, Florida, was seeking an everyday player. Helped by Odermann's Education Fund, Bautista went there and played for two years until being drafted.

I mention this because while working at my alma mater, Santa Clara University, back in 1972 and 1973, I met Odermann, who was taking classes there on his way to becoming a stock-broker. He told me at that time about his passion for helping baseball players in Latin America and that he had started his education fund. Fast track to 2013: Bautista had met Odermann and wanted to help extend Don's program with his own resources and outreach, but because Odermann had run into some health issues, Jose wasn't sure where the program was going. He decided to create his own foundation.

Bautista not only leaves behind 10 seasons as a Blue Jay, he also leaves behind for one and all his Bautista Family Education Fund. The BFEF is dedicated to assisting and supporting young amateur athletes in all facets of their transition to college life in order to maximize opportunities both on and off the field. Jose is making a difference. "When you can help kids into not giving up their dream to continue to play sports while getting their education, I think it's a great opportunity." Odermann passed away at the age of 72 on January 10, 2017, due to Alzheimer's disease. With his passion for helping others, Bautista continues to repay the favour he received from Don. Nicely done, Jose.

CHAPTER 24

QUITE A RIDE

The 2016 season stood out for two reasons: it marked the 40th season in franchise history, and it featured one of the most memorable playoff home runs ever, when Edwin Encarnacion ended the Wild Card Game in the 11th inning at the Rogers Centre with a 5–2 victory against the Baltimore Orioles. The club would beat the Texas Rangers for a second straight year in the American League Division Series before losing to Cleveland in five games in the American League Championship Series.

Everything but the Cape

It was a super season that featured "Superman" in centre field. I first met Kevin Pillar in 2013. Kevin was born in Southern California in the Los Angeles district of West Hills. What intrigued me right away in his background was the phenomenal NCAA Division II–record 54-game hitting streak he had put together at Cal State Dominguez Hills in 2010. When it comes to the top two NCAA Divisions, this was only four games shy of the NCAA Division I all-time record of 58 games, set by former major league star and White Sox manager Robin Ventura. Eight different times during Kevin's streak, he came to the plate needing a base hit in his last at-bat, and he got it. I asked him how the streak ended. "They walked me three times, and so I had only one at-bat. They never really gave me a chance to hit." That conversation defined for me Pillar's quiet and understated personality. He was the Blue Jays' 32nd-round pick (979th overall) in June 2011 and someone who has been anything but quiet playing centre field.

Pillar was blessed with the "competitive gene," as I like to call it, early on in his life. Sportsnet's Kristina Rutherford wrote a very insightful article on Kevin's childhood. His dad, Michael, was a professional motocross racer, so at age three, Kevin rode his first motorcycle on the desert and dirt paths near the family home in West Hills. He was in his first race at age six. He said he was fearless, which is not a surprise to hear, but it also scared his parents to death. By age 10, here was a kid on the adult motorcycle tracks, ripping over jumps while his dad followed him around trying to keep him safe. Family and friends called him "Crash." When Troy Tulowizki arrived in the Blue Jays clubhouse in July 2015, he quickly assessed Pillar in his own quiet way, and "Crash" became "Crash Dummy," adding a lot of laughter in the Blue Jays clubhouse.

During batting practice, whenever there was a discussion going on about the game, Kevin would come over between his swings to quietly listen. He loved playing observer, picking up little bits of information from veterans like Josh Donaldson, Russell Martin, and Tulowitzki or hearing what Buck Martinez, Pat Tabler, and Joe Siddall had to say, assessing key aspects of the game the night before.

Being a good listener has helped Pillar to maximize his abilities. He likes to say that he "lives in the moment," which is a trait I have always respected in people. Another person who does that is manager John Gibbons. Coincidentally, there was a live-in-the-moment incident between the two on June 24, 2014, when Kevin was lifted for pinch hitter Anthony Gose. Pillar tossed his bat in anger in the dugout. Gibbons told Pillar to go to the clubhouse and after the game told him he was going back to Triple-A. It was a moment of truth for Kevin. Much to his credit, he went to Buffalo with the goal of coming back better than ever and leaving this particular moment behind him. Kevin did just that, and as a result became mentally tougher in a game that demands mental toughness every single day. Good for John Gibbons, and good for Kevin Pillar.

On October 10, 2017, Kevin and his wife, Amanda, celebrated the birth of their first child, a girl they named Kobie Rae, perhaps the next "Supergirl." Amanda was a terrific guest for us on radio during the annual Lady Jays Food Drive each season. We all laughed out loud at her funny remarks about her husband. I asked her how she felt about seeing him crash against the wall seemingly every game at the Rogers Centre. "Kevin will come home after a game and I'll say, 'How's your knee?' and he'll say, 'It's my shoulder.' Then the next game it'll be, 'Kev, how's your shoulder?' and he'll answer, 'It's my back.' But I don't worry because that's my husband, and I have seen him play like this his whole career, going back to when we were in college together. I know he is hurting all over." When I mentioned what a great job Amanda did on the radio, Kevin told me he always jokes around with his wife: "Do you ever think I'm gonna die out there? And she's like, 'I don't know, maybe.'"

The Stro-Show in the 6

Pitcher Marcus Stroman was called up to the Blue Jays on May 3, 2014. He was already beginning to make an impression with his intensity and outspoken passion for the game he loves. When he arrived in spring training the following season, we were talking in the clubhouse when I made a comment about his height being five-foot-nine. "Jerry, I'm five-foot-eight. I know the media guide lists me at five-foot-nine, but I am five-foot-eight." That little exchange told me a lot about this pitcher's makeup and his ability to proudly compete with that chip on his shoulder. He has HDMH, which stands for "Height Doesn't Measure Heart," tattooed on his body. How sensitive is he to his height? In 2016, at a Nike physical examination, Stroman afterwards proclaimed to one and all, "I was measured today at exactly five-foot-seven-and-one-quarter-inch."

Marcus also has a compassionate side. He came to the Blue Jays in 2014 wearing No. 54 and asked to begin the 2015 season with No. 6 in honour of his grandmother, Gloria Major, who had attended all of his high school games. She passed away while he was studying at Duke University. Gloria was born on March 6, 1943. Her number accompanied her grandson to the 2017 World Baseball Classic, in which he was selected as MVP from the winning Team USA. Also, as Marcus points out, he proudly wears 6 in "the 6," which has become synonymous with Toronto, thanks to world-famous recording artist Drake, who proclaimed that it derived from the city's 416 area code and the six municipalities that amalgamated into the modern City of Toronto in 1998.

Stroman injured his left knee in a 2015 spring training pitcher's fielding drill and had to have surgery. As he was rehabbing at Duke under the watchful eye of physical therapist and athletic trainer at Duke Sports Medicine, Nikki Huffman, Marcus earned his bachelor's degree in sociology. As for Huffman, the Blue Jays were impressed enough not only to hire her after her work with Marcus but to name her head trainer in 2018, making her just the second woman to hold that position in any of the North American top four sports leagues.

Most everyone had written off Marcus in the 2015 season — except for Marcus. The "Stro-Show" truly began when he was activated from the 60-day disabled list on September 11 and started the second game of a doubleheader the following day. Stroman pitched five innings to earn the win. He would go on to make three more starts, finishing the 2015 regular season with a September mark of 4-0 and an ERA of 1.67. He wasn't finished. Not by a long shot.

Marcus pitched in his first career postseason game in Game 2 of the 2015 American League Division Series against the Texas Rangers, going seven innings with a no-decision. He started again in Game 5, the famous "bat flip" game, allowing six hits and two earned runs over six innings in an eventual 6–3 Blue Jays victory. The following season, Marcus pitched a career-high 204 innings and again had his mettle tested. The Blue Jays announced he would start the Wild Card Game against the Baltimore Orioles at the Rogers Centre. In that famous game, the fans saw him produce six strong innings, allowing just two earned runs while striking out six and leaving to a standing ovation. Marcus Stroman just happened to be on the hill in back-to-back years for two of the biggest playoff games in franchise history. And all at five-foot-seven and a quarter.

Biagini Was a Genie

And then there was Joe. On March 30, 2016, manager John Gibbons announced that a Rule 5 Draft pick, Joe Biagini, had made the Opening Day roster and would pitch out of the bullpen. Joe made his major league debut on April 8, pitching a perfect 9th inning against the Boston Red Sox, striking out David Ortiz for his first career strikeout. A Genie had struck out a Big Papi. Joe did not yield a home run until September 3, and finished his first season with a 4-3 record, 3.06 ERA, and 62 strikeouts in 67 and two-thirds innings. Coming from the San Francisco Giants in December 2015, Joe is one of the best Rule 5 Draft picks the Blue Jays have made.

We were two kids from San Francisco who both started out living in Redwood City. His dad, Rob, pitched in the Giants organization in 1981 and 1982. I hit it off with Joe right from the start. He is a kidder, and so am I. When I first met Joe before a game, I playfully said, "Now go be-a-genie on the mound."

"Oh, like I didn't hear that . . . in the third grade."

Joe has a deadpan sense of humour that can seemingly take hours to come out when he talks. Our engineer, Tom Young, who always does a great job and is responsible for the public address announcer's voice each game for our listening audience to enjoy, asked me one day if Biagini would be a good guest for our five-minute pregame show. I said, "Sure. Good idea." So, with microphone in hand, down I went to the field for our interview. It is the only time in his career that Tom has ever had to edit down a 20-minute interview into a workable five minutes. Joe is all over the map with his dry sense of humour and can be very wordy, to say the least. I told Joe later about what our engineer had had to do with our interview, but added,

"Don't ever change. You be your quirky self here on interviews and with the media, but also be yourself on the mound. You are one of the most competitive players I have ever seen put on a Blue Jays uniform, with a daily routine and discipline that is outstanding. It is okay to be two people, which you clearly are."

May 9 saw the Blue Jays travel to Biagini's hometown in San Francisco for a three-game series. "My whole idea of baseball was very much constructed by the Giants and AT&T Park. Getting drafted by the Giants, the hope was I'd play there one day. Ironically, I'm now about as far away from there as you can get, but I'll hopefully get to pitch in the series, and I am excited about that." In the final game of that series, manager John Gibbons made sure that Joe did. In front of his mom and dad and many friends, Biagini was a genie: on two pitches he retired the only batter he faced, Matt Duffy, on a groundout to second base to end the 7th. He received a "standing family ovation" as he left the mound.

Edwing's Walk-Off

The 2016 regular season came down to the last six games. With the Red Sox leading the second-place Blue Jays by six games with six to play, it was a foregone conclusion that Boston would win the A.L. East. When the Orioles arrived at the Rogers Centre Tuesday, September 27, to begin a three-game series, they were 85-71, trailing the Blue Jays by one game in the chase to the Wild Card finish line. There was a lot at stake, including home field advantage, if the two teams were tied for the Wild Card spot after Sunday. The Blue Jays stood 9-7 in the head-to-head season series.

Aaron Sanchez beat Baltimore, 5–1, Tuesday night to clinch the tie-breaker. The Blue Jays had a two-game lead with five games to play. However, the Orioles took the next two games to tie up the Wild Card race with three games to play. The Red Sox beat the Blue Jays Friday night at Fenway Park, 5–3, while the Orioles defeated the Yankees in New York, 8–1, to take a one-game lead. On the postgame show with Joe Siddall, I put into perspective what I had heard back in 1985 from Kansas City's John Wathan: "In baseball a three-game winning streak is nothing. It looks like that is what it is going to take to have the Blue Jays go back to the American League Division Series against Texas."

On Saturday, the Blue Jays scored a run in the top of the 9th off Red Sox closer Craig Kimbrel to win, 4–3, while the Orioles lost to the Yankees, 7–3. Both teams were 88-73 with one game to play. To add to the drama, Major League Baseball had instituted a new 3:00 p.m. ET start time for all games on the last day of the season. Sunday, in 2:32, the Orioles beat the Yankees, 5–2, to clinch a tie for the Wild Card. The Blue Jays game was in the 7th inning at Fenway Park tied, 1–1. When you talk about scoreboard watching and feeling the pressure, this was it.

In the top of the 8th inning, two veterans teamed up to take the lead. Troy Tulowitzki singled to centre to drive home Edwin Encarnacion and take a 2–1 lead. That was the final score. Aaron Sanchez went 7 innings allowing only one run to finish the season with an American League–leading 3.00 ERA. Brett Cecil and rookie Biagini blanked the Sox in the 8th. Roberto Osuna pitched a scoreless 9th for his 36th save. The Blue Jays had won two in a row to finish the season 89-73, tied with the Orioles for the Wild Card spot. Now they needed that third straight win as they headed home for a Tuesday night winner-take-all game against the Orioles.

Without a doubt, Edwin Encarnacion's biggest and most dramatic career home run occurred October 4, 2016, at the Rogers Centre. The Wild Card Game was tied, 2–2, after 10 innings. In the top of the 11th, Francisco Liriano came out of the Blue Jays bullpen and retired the Orioles in order. In the bottom of the inning, Orioles reliever Brian Duensing struck out Ezequiel Carrera for the first out. Manager Buck Showalter then went to his bullpen for veteran right-hander Ubaldo Jimenez instead of his closer Zach Britton, who had been perfect in the regular season, saving 47 games in 47 save opportunities.

Jimenez threw only five pitches before it was over. Devon Travis singled to left on the third pitch he saw. Josh Donaldson followed with a first-pitch single to left, moving Travis to third. Edwin then crushed the first pitch he saw to deep left-centre field for a no-doubter walk-off three-run home run. Almost upon impact, I said, "Yes, sir! The Blue Jays are going to Texas!" For nearly a minute on radio, all you heard was the roar of the crowd before I got back on the air. "The Blue Jays win it, 5–2, in 11 innings as Edwin Encarnacion disappears into a sea of blue at home plate, mobbed by his teammates."

Edwin became only the fourth player in major league history to end a winner-take-all postseason game with a walk-off home run, joining Pittsburgh's Bill Mazeroski in the 1960 World Series, Kansas City's Chris Chambliss in the 1976 ALCS, and the Yankees' Aaron Boone (now their manager) in the 2003 ALCS. (Joe Carter's walk-off home run in Game 6 of the 1993 World Series was not in a winner-take-all postseason game.) The Blue Jays would go on to sweep the Rangers in three games in the American League Division Series before losing the Championship Series to Cleveland in five games.

Thanks for the Memories

Looking back at 2015 and 2016, I had the distinct pleasure to make my two favourite calls as the lead announcer for Blue Jays fans across Canada: Jose Bautista's bat-flip home run in the playoffs against Texas and, a year later, Edwin's walk-off playoff home run to beat Baltimore in the Wild Card Game. *"Call it two!"*

It was so much fun being around "Joey Bats" and listening to the crowd's "JOSE! Jose, Jose, Jose!" with his every home run; hearing "MVP" chants whenever Josh Donaldson stepped to the plate; seeing Troy Tulowitzki standing at second while "TU-LO! TU-LO! TU-LO!" rocked the Rogers Centre; being able to say, "Yes, sir! The Blue Jays are going to Texas!" as Edwin's mammoth blast brought down the house; witnessing the "Stro-Show" every five days; seeing the "Genie" pitch both as a reliever and a starter; following the development of the "Sanchize," Aaron Sanchez, who came up through the system labelled as the "franchise" and led the American League in 2016 with his 3.00 ERA; observing J.A. Happ work with Pete Walker in 2016 and become only the sixth Blue Jays starter in franchise history to have a 20-win season; marvelling in 2017 at Ryan Goins a.k.a. "GoGo," hitting .714 with the bases loaded, including two grand slams, on his way to a career-high 62 RBIs, all with a sense of humour: "When the bases are loaded, I get lucky. When there's no one on base, I get out."

And it continued: standing in awe as Steve Pearce hit two historic walk-off grand slams on the same homestand four days apart; cringing as "Superman" Kevin Pillar literally hit the ivy-covered brick wall at Wrigley Field to make yet another amazing face-plant catch; flabbergasted at countless slow-motion replays of Chris Coghlan's acrobatic somersault over bent-over catcher Yadier Molina to score a run against the St. Louis Cardinals; applauding Justin Smoak for his breakout All-Star season in 2017, with 38 home runs and 90 RBIs.

It was so much fun appreciating Russell "The Muscle" Martin and his nine playoff appearances in his 12-year career despite injuries — "It wasn't that I was hurt catching. It was that I was catching hurt."; remembering when Gold Glover and versatile player Darwin Barney, who had already won two World Series at Oregon State, once told me, "I try to prepare my body to play every day. I never know what my role might be so I have to be ready for whatever my manager asks."; getting to know Kendrys Morales, who defected from Cuba in 2004 after 11 failed attempts and arrived in Miami on a speedboat along with 18 other Cubans; respecting Troy Tulowitzki's outstanding makeup as a professional trying to stay healthy while doing his best to get back to the World Series for the first time since he was a rookie with Colorado in 2007; hearing Devon Travis's teammates tease him and call him "The Baby" because they say all he does is eat, sleep, and play baseball; and being touched by Marco Estrada's deep love for his mother, Sylvia, who provided him with the opportunity to achieve his goals.

Justin Smoak followed up his outstanding 2017 All-Star season by being named a finalist in 2018 for the Gold Glove Award for fielding excellence at first base. And he was not traded at the July 31 trade deadline, which obviously had been talked about by Justin and his wife, Kristin, and overheard by their adorable three-year-old daughter, Sutton. When visiting the Toronto Zoo on August 2, Sutton said, "Mama, we didn't see the elephants today . . . maybe they got traded." Ah . . . out of the mouths of babes.

AFTERWORD

Signature Calls

Many times, I have been asked how I came up with some of my "signature calls." I can honestly say none of them were planned. They were all just naturally a part of my flow and delivery in the moment. The irony is that I am not a big believer in signatures. However, I am a staunch believer in being yourself. I tell that to young aspiring broadcasters all the time. Better to let it happen and enjoy that comfort the rest of your career. That is exactly what happened with my home-run call.

Over my five years calling Triple-A games, I did not have a "home-run call," nor did I try to invent one. The same held true when I came to Toronto to begin broadcasting full-time in 1982. Then one afternoon at Exhibition Stadium in 1983, a Blue Jay hit a third-inning leadoff home run into the left-field bleacher seats. "There it goes!" After that call, I said to myself, "That was good. I liked that. Maybe someday that could be a home-run call for me." The very next inning, another Blue Jay hit a home run to left field, but this time with runners on base to take the lead. My excitement was obvious in the call. "*There she goes!* The Blue Jays take the lead!" When that Blue Jay touched home plate, and I do not remember who it was, I said to myself: *That's my home-run call from now on. It feels so comfortable.*

It was my dad who, in 1983, suggested that I say, "The Blue Jays are in flight," when I call the team's first run of the game. I have done that for him ever since. It was my wife, Mary, who said, "When the Blue Jays score, why don't you have those runs stand out from the other team's by emphasizing the word 'SCORES,' so that listeners always know when a Blue Jay has crossed home plate." Put the two together, and it has a nice ring to it. "Donaldson lines a base hit to left! Bautista rounds third heading home. Here's the throw . . . the slide . . . the tag . . . he SCORES! The Blue Jays are in flight, leading the Yankees, 1–0!"

When I grew up listening to broadcasters, it was always "Hi, Everybody." After Tom was diagnosed with brain cancer and had to leave the booth, I knew I would be moving into the lead seat. I did not want to be like everyone else. We had lived in Toronto for years and made many friends. I consider every listener a friend. So it was very natural to come on the air with "Hello, Friends! This is Jerry Howarth."

Another favourite call of mine is "*Call it two!* A double play!" When I first used it, I liked it immediately. It's spontaneous and excitedly draws the audience in, meeting with their loud and happy approval.

Dick Enberg — An Inspiration to Me

Legendary broadcaster Dick Enberg passed away at the age of 82 on December 21, 2017. In 1976, Dick was the California Angels' radio broadcaster, working with his partner and former pitcher and Hall of Famer, Don Drysdale. The Angels' Triple-A club was in Salt Lake, where I was broadcasting their games from 1976 to 1978. One day in our clubhouse after a game, they had the Angels broadcast on with Enberg at the mic. As I listened, I heard him say, "There's a line drive into deep left-centre field. Mickey Rivers is running, running, running . . . and he makes the catch! The Angels keep the lead as Rivers steals a run away from the A's." I could "see" Rivers making that catch because of how Dick made that call. I had never before heard a broadcaster repeat words like that for effect on radio. Thus was born for me "hooking, hooking, hooking; dropping, dropping, dropping; slicing, slicing, slicing; and running, running, running." I never know what the end result will be, which adds to the suspense for both the audience and me.

I had the pleasure of meeting Enberg a few times in my career. On one occasion, I told him how much I had enjoyed hearing him work with Drysdale. "Jerry, I am fortunate in my career to have had great partners to work with. Don here with the Angels and Merlin Olsen when we call Los Angeles Rams games together. I have always felt if I highlight my partner — the former player — and put him first, it highlights the broadcast for our listeners."

I have tried to do that with all the former players I have worked with in my career because of what Dick shared with me that day on the field in Anaheim.

Interviews and a Notebook

Listening has been such an important element in my career. First, listening closely to my partners on radio, so I don't repeat what they just said. And, second, intently listening as an interviewer to then ask the best follow-up questions. I love walking up to a guest with only my recorder and spending five minutes finding out about that person for our audience. If you Google *Five Minutes with Jerry*, you will hear guests that go all the way back to March 2016 and my first visit with third-base coach Luis Rivera. I encourage young broadcasters to ask short questions and then listen. Your guest's answer will dictate your next question.

I have always carried a notebook. Before every season starts, I write down the name of every player that I will see that spring training alphabetically, with their complete biographical profile. This has proven invaluable for me over my career, helping me when I meet new players in spring training or am simply renewing acquaintances with the veterans. A glance at my notebook brings me right up to date with the names of their family members, plus baseball statistics from the season before. I keep that notebook with me on the field throughout the entire season. It helps me to tell stories during the broadcast. After I hear a story down on the field, I quickly jot down a few notes to remind me about the details when I'm on the radio that night or in the weeks to come. Writing everything down became my photographic memory. After the season is over, I toss the notebook and start all over again the following season. That simple approach has worked for me since 1974.

Famous People

We have had many interesting guests in the radio booth over the years. Even I cannot believe that I have literally sat down right next to and had conversations with Robert Duvall, Meat Loaf, Alice Cooper, and former U.S. President Richard Nixon, to name a few. There have been visits with so many Toronto personalities, like 98.1 CHFI's *Morning Show* co-hosts Erin Davis and Mike Cooper, Howie Mandel, and Bryan Adams. The radio booth was also a great way to get to know the Blue Jays' wives and girlfriends, who would come on the radio annually to help promote the Lady Jays Food Drive. Many Blue Jay alumni have visited with us, but Tom Henke's outrageously funny inning, when he talked about being a hockey coach, tops the list. You had to hear it to believe it.

Remembering Roy Halladay

Roy Halladay, at the age of 40, died in a plane crash on November 7, 2017, off the coast of Florida. The grief felt by so many was overwhelming. His wife, Brandy, was unbelievably strong as she stood at the microphone on the playing field at Clearwater's Spectrum Field in Florida, sharing her thoughts about her husband on the day they formally honoured him in a celebration of his life. I was Roy's friend for nearly 20 years. Everything that was said about him was so true, from his discipline and work ethic on the field to his charitable acts off it.

I can vividly remember interviewing Halladay out in Anaheim in the first-base dugout one night. "Roy, do you think if pitchers followed your routine they would get better?"

"Jerry, you have to listen to your own body. What I do works for me, and I wouldn't change a thing. But other pitchers have to listen to their own bodies on how hard they can push themselves and do what's best for them. Just copying my routine wouldn't be them."

From a "philosophy of life" perspective, there is one other moment I had with Roy that gave me an outlook on life that I have used to this very day. He was reading a book in the clubhouse during spring training when I came up to him and asked what he was reading.

"It's called *The Mental ABC's of Pitching* by Harvey Dorfman. I read it five times a season."

I was stunned to hear that last sentence. "I read it that many times each season to continue to stay focused and disciplined on what I am doing on the mound."

We continued to talk. "Roy, reading it that many times, what is the one thing you have taken out of this book?"

"Two words: 'next pitch.' Harvey stresses those two words so that you stay focused strictly on that catcher's glove. This way you do not allow yourself to be distracted by an error that might have just occurred behind you or a plate umpire's call that you didn't agree with. Those two words have helped me so much as a pitcher."

I reached out to Brandy after Roy's death: *Roy has been an influence in my life with his next-pitch philosophy that he used so well to concentrate on staying in the moment out on the mound. I have used those two words when things have gotten rough in my life, in order to move forward instead of negatively looking back. That has been so valuable. It is his legacy for me. I not only use it every day but I share it with others so that they can use it, too. Roy was special, Brandy, and so are you.*

POSTSCRIPT

If someone had told me growing up in California that I would spend more than half my life living and broadcasting major league baseball games in Canada, I would have laughed and said, "No way." The answer was "Yes, way." I was blessed with a loving wife, two wonderful sons, a love for sports, and an openness to God that helped me to listen and then follow my heart. Turning a hobby into a career has proudly allowed me to bring the Blue Jays and the game of baseball on the radio to everyone across Canada for 36 years. I am so grateful.

On February 13, 2018, I announced my retirement on *The Jeff Blair Show* in downtown Toronto at the Sportsnet Studios. I knew it was time. I just did not think I had the voice or the stamina to continue at the level I had set for myself over the years. I did so with no regrets.

It was a wonderful ride.

ACKNOWLEDGEMENTS

I would like to start by thanking my lovely wife, Mary, who for 47 years has been right by my side, helping me be the best husband, father, grandfather, and broadcaster I could ever imagine. She worked as a lawyer, in a profession she enjoyed, but she always allowed me to pursue my career aspirations first. For that and all her love, I am so appreciative. Mary is that "rock" you so often hear about. Our two sons, Ben and Joe, are always loving and supportive and now have families of their own. Ben and Megan live in Chicago with their sons, Coleson and Emmett. Joe and Kathy live in Toronto and are blessed with their son, Wesley. Joe is our professional photographer and is responsible for submitting all the pictures for this book, including taking the one for the cover. A job well done. A special thanks to all the wives of the players, managers, and coaches, the training staff, equipment managers, clubhouse attendants, and front office personnel who spend countless hours helping to bring the Blue Jays to their fans. We couldn't do it without you.

There are so many other people to thank. Buck Martinez suggested I write a book on my life and career with the Blue

Jays. About that same time, a lovely woman named Joan Levy Earle from Cornwall, Ontario, came into my life for a second time. In 2009, Joan had come to a Blue Jays game with her husband, Jack Mann, who was an ardent Blue Jays fan. The author of 13 books and a well-known artist, too, Joan dropped off one of her books for me at Gate 9. I quietly dismissed it without ever reading it. In 2015, at another game, Joan left me another one of her books. Well, I read that book, and I thoroughly enjoyed it. Though we had not yet met, Joan felt inspired to suggest I write a book. She has been a faithful and constant companion ever since and has helped and encouraged me to make this book the best it can possibly be.

Ann Tersigni is a wonderful and loving friend and passionate Blue Jays fan. She read and reread the words in this book countless times to help highlight the stories and streamline the pages before I even submitted it to ECW Press. Her perspective as both a longtime baseball fan and an accomplished editor has helped me write a book for everyone, sports fans or not. Annie and her husband, Ange, are special people.

I would like to thank five people I started with at the HEWPEX Sports Network back in 1980, which was later renamed the Telemedia Sports Network. Tom Cheek was a great partner, and together "Tom and Jerry" took on a whole new meaning over the years in Canada. The two of us worked together for over 22 years to bring the sounds of the game to the fans. Len Bramson hired me in 1982 to join Tom on the radio. He heard something in me that told him I would be a great fit with Tom, and for that I am eternally grateful. Sue Rayson, who worked with Len for years, was a tremendous friend and ally for me in our business. Without her phone call to me in Salt Lake City back in 1980, there would not have been a Blue Jays career.

Paul Williams was there as a close friend and made my job so much easier with his guidance and support. Nelson Millman, who would later head up our broadcasts, always gave me help and assistance. He believed in me when I succeeded Tom in the lead role, and I always knew he was there for me.

A special thanks to Scott Moore, president, Sportsnet & NHL Properties, who has been a longtime friend and supporter of mine. Scott gave me the opportunity to work with Rob Faulds on TV for part of a Blue Jays season back in 2002, which led to many friendships for me on the television side. I also very much appreciated Dave Cadeau and Don Kollins, the program directors at Sportsnet 590 The Fan, and his assistant, Jason Rozon, along with Allegra Lindala.

On the Blue Jays side, I would first like to thank Paul Beeston, who gave me his backing and friendship from the very beginning. He was loyal, friendly, and supportive. I knew I could go to him anytime to talk about what was happening in my world. He made every situation better. Pat Gillick formed a special friendship with me. He saw the big picture. Public relations director Howie Starkman always gave me his undivided attention, providing me with many interesting pieces of information for our radio audience. Blue Jays director of team travel Mike Shaw made time for me no matter how busy he was. So many details have to be addressed each season. Mike helped me with all of them. I owe a debt of gratitude over my entire career to all those who worked in the Blue Jays front office who helped me to reach out to the fans: Sue Mallabon, Mal Romanin, Erik Grosman, and Jay Stenhouse. Paul Godfrey and his family were always loyal and supportive friends. A special thanks to trainers Ken Carson, Tommy Craig, Brent Andrews, George Poulis, and Mike Frostad, among others, who continually made sure I was okay, especially on the road, whenever health questions arose. Sheila Stella in the ticket office has been a loyal friend since she started back at Exhibition Stadium. Along with her staff, I appreciate all Sheila did for me.

I would like to thank four Blue Jays managers. Jimy Williams taught me not to jump to conclusions on the radio but rather to wait until the next day to talk about interesting situations and why decisions were made. Jimy later gave the network the glowing recommendation I needed for them to bring me into the booth as an unknown. Bobby Cox was the first major league manager I worked with in radio. For four years, he shared with me a lot of his thoughts, bringing me closer to the game. Cito Gaston would openly talk with me about his philosophy of life and how he'd lived through many difficult personal experiences growing up in the South, some of which had nothing to do with baseball. I learned so much from him. John Gibbons taught me how to see the game in its proper perspective and be open to any and all conversations about it. Patience is a virtue, and John has it in spades.

I was fortunate to be a spokesperson on radio for many businesses. Ron Hoare was one who asked me to write two Blue Jays booklets entitled *Where are They Now?* that were distributed all across Canada. Bob Johnston became a lifelong friend and supporter of my work. Bill Hall and his family were always there for me and were loyal sponsors, providing various promotions on the air for our fans. Bill Sheine continued these promotions for years. Jack and Marg Rider and their daughter, Fran, loved both the Blue Jays and my family.

I was blessed with one of the greatest avocations a person could have: being a basketball coach for 25 years. It started in the Etobicoke Basketball Association, where I began coaching my own two sons on Saturdays alongside co-coach Marsha Gettas, whose son, Griffin, was on those teams. It was Marsha who called Islington Middle School back in 1991 to recommend me as their new basketball coach, and that started my basketball career. Nick Christian was my first basketball mentor when I was at Islington. He coached at nearby Bloordale Middle School and spent countless hours of his time teaching me the fundamentals of the game that I used for 25 years. My last 20 years coaching were spent at Etobicoke Collegiate Institute. ECI coaches Paul Dias, Paul Pearson, Elias Paisley, Andy Van Dyke, Hank Spencer, and many others in the front office were instrumental in helping me each season. They were my "basketball family." A thank you as well to all the coaches and referees I met who were great teachers and mentors, and who helped make me a better coach.

I had the distinct pleasure working with Special Olympics Canada for 29 years. Each December, I would co-emcee with my friend Brian Williams a breakfast before approximately 1,500 people in downtown Toronto. The room was filled with Special Olympians and donors who gave so much of their time and money to help others. This whole endeavour was run by the Etherington family, headed by Joe Etherington, who later passed the torch to his sons, Brian and Bruce. Brian's sons Paul, Mark, and Sean continued that tradition, along with Lea Parrell, who with her husband, Vince, put all the fundraising details together for a great cause. For 20 years, I was the guest speaker at a Special Olympics Bowling tournament held in Etobicoke each November. Walter Heeney was the architect. His daughter, Jan, was a very good Special Olympian bowler with easily the best smile. In St. Thomas, Ontario, I was the emcee for 20 years at their annual January Sports Spectacular Dinner. The head table each year featured 10 outstanding athletes, including the guest speaker. Thanks to Gary Clarke and Jerry O'Brien, I was able to meet and interview hockey legends, such as Bobby and Dennis Hull, Frank Mahovlich, Jean Beliveau, Marcel Dionne, Red Kelly, and Yvan Cournoyer. There were Olympians and Blue Jays and so many others from all sports at the head table. Brent Lale put it all together.

For 10 years, I was the emcee for the Etobicoke Sports Hall of Fame dinner. I was proudly inducted in 2000, and it is one of the nicest honours I have ever received. A big thanks to Jim Sturino and Joanne Noble for all the work they did to make that Hall of Fame one of the best in Canada. For another 10 years, Greg Hamilton, the director of Baseball Canada, asked me to emcee their January baseball dinner at the Rogers Centre. This allowed me to meet and get to know so many Canadians who starred on the diamond from the major leagues to Team Canada competitions around the globe. In 2018, I proudly received the Order of St. Michael's, a distinguished honour from St. Mike's High School, where my two sons graduated in 1996 and 1997.

I am fortunate to be in an industry with a very small fraternity, where we all get to know and appreciate each other. I have been blessed with friendships with so many fellow broadcasters, as well as members of the media, both in Toronto and in cities across Major League Baseball. That interaction has paved the way for countless stories and interesting information that made my job easier. Veteran journalists like Bob Elliott, Milt Dunnell, Trent Frayne, John Robertson, Pat Marsden, and Larry Millson all befriended me early in my career, making my transition to the radio booth and a new country so much smoother. From the beginning in 1982, John Iaboni, Brian Williams, and Fred Anderton made sure I felt comfortable in my new city and country. Buck Martinez, Jeff Blair, Richard Griffin, Dan Shulman, Pat Tabler, and Jamie Campbell head up a long list of baseball friends who have continued that for me to this very day.

I would like to thank Dr. Rob Nam at Sunnybrook Hospital, who on November 22, 2016, surgically removed my cancerous prostate gland with a tumour at the stage-one level. Thanks as well to my personal physician, Dr. James Choe, who referred me to Dr. Nam. My ENT, Dr. Adam Toth, was most instrumental in helping me cope with voice issues to keep me on the air. Dr. Vince Sinclair, who is like a brother, kept my back adjusted at his Streetsville Chiropractic Clinic for 35 years and, after that, Dr. Sam Abbruzzino in Etobicoke. Blue Jays longtime orthopaedic surgeon, Dr. Allan Gross, was another who has always made time for me, watching out for my health and well-being.

We have had so many friends and family members along the way who have added much to our lives, in both the U.S. and Canada. I cannot begin to name them all, but each one has made this journey so wonderful for me and my family.

Finally, a very special thanks to ECW Press. Without Michael Holmes and his staff, this book would not exist. Laura Pastore did an excellent job as the editor, and because she is an ardent Blue Jays fan, my job was made so much easier in finalizing this book with her. I have become a part of ECW's family. That was very evident when our son, Joe, took the pictures for this book's cover and was made to feel so welcome on that joy-filled day.

THANK YOU, FRIENDS!

At ECW Press, we want you to enjoy this book in whatever format you like, whenever you like. Leave your print book at home and take the eBook to go! Purchase the print edition and receive the eBook free. Just send an email to ebook@ecwpress.com and include:

- the book title
- the name of the store where you purchased it
- your receipt number
- your preference of file type: PDF or ePub

A real person will respond to your email with your eBook attached. And thanks for supporting an independently owned Canadian publisher with your purchase!

At ECW Press, we want you to enjoy this book in whatever format you like, whenever you like. Leave your print book at home and take the eBook to go! Purchase the print edition and receive the eBook free. Just send an email to ebook@ecwpress.com and include:

Get the eBook free!*
*proof of purchase required

- the book title
- the name of the store where you purchased it
- your receipt number
- your preference of file type: PDF or ePub

A real person will respond to your email with your eBook attached. And thanks for supporting an independently owned Canadian publisher with your purchase!